# COUGHING AND CLAPPING: INVESTIGATING AUDIENCE EXPERIENCE

# SEMPRE Studies in The Psychology of Music

Series Editors
Graham Welch, *Institute of Education, University of London, UK*
Adam Ockelford, *Roehampton University, UK*
Ian Cross, *University of Cambridge, UK*

The theme for the series is the psychology of music, broadly defined. Topics include: (i) musical development at different ages, (ii) exceptional musical development in the context of special educational needs, (iii) musical cognition and context, (iv) culture, mind and music, (v) micro to macro perspectives on the impact of music on the individual (such as from neurological studies through to social psychology), (vi) the development of advanced performance skills and (vii) affective perspectives on musical learning. The series presents the implications of research findings for a wide readership, including user-groups (music teachers, policy makers, parents), as well as the international academic and research communities. The distinguishing features of the series is this broad focus (drawing on basic and applied research from across the globe) under the umbrella of SEMPRE's distinctive mission, which is to promote and ensure coherent and symbiotic links between education, music and psychology research.

Other titles in the series

*Embodied Knowledge in Ensemble Performance*
J. Murphy McCaleb

*Developing the Musician*
*Contemporary Perspectives on Teaching and Learning*
Edited by Mary Stakelum

*Music and Familiarity*
*Listening, Musicology and Performance*
Edited by Elaine King and Helen M. Prior

# Coughing and Clapping: Investigating Audience Experience

Edited by

KAREN BURLAND
*University of Leeds, UK*

STEPHANIE PITTS
*University of Sheffield, UK*

**ASHGATE**

© Karen Burland and Stephanie Pitts 2014

All rights reserved. No part of this publication may be reproduced, stored in a retrieval system or transmitted in any form or by any means, electronic, mechanical, photocopying, recording or otherwise without the prior permission of the publisher.

Karen Burland and Stephanie Pitts have asserted his/her right under the Copyright, Designs and Patents Act, 1988, to be identified as the editors of this work.

Published by
Ashgate Publishing Limited
Wey Court East
Union Road
Farnham
Surrey, GU9 7PT
England

Ashgate Publishing Company
110 Cherry Street
Suite 3-1
Burlington, VT 05401-3818
USA

www.ashgate.com

**British Library Cataloguing in Publication Data**
A catalogue record for this book is available from the British Library

**The Library of Congress has cataloged the printed edition as follows:**
Coughing and Clapping: Investigating Audience Experience / edited by Karen Burland and Stephanie Pitts.
    pages cm. – (SEMPRE Studies in the Psychology of Music)
Includes bibliographical references and index.
1. Music audiences – Psychological aspects. 2. Concerts – Psychological aspects.
I. Burland, Karen. II. Pitts, Stephanie.
ML3830.C66 2014
780.78–dc23
                                                                                                           2014017419

ISBN: 9781409469810 (hbk)
ISBN: 9781472410283 (ebk-PDF)
ISBN: 9781472410290 (ebk-ePUB)

Printed in the United Kingdom by Henry Ling Limited,
at the Dorset Press, Dorchester, DT1 1HD

*For Isobel Holly Clark*

# Contents

| | |
|---|---|
| *List of Figures* | *ix* |
| *List of Tables* | *xi* |
| *Notes on Contributors* | *xiii* |
| *Series Editors' Preface* | *xix* |
| *Acknowledgements* | *xxi* |

| | | |
|---|---|---|
| 1 | Prelude<br>*Stephanie Pitts and Karen Burland* | 1 |

**SECTION 1: BEFORE THE EVENT: PREPARING AND ANTICIPATING**

| | | |
|---|---|---|
| 2 | Marketing Live Music<br>*Daragh O'Reilly, Gretchen Larsen and Krzysztof Kubacki* | 7 |
| 3 | Musical, Social and Moral Dilemmas: Investigating Audience Motivations to Attend Concerts<br>*Stephanie Pitts* | 21 |
| 4 | Safe and Sound: Audience Experience in New Venues for Popular Music Performance<br>*Robert Kronenburg* | 35 |

**SECTION 2: DURING THE EVENT: LISTENING AND CONNECTING**

| | | |
|---|---|---|
| 5 | Interlude – Audience Members as Researchers<br>*Stephanie Pitts and Karen Burland* | 53 |
| 6 | The Value of 'Being There': How the Live Experience Measures Quality for the Audience<br>*Jennifer Radbourne, Katya Johanson and Hilary Glow* | 55 |
| 7 | In the Heat of the Moment: Audience Real-time Response to Music and Dance Performance<br>*Catherine J. Stevens, Roger T. Dean, Kim Vincs, and Emery Schubert* | 69 |

| 8 | Texting and Tweeting at Live Music Concerts: Flow, Fandom and Connecting with other Audiences through Mobile Phone Technology<br>*Lucy Bennett* | 89 |
|---|---|---|
| 9 | Moving the Gong: Exploring the Contexts of Improvisation and Composition<br>*Karen Burland and Luke Windsor (with Christophe de Bézenac, Matthew Bourne, Petter Frost Fadnes and Nick Katuszonek)* | 101 |
| 10 | Context, Cohesion and Community: Characteristics of Festival Audience Members' Strong Experiences with Music<br>*Sidsel Karlsen* | 115 |
| 11 | Interlude – Lasting Memories of Ephemeral Events<br>*Karen Burland and Stephanie Pitts* | 127 |
| 12 | 'The Gigs I've Gone To': Mapping Memories and Places of Live Music<br>*Sara Cohen* | 131 |
| 13 | Warts and All: Recording the Live Music Experience<br>*Paul Long* | 147 |
| 14 | Staying Behind: Explorations in Post-performance Musician–Audience Dialogue<br>*Melissa C. Dobson and John Sloboda* | 159 |
| 15 | Postlude<br>*Karen Burland and Stephanie Pitts* | 175 |

*References* *181*
*Index* *201*

# List of Figures

| | | |
|---|---|---|
| 2.1 | Music Brands Framework ( Adapted from O'Reilly, 2011) | 17 |
| 4.1 | Entertainment Avenue, the retail street at the O2 Greenwich, London (©Robert Kronenburg) | 47 |
| 4.2 | Phoenix on stage at The Joint by Vogue, Las Vegas (©Robert Kronenburg) | 49 |
| 7.1 | Two-dimensional representation of emotion on the portable Audience Response Facility (pARF) | 75 |
| 7.2 | Mean arousal response and standard deviation across the 25-minute performance from 10 audience members | 76 |
| 7.3 | Mean valence response and standard deviation across the 25-minute performance from 10 audience members | 76 |
| 7.4 | Mean arousal and mean valence continuous ratings recorded in section 2 of *Glow* | 81 |
| 7.5 | Mean arousal and mean valence continuous ratings recorded in section 5 of *Glow* | 81 |
| 7.6 | Photographs of a 'test' audience watching a film at two points in time | 84 |
| 9.1 | View of the performing space from the balcony | 91 |
| 9.2 | Factors influencing live performance/improvisation in context | 113 |
| 12.1 | Les's memory map | 134 |
| 12.2 | Close-up image of Les's memory map | 135 |
| 12.3 | Ian's memory map | 136 |
| 15.1 | The cyclical process of being an audience member | 177 |

# List of Tables

| | | |
|---|---|---|
| 3.1 | Audience studies 2003–2010 | 23 |
| 7.1 | Mean usability ratings for the pARF | 73 |
| 10.1 | Factors reported to have impacted on occurrences of festival attendees' SEM | 117 |
| 14.1 | The positioning of the present research and the 'dominant' model on four key research dimensions | 162 |
| 14.2 | Details of the five pilot research events | 163 |

# Notes on Contributors

**Lucy Bennett** completed her PhD in online fandom at JOMEC, Cardiff University. Her work on digital culture, fans and audiences appears in journals such as *New Media & Society, Transformative Works and Cultures, Social Semiotics, Continuum, Cinema Journal, Celebrity Studies* and *Participations*. She is the co-founder and co-chair of the Fan Studies Network and is currently co-editing a special issue of *New Media & Society* and a forthcoming anthology on crowdfunding.

**Matthew Bourne** is a pianist and composer living on a remote hillside somewhere in West Yorkshire. Bourne studied Jazz performance at Leeds College of Music before concluding his postgraduate studies at the University of Leeds. Bourne's highly-individual work as a pianist has earned him numerous accolades and awards. Working for artists and organizations as diverse as the London Sinfonietta, Amon Tobin, John Zorn and inventor of the Fluid Piano™, Geoff Smith, Bourne continues to be an active presence in the fields of improvised and contemporary music. (http://www.matthewbourne.com)

**Karen Burland** is an Associate Professor in music psychology at the University of Leeds. Her published research focuses on jazz audiences and their engagement in live performances in different contexts; the environmental conditions leading to childhood musical success and the professional development of musicians during career transitions; professional and amateur musical identities; and music therapists' use of music technology in therapeutic settings. Karen is a member of the SEMPRE committee and Reviews Editor for the *British Journal of Music Education*.

**Sara Cohen** works at the School of Music at the University of Liverpool and is Director of the Institute of Popular Music. She has a DPhil in Social Anthropology from Oxford University and is the author of *Rock culture in Liverpool: Popular music in the making* and *Decline, renewal and the city in popular music culture: Beyond the Beatles* (Ashgate).

**Roger Dean** is a composer/improviser, and since 2007 a research professor in music cognition and computation at the MARCS Institute, University of Western Sydney. He founded and directs the ensemble austraLYSIS, and has performed as bassist and pianist in contexts from the Academy of Ancient Music and the Australian Chamber Orchestra, to the London Sinfonietta and the Hoarded Dreams Jazz Orchestra. His creative work is on 50 commercial audio CDs, and he has released many digital intermedia pieces and, recently, sound installation works. His main current research is on perception of affect in music, the role of acoustic intensity and timbre, and rhythm generation and perception. His 400 substantive research publications include seven humanities books. Previously he was foundation CEO of the Heart Research Institute, Sydney, researching in biochemistry, and then Vice-Chancellor and President of the University of Canberra.

**Christophe de Bézenac** is a musician, researcher and lecturer based in the UK. After studying at the Conservatoire de Strasbourg, he completed a PhD which examined perceptual ambiguity in music, taking an ecological approach. During this time he became actively involved in the European experimental jazz/rock scene, where he performs at international festivals/venues. Christophe's musical research interests have also led him to work in the field of cognitive neuroscience, examining the neural correlates of ambiguity between self and other in perception and action. The aim of this work is to shed light on mechanisms at work in psychosis, where self/other boundaries can become blurred.

**Melissa Dobson** received her doctorate from the University of Sheffield in 2010, with a thesis investigating audience experience and enjoyment of classical music concert attendance. She has since worked as a post-doctoral Research Assistant at the Guildhall School of Music & Drama, where she contributed to the 'Orchestral musicians in the twenty-first century' and 'Understanding audiences' research programmes. Her research interests lie broadly in the social psychology of music, with a particular focus on audience and performer perspectives on live music-making.

**Petter Frost Fadnes** has parallel careers in performance and academia, and his research interest is centred on improvisational thinking within a practical context, specifically looking at improvisational processes through musical performance. His overall mission is to demystify improvisational music-making, and reveal the *musical thought* within the performance. Frost Fadnes is Associate Professor at The Department of Music and Dance, University of Stavanger, and former principal investigator for the HERA-funded research project *Rhythm Changes: Jazz Cultures and European Identities*. He performs with players from mainly Norway and the UK, and continues to seek 'the perfect melody' through eclectic musical approaches within the settings of improvised music. Frost Fadnes performs regularly with *The Geordie Approach*, *The Thin Red Line*, and *Kitchen Orchestra*.

**Hilary Glow** is Associate Professor and Director of the Arts and Entertainment Management Program at Deakin University. Her research focuses on the relationships between cultural policy, the performing arts and its audiences. She is the author of *Power plays: Australian theatre and the public agenda*.

**Katya Johanson** is Senior Lecturer in the School of Communication and Creative Arts at Deakin University. She is the author of many book chapters and journal articles on cultural policy and audiences for performing arts and festivals.

**Sidsel Karlsen** is professor of music education at Hedmark University College in Norway as well as adjunct professor at the Sibelius Academy in Finland. She has published widely in Scandinavian and international research journals and is a contributor to international anthologies such as *Sociology and music education* and *Learning, teaching, and musical identity: Voices across cultures*. Her research interests cover, among other things, the social and cultural significance of music festivals and multicultural music education.

**Nick Katuszonek** is a senior lecturer at Leeds College of Music and is a drummer/ educator working at the forefront of contemporary pop and Jazz. He has both a BA (Hons) and MMus degree in Jazz studies and he also has PGCert PAE from Manchester's Royal Northern College of Music. In 2010 Nick was awarded a PhD scholarship as part of the HERA sponsored *Rhythm Changes* Project. His research is performance based and is focused on a practical examination of the relationship between contemporary jazz, improvisation and popular music in various European settings. His two current projects involve working with Norwegian musicians on interpretations of the music of A-ha and a comparative project in the UK using the music of The Smiths. Nick has performed professionally throughout the UK and Europe for over fifteen years. He has worked, recorded and performed with a number of musicians operating on the cutting edge of contemporary music. He is a founding member of the critically acclaimed Metropolis, a group in its eleventh year, with three album releases. The Norway based 'A-ha project' and the UK based 'The Smiths Experience' both led by Nick, have recently recorded albums and continue to perform throughout Europe.

**Robert Kronenburg** PhD RIBA is an architect and holds the Roscoe Chair of Architecture, University of Liverpool, UK. His research engages with innovative forms of architectural design, film and popular music. His books include *Spirit of the machine* (2001), *Flexible: Architecture that responds to change* (2007), *Portable architecture* (2008), *Live architecture: Venues, stages and arenas for popular music* (2012) and *Architecture in motion* (2014). He is a past Fulbright fellow, visiting fellow at St Johns College, Oxford University, and British Academy/Leverhulme Trust Senior Research Fellowship holder.

**Krzysztof Kubacki** is a Social Marketing Research Practice Fellow (VicHealth) and a Senior Lecturer in Marketing at Griffith University. He has been involved in academic and market research for over 10 years, he has published over 35 journal articles and book chapters. The broad area of his research interests could be defined as 'cultural consumption' and includes projects exploring areas such as relationship between marketing and cultural industries, influence of national culture on national brand, and cross-national comparisons between consumers in the European Union. Woven throughout his research is an interest in the relationship between social marketing and consumer culture, with his most recent work focusing on alcohol consumption among young people.

**Gretchen Larsen** is a senior lecturer in marketing at Durham University. Her main research interests lie in arts consumption, focusing specifically on the intersection of music, consumption and markets. She is the founding co-editor of *Arts Marketing: An International Journal*. Gretchen has published her research in a book, *Music, Markets and Consumption* (with Daragh O'Reilly and Krzysztof Kubacki), in several book chapters and in a range of journals including the *European Journal of Marketing, Journal of Marketing Management, Journal of Business Ethics, Marketing Theory* and the *Journal of Consumer Policy*.

**Paul Long** is Reader in Media and Cultural History at Birmingham City University and Associate Director of the Birmingham Centre for Media and Cultural Research. He is the author of *'Only in the common people': The aesthetics of class in post-war Britain* (2008). He has written widely on media history including studies of BBC4's *Britannia* series and Tony Palmer's TV series *All You Need is Love* as well as the role of student unions in UK popular music cultures. His research on creative industries includes contributions to the EU-funded projects 'Creative Metropoles' and 'Cross-Innovation'. He is part of the AHRC-funded project 'Cultural Intermediation and the Creative Economy' where he researches the relationship of 'hard to reach' communities with the cultural sector (http://culturalintermediation.wordpress.com). He is currently developing research concerning the role of class, ethnicity and gender in creative industries work.

**Daragh O'Reilly** is a Senior Lecturer in Creative and Cultural Industries at Sheffield University Management School. He is the co-editor, with Ruth Rentschler and Theresa Kirchner, of the *Routledge companion to arts marketing* (2014) and the co-author, with Gretchen Larsen and Krzysztof Kubacki, of *Music, markets and consumption* (2013).

**Stephanie Pitts** is Professor of Music Education at the University of Sheffield, with research interests in music education and the social psychology of music. She is the director of the Sheffield Performer and Audience Research Centre (SPARC), and currently working on an investigation of 'lapsed' arts engagement with out-of-practice amateur musicians and infrequent audience members. She is the author of books including *Valuing musical participation* (Ashgate, 2005), *Chances and choices: Exploring the impact of music education* (Oxford, 2012) and, with Eric Clarke and Nicola Dibben, *Music and mind in everyday life* (Oxford, 2010).

**Jennifer Radbourne** is Emeritus Professor and former Dean of the Faculty of Arts and Education at Deakin University. Her research and consultancy in arts marketing, arts governance and business development in the creative industries has been published in international journals, books and conferences. She is on the editorial board of two international journals and has been the recipient of four Australian Research Council grants.

**Emery Schubert** is an Associate Professor in Music and an Australian Research Council Future Fellow. He is co-leader of the Empirical Musicology Group, and Music-Science, both at the University of New South Wales. His primary research area is in music psychology and emotional responses to music. He was President from 2008 to 2009 of the Australian Music and Psychology Society (AMPS) and serves on the editorial board of key journals in the field of music psychology.

**John Sloboda** is Research Professor at the Guildhall School of Music & Drama where he leads their 'Understanding Audiences' Research Programme. He is also deputy leader of the 'Capturing London's Audiences' research strand of CreativeWorks London, one of four AHRC-funded Knowledge Exchange Hubs for the Creative Economy (2012–16). He is author of over 150 publications in the field of music psychology, and his most recent book, co-edited with Patrik Juslin, is *Handbook of Music and Emotion* (2010).

As a cognitive psychologist, **Catherine Stevens** investigates the learning, perception, creation and cognition of complex, non-verbal sequences using the familiar and universal contexts of music and dance. She holds BA (Hons) and PhD degrees from the University of Sydney. Kate is Professor in Psychology and leads the Music Cognition and Action research program in the MARCS Institute at the University of Western Sydney (http://marcs.uws.edu.au; http://katestevens.weebly.com).

**Kim Vincs** is the Director of the Deakin Motion.Lab, Deakin University's motion capture studio and performance technology research centre. Her research focuses on applied, practice-based artistic research in dance and technology. She is also a choreographer and transmedia artist. She is a member of Deakin University's Centre for Intelligent Systems Research.

**Luke Windsor** has been researching and teaching psychological, aesthetic, analytical and semiotic aspects of music since the mid-1990s. In particular he has published on rhythm and timing in performance, the sources and modelling of musical expression, ecological approaches to the perception and production of musical performances, and musical gesture. He has supervised doctoral work on a range of music-psychological and practice-led topics including musical improvisation. Luke is a Senior Lecturer in the School of Music at the University of Leeds in the UK, where is he is also Pro-Dean for Student Education for the Faculty of Performance, Visual Arts and Communications. He has previously worked and studied at City University, London, the University of Sheffield, and at Radboud University, in the Netherlands.

# Series Editors' Preface

The enormous growth of research that has been evidenced over the past three decades into the many different phenomena that are embraced under the psychology of music 'umbrella' continues, with new journals, books, media interest, an expansion of professional associations (regionally as well as nationally) and increasing and diverse opportunities for formal study, and not just in English-speaking countries. Such interest is not only from psychologists and musicians, but also from colleagues working in the clinical sciences, neurosciences, therapies, lifelong health and well-being, philosophy, musicology, social psychology, ethnomusicology and education across the lifespan. The Society for Education, Music and Psychology Research (SEMPRE) recently celebrated its 40th Anniversary (2012) as one of the world's leading and long-standing professional associations in the field. SEMPRE continues to be the only international society that embraces an interest in the psychology of music, research and education, seeking to promote knowledge at the interface between the social sciences of psychology and education with one of the world's most pervasive art forms, music. SEMPRE was founded in 1972 and has published the journals *Psychology of Music* since 1973 and *Research Studies in Music Education* since 2008, both now produced in partnership with SAGE (see www.sempre.org.uk). Nevertheless, there is an ongoing need to promote the latest research findings to the widest possible audience through more extended publication formats, especially books, if we are to fulfil our mission of having a distinctive and positive impact on policy and practice internationally, within and across our disciplinary boundaries. Hence the emergence of the strong collaborative partnership between SEMPRE and Ashgate.

The Ashgate 'SEMPRE Studies in The Psychology of Music' has been designed to address this international need since its inception in 2007. The theme for the series is the psychology of music, broadly defined. Topics include (amongst others): musical development and learning at different ages; musical cognition and context; culture, mind and music; creativity, composition and collaboration; micro to macro perspectives on the impact of music on the individual (such as from neurological studies through to social psychology); the development of advanced performance skills; musical behaviour and development in the context of special educational needs; and affective perspectives on musical learning. The series seeks to present the implications of research findings for a wide readership, including user groups (music teachers, policy makers, parents and carers), as well as the international academic teaching and research communities. A key distinguishing feature of the series is its broad focus that draws on basic and applied research from across the globe under the umbrella of SEMPRE's distinctive mission, which is to promote and ensure coherent and symbiotic links between education, music and psychology research.

It is with great pleasure that we include *Coughing and Clapping* in the SEMPRE series. This engaging edited collection takes a novel and through-designed empirical approach to the diversity of audience experience that relates to attendance at live performances, particularly concert-going. The authors illustrate how the act of concert attendance is closely interwoven with attendee biography, as well as with experiences and expectations of, for example, the venue, repertoire, social context and artists. Modern communication technology is also a focus, such as in understanding how this can mediate and extend the situated audience experience. There is a clear sense that the 'experience' of a live music event extends temporally beyond the performance itself to include anticipation (often collective) and post-event reflection and emotion-imbued memories. The authors provide us with a comprehensive sense of the value of live performance, both to the individual audience member and also collectively to the group. The book is essential reading for anyone who is interested in why live music matters.

Graham Welch
*Institute of Education, London, UK*
Adam Ockelford
*Roehampton University, UK*
Ian Cross
*University of Cambridge, UK*

# Acknowledgements

We would like to thank the authors for their contributions and enthusiasm and for sharing our vision for the book. We are very grateful to the hundreds of research participants who appear within the book for sharing their musical experiences with us. Thank you to Rich for being there from the beginning of our collaboration, carrying boxes, making coffee and proofreading, and to Oscar and Isobel for providing fun and smiles. Thanks also to Ashgate and SEMPRE for supporting the project and helping with the final stages of the book's creation.

# Chapter 1
# Prelude

Stephanie Pitts and Karen Burland

When Christopher Small invented the useful word 'musicking' to describe the many forms of taking part in music, he did so through a rhetorical deconstruction of the classical symphony hall and its ritualized performance events, in which he perceived there to be 'a dissonance between the meanings – the relationships – that are generated by the works that are being performed and those that are generated by the performance events' (Small, 1998: 14). His evidence was gathered as an ethnomusicologist, applying the techniques of close observation and rich description to a musical setting close to home, in ways that have since become more widespread within that discipline. For music psychologists, however, Small's account of the concert hall raised more questions than it answered, and perhaps contributed to the growth in empirical investigations of listener experience that have flourished in the last decade or so, many of whose authors are represented or referenced in this book.

In *Coughing and Clapping*, we take Small's framework of exploring the many facets of concert attendance – the venue, the decisions and rituals of ticket purchasing, the interaction with other audience members, the expectations of listener behaviour, and the music 'itself', encompassing repertoire and performance – and examine fresh evidence for how these elements are experienced and understood by concert-goers. Rather than focusing exclusively on classical music, as Small did on that occasion, our authors examine a range of classical, jazz and popular music audiences, whose varied experiences help to illuminate what is distinctive about listening in different genres, and also what is similar about the pleasures and purposes of live music listening. Some of the case studies reported here (see chapters by Radbourne et al., and Stevens et al.) venture into other art forms, particularly contemporary dance, raising questions about whether the experience of live arts consumption is different across genres. Many of the chapters show how live listening is made distinctive by its listeners, as each person's connection with the event is shaped by expectations, prior experiences, mood and concentration. This variety of experience suggests that while Small's rhetoric about the concert hall remains a useful polemic against which empirical evidence can be compared, the need for an updated view of the purposes and practices of the concert hall and other musical venues is long overdue.

The decision to call this collection *Coughing and Clapping* arose during one of the many coffee and biscuit sessions that have gone into the making of this book. The suggestion was at first light-hearted, but as our prospective authors and commissioning editors responded positively to the idea, we came to appreciate the way that the title puts the audience at the heart of the live music experience. However extensive the preparation that goes into a musical event – from fire extinguishers (Kronenburg) to repertoire (Burland and Windsor), and from marketing (O'Reilly et al.) to tweeting (Bennett) – it is the audience, through the quantity of their attendance and the quality of their response, who make each performance distinctive. A long-time collaborator of ours on audience research, Chris Spencer, drew our attention to a report on BBC Radio 4's *Today* news programme (29 January 2013), in which pianist Susan Tomes and economist Andreas Wagener were discussing recently published statistics to suggest that people cough twice as much during performances than they do in everyday life. Contemporary music and quiet, slow movements were most likely to attract such a response, and coughing in the concert hall followed predictable patterns, one person's coughs setting off a wave of similar events (Wagener, 2012). While Tomes observed that the concert hall cough also seemed more vigorous and unrestrained than its real life counterpart, and was therefore 'really quite distracting and startling to performers', Wagener suspected a deliberate motivation to be heard in the concert hall: coughing has an ambiguity such that 'you cannot really distinguish whether it is a deliberate thing that happens, a sort of comment that you wish to make on the music, or whether it's something that is just a reflex because you have an itching throat […] and this ambiguity makes a cough a rather attractive way to comment on the music, to participate in the performance, to show your existence in the concert and to break this concert etiquette'.

Wagener may be right in his supposition that audience members want to find a voice in the concert hall, and several of the chapters in this collection show how new technology is enabling them to do exactly that, by tweeting and texting during performances (Bennett), and through blogging (Long), archiving and mapping (Cohen) after the event. Audiences themselves are becoming increasingly public commentators on live music, through online fan forums, Twitter feeds and other evolving technology. A response to a concert can now go far beyond conventional, polite applause – coughing and clapping are only the start of the audience's expression of their appreciation (or otherwise). Their experience is therefore more available to researchers, acting as a resource to both inform research and to measure against data collected in other, more researcher-directed ways. In compiling some of the more technology-focused chapters in the book, we have been aware of the danger that these will date quickly, so that what sounds like cutting-edge practice now will no doubt be superseded in a few years' time. Similar challenges have been seen in the research on listening to recorded music, where Walkmans have been replaced by iPods, and CDs by downloads, almost more quickly than commentators can publish their response (cf. Bull, 2000; 2005). Nonetheless, these chapters have lasting messages about the urge to document and react to a temporal arts experience: in the same way that researchers grapple with ways of understanding the fleeting nature of live listening, audiences too are seeking to secure their musical memories, to make them part of their musical narrative and identity.

Our authors come from a wide range of disciplinary backgrounds, including music, architecture, psychology, cultural studies, media, arts marketing and management. Within each of those disciplines, research on the qualitative experience of live arts engagement is relatively new, and brings with it a search for effective methods that capture the immediacy and individuality of audience experience. Some of these are audience-led, such as the tweeting and blogging of Tori Amos fans in Lucy Bennett's chapter, and the fan forums used by Robert Kronenburg and Paul Long: here the audience members provide the research 'data' unsolicited, and the researchers interpret this naturalistic evidence to gain a sense of what audience experience means, within and after the musical event. Other evidence is more directly prompted by the researchers, through discussions between audiences and performers (Burland and Windsor; Dobson and Sloboda), and widespread use of interviews, questionnaires and focus groups (Pitts; Karlsen; O'Reilly et al.), with Sara Cohen's invitation to make 'maps' of musical memories showing how visual prompts can enrich these verbal responses. Some authors tackle the challenging question of how to capture a time-specific experience by using 'in the moment' response tools with their audiences (Stevens et al.), measuring emotion and arousal during the course of a performance and so advancing understanding of what people are doing when they listen. Taken together, these chapters show the state of audience research to be still a relatively exploratory one, but one which is gathering pace and providing new insight on the contribution of live music to individual and social experience.

We have divided the book into three sections, and will introduce the later sections in more detail as they begin. Drawing on the diverse range of disciplines and methods represented by our authors, we have aimed to provide a closer empirical examination of Small's (1998) portrayal of the concert hall, broadened here to include a range of venues and genres. In the first section, 'Before the event', the focus is on preparing for and anticipating the live music experience, and perspectives include those of the marketing and branding experts who make decisions about how to portray music to its potential audiences (O'Reilly et al.), the audiences who interpret those marketing materials and weigh them up against their own musical and social preferences and priorities (Pitts), and the architects and venue managers who prepare the spaces in which live music is heard (Kronenburg). Despite the focus on anticipation, the cycle of audience engagement quickly becomes clear: decisions about attendance are informed by previous experiences, and marketing and venue design are shaped by past as well as future audiences. In the third section of the book, this loop is closed and the cycle continued with a focus on capturing the ephemeral experiences of live arts attendance, through mapping (Cohen), recording (Long) and discussing events (Dobson and Sloboda). These are all processes of audience engagement that help to articulate the experience of live listening in ways that, as well as being informative for researchers and concert promoters, provide the audiences with ways of assimilating a musical life narrative from the fragmented and transitory nature of being an audience member. Between these two stages in the continuous process of audience engagement, the second section of the book considers all that goes on in the event itself: the acts of evaluating and responding to an event (Radbourne et al.; Stevens et al.), the decisions or invitations to make these evaluations public (for audiences in Bennett's chapter, and for performers in Burland and Windsor), and the sense of belonging and identity that can result from being part of an audience (Karlsen). The book as a whole shows the multiple meanings of live listening amongst varied audiences, and we reflect in a final chapter (Burland and Pitts) on what it means to be an audience member – and why that matters, for researchers, performers and promoters, and future listeners.

# SECTION 1
# Before the Event: Preparing and Anticipating

# Chapter 2

# Marketing Live Music

Daragh O'Reilly, Gretchen Larsen and Krzysztof Kubacki

In this chapter, we review issues relating to the marketing of live music and suggest a way of thinking about it which emphasizes the contributory role of audiences/fans/consumers, as well as live music's symbolic or cultural aspects. The marketing of live music is an intensely practical exercise for the promoter. However, rather than providing an event management, project management or other mainly operational perspective, we go back to the 'official' definition of marketing and seek to move beyond current 'mainstream' notions. This is not to downplay the importance of operational issues, such as health and safety or licensing laws. It is more a case that this edited collection affords an opportunity for rethinking tired ideas which do not relate well to the realities of live music markets. There is no guaranteed formula for live music marketing. If one asks the question, 'How should live music be marketed?', the only sensible answer is: 'It depends'. Live music marketing occurs in so many different contexts and forms and on so many widely differing scales and occasions that it would be unwise to impose a universal law-like view. In any case, the real question that matters from a marketing practitioner's point of view is 'How can live music be marketed *successfully*?' There are many musical concerts and festivals which have lost money for their promoters, and there are plenty of musical venues, once famous and thriving, which are no longer in operation. Apart from getting the operational details right, we believe that a consideration of some of the wider, strategic issues can be very helpful in successful live music promotion.

The chapter begins with a review of the 'official' definition of marketing. As we aim to show, a discussion of live music marketing may benefit from adjusting the institutional definition of marketing. To that end, we offer a simple definition which lends greater weight to the role of music consumers, and to the processual and symbolic aspects of this important commercial and cultural phenomenon.

**Problematising 'Marketing'**

Classic marketing objectives are to recruit and retain customers, with retention of existing customers usually being regarded as cheaper than recruiting new ones (Kotler et al., 2013, p. 19). This sits well enough with the idea, more widely used in the arts, including music, of audience development. The need to recruit and retain means that live music promoters must have strong competences in originating and sustaining relationships beyond a single transaction. This is about building a dynamic connection with customers over a longer period. For example, a pub venue may need to develop strong local relationships based on weekly events, whereas a festival organization will want people to return in the following years.

Another key aspect of marketing is the exchange relationship between a provider and a purchaser, a seller and buyer, a marketer and a consumer. Within live music, this translates into the commercial relationship between a performer and their audience. All of this is readily understandable, but if one returns to basic definitions of marketing, it can quickly be seen that there are problems in applying it to music.

The American Marketing Association (AMA)'s definition of marketing is as follows: 'Marketing is the activity, set of institutions, and processes for creating, communicating, delivering, and exchanging offerings that have value for customers, clients, partners, and society at large' (AMA, 2007 [online]). There are a number of points worth teasing out in this definition. Firstly, the players or stakeholders it mentions include customers, clients, partners and society at large. This is very odd indeed, in so far as it completely fails to mention shareholders and executives as beneficiaries of the value which arises from market exchanges. Within the capitalist system – and certain parts of the music industries can be read as a very pure (or should that be impure?) form of capitalism – it is the owner of capital who is the key player, and marketing is usually seen as a highly important part of his/her behaviour. So, why this omission? Secondly, the AMA definition positions customers, clients, partners and society at large as people for whom something is done, and value is provided, as if marketing were an altruistic act, and profit were irrelevant. This is a significant – and perhaps ideologically convenient – elision of music commerce. The law of market investment says that capital will have its return, and marketing claims the intellectual authority for the best means of securing it. These points apply to music marketing as well as to other offerings. Thirdly, the AMA definition, with its emphasis on consumers as people for whom something is done, reduces them to being always only consumers and never also active participants. The danger in this formulation is that it ignores consumer agency. This is a fundamental issue. In the past, it has been taken for granted by marketers, and by many marketing scholars, that marketing is something done by marketers, and marketers only. This view privileges the agency of the seller. Yet a sales transaction requires a buying transaction. The two are mutually constitutive, two sides of the same coin. They have a financial effect on both parties to the deal. A market is made by the junction of offerors and purchasers. Therefore, arguably, marketing, in the sense of market-making, is better read as an activity or process carried out by both parties to a deal, one party behaving as a seller and the other as a buyer in that particular moment, each with their own set of associated practices. This view of marketing, which is, admittedly, not widely shared, has at least the merit of acknowledging the important role which the buyer or consumer plays. It seems very odd indeed that marketing, with its long-standing emphasis on the sovereignty of the consumer, client or customer, should not acknowledge in its primary institutional definition the co-agency of both the buyer and the seller.

Finally, an important strand of thinking in consumption studies – nowhere referenced in the AMA definition – is that consumers no longer consume products simply for their functional value, but also for their symbolic value, for what they mean to themselves and to others: 'Central to postmodern theories of consumption is the proposition that consumers no longer consume products for their material utilities but consume the symbolic meaning of those products as portrayed in their images; products in fact become commodity signs' (Elliott, 1997). There is a long-standing argument that consumers use brands as resources to construct identities (see Elliott and Wattanasuwan, 1998). This view sees social subjects as active agents who play a crucial role in creating their own identities through consumption. This idea of meaning-making consumer projects, in which identity is a key focus of attention, has particular relevance to the symbolic consumption of music (Larsen et al., 2010; Larsen, 2014). Music can be read as a multisensory experiential resource for the construction of identity. We can conceive of consumption as a process of meaning-making, and the notion of 'active' or 'creative' consumption recognizes that consumers are reflexive about their consumption activities, actively interpreting or judging, appropriating or resisting the texts offered for consumption. The meaning of the music is not only 'in' the music itself as coded, performed and decoded aurally, but in the consumers' acts of engagement with it, the accounts which they give of it and the cultural categories which they use to talk about it.

Another aspect of agency which is obscured by the conventions of financial management discourse is the question of who is the investor in the music business. In the case of an international organization like Live Nation (www.livenation.co.uk), the answer might seem straightforward, according to current conventions at least. Certain people invest in Live Nation as shareholders, and Live Nation invests in the promotion of live music. Audiences who attend concerts and festivals, however, are not usually seen as investors in the same way. The money from ticket and subscription sales is posted to the revenue account and seen as forming the stream of money which contributes to the return on investment. Yet from the point of view of a fan or audience member, arguably they are also investing in the artists who are playing live music. Their money is the same unit of account and is just as necessary to the economic sustainability of the musician as that of the marketer, as well as the person or company who is normally regarded as the investor – in this case the promoter or record label.

If the above AMA definition were applied directly and unreflexively to live music, it would read as follows: '[Live music] marketing is the activity, set of institutions, and processes for creating, communicating, delivering, and exchanging offerings that have value for customers, clients, partners, and society at large'. If this definition were adopted, there would be no acknowledgement here of, for example, the festival organizer, the impresario, or the chamber music promoter, or anyone else who might be involved in marketing of live music, even ... musicians.

This would clearly be a fatal weakness in the definition. Nor does it offer any role for music consumers in the making of live music markets. Live music consumers also help to construct the market by providing money through their ticket purchases or subscriptions. Audiences, through their engagement, participation and quality of attention, help to add or co-create value in the concert or festival experience.

We argue, therefore, for a view of live music marketing that remedies the flaws in the AMA definition of marketing by acknowledging the role of the marketer, the interest in profit, the agency of both producers and consumers and the meaning-making processes by which live music brands are made.

## What is Live Music?

Live music is a multisensory, immersive, aesthetic, musical and social experience. The theorization of the consumption of live arts performance, in particular, is very underdeveloped within marketing and consumption studies (Minor et al. 2004), although a considerable amount of work has of course been done on consumer experiences and experiential marketing (e.g. Holbrook and Hirschman, 1982; Kozinets, 2002). An interesting and helpful paper by Joy and Sherry (2003, p. 280) on multisensory embodied arts consumption experiences, is, the authors argue, 'a corrective to the producer's perspective of consumption that dominates the discourse of experience'. Live music is a unique form of musical experience spontaneously co-created by musicians and their audience. These experiences are produced through the interaction between musicians, audiences and the environment, and the experience itself cannot be separated from the music. The live music experience is ephemeral, and variable in terms of quality. Two concerts from the same artist can never be quite identical. Live music experiences are also perishable, once produced and consumed.

The words 'live music' can refer to a very wide range of experiences, for example, a long-standing music festival like Glastonbury or Bayreuth, a group of amateur musicians playing at a wedding, an organist playing at a funeral, an orchestra playing in a prestigious national venue, a rock band playing a gig on a worldwide tour, a brass band playing at a seaside resort, a choral concert, or a recital by a celebrated musician. It follows that those who are involved in putting on or promoting live music may include, for example, a local pub landlord, a student union entertainments officer, a large international organization like Live Nation, a successful festival organizer like Michael Eavis, the organizers of public concerts for municipal or national venues, a Broadway impresario, a rural ballroom operator, a rave organizer, radio DJs, tour managers, ticketing operations, music video directors, P.T. Barnum selling Jenny Lind (Waksman, 2011), musical artists themselves, record labels, artist managers, booking agents, and of course fans who spread word of mouth online and offline about forthcoming events. Live music brings together musicians and music consumers, and often many of the relevant stakeholders, into a physically and socially defined space such as a concert hall, field or stadium. Because of their scale and spectacle, important live music events are usually heavily mediated by different kinds of technology, whether audio-visual or digital. Even at small popular music gigs, it is very common to see people capturing video footage for use on band websites and social media. At larger venues, performer and audience interaction can be beamed live onto screens on or to the side of the stage, a practice akin to turbo-charging the co-created musical and visual spectacle.

The history of live music venues and public concerts is centuries long: the Teatro San Cassino opera house in Venice, opened in 1637, was one of the first venues to fully rely on the box office, rather than direct musical patronage (O'Reilly, Larsen and Kubacki, 2013, p. 203). Harbor (2013) shows how live music began to be organized professionally by musicians themselves when the systems of court and ecclesiastical patronage broke down in seventeenth-century London. Live music was promoted by advertisements placed in newspapers. The first public concert in London was given by violinist John Bannister in 1672. In fact, before Thomas Edison invented the gramophone in 1877, all music was live music. Throughout the twentieth century, the increasing importance of recorded music negatively affected opportunities for musicians to perform live (Frith, 2007). The more recent influence of the internet has resulted in a major shift in favour of live performance, largely for reasons of economics. For many musicians, live concerts have become the main source of income (Connolly and Krueger, 2006); and a broad range of ancillary products, such as t-shirts and programmes, can also be sold to fans at live performances, thereby generating additional revenue. Live music has acquired a cultural and economic significance that has rarely been seen since the beginning of the music industry, but there is still little research into the market for live music (Holt, 2010; Oakes, 2003). In a number of musical genres, particularly folk, jazz and rock, live music remains the test of quality and authenticity, as well as an important developmental experience for musicians. As Frith (2007) suggests, live performance can be seen by fans as something that enables them to witness the extraordinariness and uniqueness of musical talent and hard work.

Live music is also big business, part of the entertainment industry, or show business. The growth of Live Nation and AEG Live as key international players in the industry is a clear indication of the commercial importance of live music promotion. These companies' roles go beyond the traditional functions of booking agents or promoters, since they also act as intermediaries between artists and venues and organize live music events themselves. They have acquired different elements of the live music value chain, from venues, through organization and management of tours, ticket sales, merchandise, and sponsorship deals, to recordings (Holt, 2010). The live music business is also based around the degree of scarcity of the opportunity to see and hear specific musicians playing live.

## Live Music as a Product

Marketers need a product or offering to market to buyers. Marketing is fundamentally about the exchange relationship between buyer and seller. The notion of exchange is central to both markets and marketing (e.g. Bagozzi, 1975). For some musicians and fans, to call music a product can be problematic, and raises questions of commodification and selling out. However, O'Reilly, Larsen and Kubacki (2013) argue that there is a way in which music may be conceptualized as a product, and that this notion is closely connected to the question of value. When we talk about music as a product, therefore, we are talking about something market-driven and extrinsic. The value of 'music as a product' is based on its economic exchange value. For the holders of legal music ownership rights, the value lies in music's ability to generate a capital surplus. The scarcer the opportunity to hear a good artist, the more potential value it holds, and the more value that may be extracted from it. From a financial point of view, the live music marketer is seeking to extract financial value in the sense of profit (or break-even) from the live concert, tour or festival. This is relatively easy to calculate, as sales revenue minus costs.

From the music consumer's point of view, the value of music is better captured by Vargo and Lusch's (2004) notion of 'value in use', which is actualized at the moment of consumption and co-created through the interaction of all those involved in the process of bringing the music to market. 'Consumers' seek a range of different kinds of value from music ranging from aesthetic pleasure to self-symbolic representation (Larsen, Lawson and Todd, 2010). Music's value is thus many-sided; it is 'joy for the creator, use-value for the consumers, and exchange value for the seller' (Attali, 1985, p. 9). In the music industry, it is cultural intermediaries who 'shape both use values and exchange values, and seek to manage how these values are connected with people's lives through the various techniques of persuasion and marketing and through the construction of markets' (Negus, 2002, p. 504).

To the extent that it is a product, live music can be a more or less scarce commodity and enable its owners to charge higher or lower prices. (Concerts are of course not always priced for sale; some are free, to the audience such as those put on by municipal authorities during holiday periods.) The rarer the opportunity to see a celebrated performer, the more likely a promoter is to be able to charge a premium price. Nowadays, for major concert or festival events, there are online ticketing systems set up to facilitate ticket purchase and the management of demand for optimal profitability.

## Live Music and Consumption

Fans use their consumption of live music to symbolize something about themselves both to themselves and to others. They will sacrifice significant amounts of leisure time and money to consume performances, seeking deep, transformative experiences, sensory pleasures, and special moments of connection with artists and fellow fans. They form strong loyalties to musicians. Live music can be an important symbolic resource for the construction of their identities, images, experiences, and relationships. There are different ways of framing people's engagement with live music. These frames emphasise different aspects of engagement with live music. O'Reilly, Larsen and Kubacki (2013, p. 155) suggest that 'the "audience" frame highlights the social situatedness of consumption, embodied consumption and consumption rituals; "fans" draws attention to brand loyalty, brand communities and tribes, co-creative practices, and deviance; and finally, "collectors" links to connoisseurship, cultural capital, identity expression, symbolic consumption, product constellations and addiction'. Live music promoters need to understand all of these frames, as well as the fact that people move in and out of these frames as part of their overall music consumption. For example, live music promoters need to understand the multiple contexts within which fandom can be performed as they offer many marketing opportunities. Different types of interaction rituals occur between fans and musicians (Löbert, 2012), with artists as the focal point of the ritual. 'Primary interaction rituals' such as concerts are the core of live music consumption as this is where fans interact between themselves and the objects of their admiration. The types of interaction most treasured by fans are 'special rites', when fans are given direct access to musicians through 'meet and greet' packages or other special tickets giving backstage access to fans. Those packages can cost significantly more than standard concert tickets, yet they offer a unique opportunity for fans to catch a glimpse of the world that's not usually available to audiences. 'Secondary interaction rituals' are performed in the absence of musicians, for example when fans meet to discuss music and their favourite artists. Those rituals can be utilized by marketers through official fan clubs offering additional privileges to its members, such as early releases of tickets.

Live music is one of the most important forms of music consumption. Earl (2001) identified a long list of reasons behind the popularity of live music, including curiosity, the desire for a deeper knowledge of the music, the shared experience among members of the audience, the risk of things which may go wrong during the performance, the opportunity to sample artists' music without having to make a commitment to buying an album, or the chance to dance, shout or sing loudly. Fans or consumers are also put off from attending by the distance to travel, work commitments, cost, crowding at concerts, unruly behaviour of other fans, and the nature or quality of the venue itself. Minor et al. (2004) list a number of factors which affect musical performances, including the musical ability and creativity of the artists, sound quality, sound volume, level of temperature, seating facilities, audience enthusiasm, song familiarity, lighting, musician's movements, physical appearance and clothing, the way the stage is dressed, and ease of access. In fact, it is worth looking at the concert process in some detail to see how all of these things can come together.

## The Concert Process

A gig is a conventionally structured cultural ritual for both band and fans. Rather than being seen as a brief event which lasts for 2–3 hours, a concert, to take one instance of live music performance, should be seen as a social communication, an affective process which begins long before the event itself and continues for a considerable time afterwards. Musical events tend to follow a set pattern, and the live music marketer needs to be aware of this social and intensely communicative process.

To understand this point more clearly, consider a popular music live concert. On the audience side, rumours may begin to emerge on the promoter's or musician's website that a gig is to take place, be it a warm-up event for a tour, part of a tour schedule, a festival performance, or a one-off charity or other event. Not uncommonly, fans who frequent a particular venue will spot this news before it is confirmed on the performer's website. The performer will not post a performance date until it is satisfied all the arrangements are in place. The confirmation of particular venues and the exclusion of others are often the subject of expressions of joy or disappointment from fans on the website. For a confirmed event, there are expressions of excitement, enquiries as to which other fans are going and the pleasures of debating which pub or restaurant to meet at before the gig. This latter issue enables some fans to display their knowledge of the locality, the suitability or quality of the ambience of different local hostelries and the range of refreshments available. Fans travelling from far away make enquiries about lifts, accommodation and directions. There is quite often a ritual moan about credit card charges associated with ticket purchasing. Some fans who have the time and money will string together several dates in succession and travel together – 'following' the musicians. It is sometimes possible to purchase 'season tickets' for a particular tour. At the event itself, there are the security and ticketing barriers to pass. Inside, the bars are open and fans begin or continue drinking while waiting for the performance to begin. There will usually be a support act which comes on before the main band. While most of the audience members remain in the bar or back from the stage during the support acts' performances, these artists are carefully scrutinized, and not infrequently mentioned online. Fans have long memories for both good and bad support acts. While waiting for the main band, fans may be sitting against a wall, drinking in the bar, standing watching, chatting, taking pictures, buying merchandise or simply talking to the band associates at the merchandise stall.

On the band side, the preparations for performance are a paradoxical mixture of calm and frenetic intensity. Every member of the crew knows their role. If the band is on tour, it will arrive at a venue on the tour bus around late morning/ lunchtime. The band might still be asleep after the previous night's performance. The equipment and merchandise is taken off the bus and into the venue. The crew work with the venue staff to get everything set up – lighting, sound, instruments, and merchandise. Depending on the complexity of the set and the quality of the local venue's sound and lighting systems, this can be either a relatively straightforward experience or a fraught one. A sound check is run by the band until they and the engineer on the sound desk are happy that everything is working satisfactorily. The band will then eat a meal and begin the final preparations for the performance. Backstage, they will be aware of the audience noise from front of house, although this may not reach them in their dressing room as they begin the very last preparations, including dressing for the stage.

Once the support act has finished, the crew dismantle their equipment and run some final checks on the set-up and instruments. From front of stage, depending on the architecture of the venue, an observer might catch glimpses of the band's manager or band members in the wings. Immediately before the gig begins, a crew member signals to the sound desk, perhaps with a thumbs-up, or by clicking a cigarette lighter, often peering out into the darkness to see if this gesture has been spotted and acknowledged. There is a sense of growing excitement and anticipation from the audience, as perhaps some lead-in music is played. The audience space fills up and the crowd density increases considerably as those who have been drinking in the bar up to the last minute join the throng. The house and stage lights then come down and the band members file onto the stage in near-darkness, greeted with whistling, calls, and stamping of feet. As the band launches into the opening number, the lights come up.

During the concert, the band members are of course engaged with their musical performance. While the band will interact among themselves, the lead singer is usually the main channel for any communication with the audience, as their role involves fronting the band and introducing songs. Meanwhile the fans are engaging in a wide range of practices – watching, listening, tapping their feet, swaying their bodies, singing along, dancing, 'moshing', making pyramids, making circles, playing ring-o-roses, jumping, pogo-ing, bouncing, sitting on shoulders, surging, pushing, barging, shoving, standing around, drinking, talking to each other, listening, shouting, whistling, cheering, coughing, clapping, laughing, heckling, calling out song suggestions, wandering around drunk or stoned, posting on social media sites, or taking photographs or video on cameras or mobile phones. The setlist usually provides for two encores, each of two or three songs. Once the band leaves the stage before the first encore, and the crew check the equipment, the fans start stamping, clapping, whistling and usually do not give up until the band re-emerges on stage. The double-encore functions as a ritual departure, signalling that the performance will be ending and preparing the audience members for the close. Once the gig is over, the house lights come back on and some recorded music is played over the PA system. The crew begin immediately to dismantle the stage set for the 'out'. The band members are in the dressing room processing the performance and experiencing the resulting adrenalin come-down before heading for the bus. Fans begin to drift towards the bars, cloakroom or merchandise booth and past the security staff to the exits. In addition, at the merchandise booth, fans may have contact with members of the crew and other band associates. Some may try to intercept the band for a chat on the way to the tour bus. They will either find somewhere to eat or drink and then head for their accommodation, or travel home. The band will drive on to the next gig and the process will repeat itself until the tour is over. The website often contains the setlist, fan accounts, and photos of the gigs quite soon after. The point is that all of these aspects of the concert process have more than operational significance. They constitute the concert "product" in the wider sense, and also involve socio-symbolic practices.

**Live Music as Symbolic Practice**

All of the elements in the processes surrounding live music performances may be read as texts, in the sense of meanings set up by participants' construing of production and consumption practices and rituals and their associated signifiers. The repertoire or setlist, the movements, appearance, sounds and gestures of the performers and audience members, the technology, the spectacle, all come together in a multisensory experience which is the basis for meaning construction, and therefore for brands when read from a sociocultural perspective (O'Reilly and Kerrigan, 2013). Musicians and their intermediaries, including promoters, contribute through their branding practices to this potential meaning. But the interaction between musicians and their audiences can also be read as an important part of the branding process. By demonstrating their skill, musicians or singers earn a reputation as a 'great live band', and this may be said to contribute to the building of the performers' brand. Of course, when booking a performer, a promoter will have regard to the strength of the performer's brand, and their associated ability to attract 'bums on seats', but a live music marketer who ignores the richness of the ritual and its meanings or the pre- and post-concert social discourse around the live music performance is failing to do their job. Many of the aspects of the music concert ritual can be used to create distinctive experiences which can be monetized. The following framework (Figure 1 below), attempts to capture this conceptually.

At the top left of the diagram, the words 'Cultural Context' indicate that all live music should ideally be analysed in relation to the specific context(s), scene(s) and business environment(s) in which it occurs. An orchestra or band conducting an international tour will bring a similar kind of repertoire into a range of differing contexts, so that it becomes necessary to analyse how the concert or gig plays in particular international venues. The four ellipses on the left-hand side of the diagram are elements adapted from du Gay et al.'s circuit of culture (1997). They indicate that meanings are produced, consumed, articulated and regulated in a 'circuit', which in the case of live music is the gig or concert and attendant ritual and marketing communications processes. The concert programme, the setlist, is encoded into musical, aural and visual texts which are simultaneously consumed by the audience members. These texts draw upon sounds, images and words which are in cultural circulation to express something about what they refer to, their referents. The composer or songwriter selects and arranges these symbols

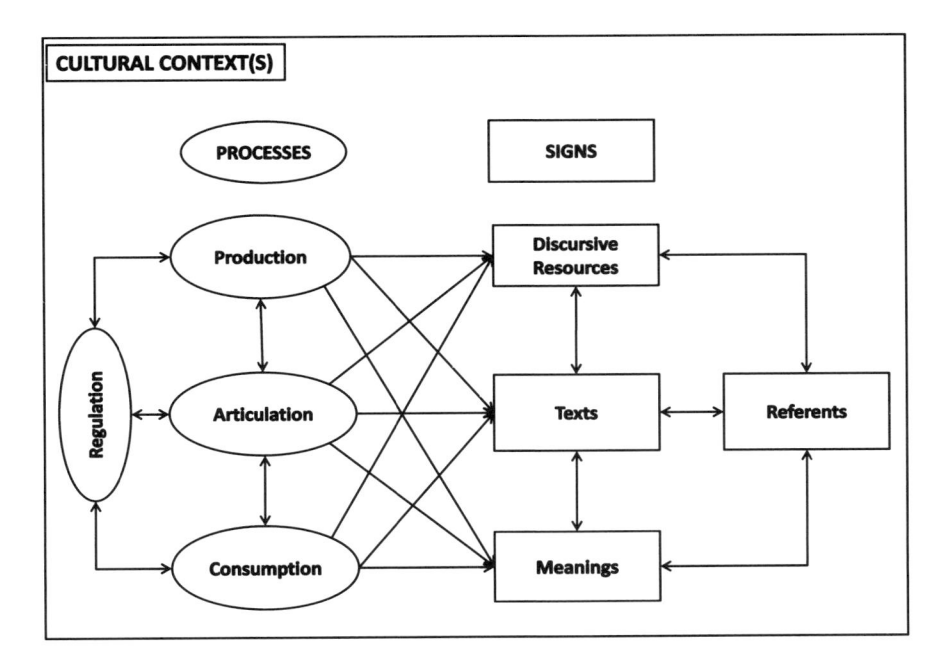

Figure 2.1  Music Brands Framework (Adapted from O'Reilly, 2011)

within the programme, placing them in a certain sequence or other relation to one another. The singing, shouting, whistling, dancing, moshing, coughing, clapping and gesturing of the audience members all signify something to those present.

## Live Music Promotion

In the live music business the word most commonly used in relation to the marketing of live music has tended to be 'promotion'. However, within commercial marketing, this is a word used for only one part of marketing activities, and is now more commonly known as 'marketing communications', or 'marcomms'. Other music marketing activities might include strategic actions such as audience development, relationship marketing, cultural strategy as well as the so-called marketing mix elements, such as the product (repertoire) in a narrow sense, price, place (route to market), promotion, people, process, and physical space.

All kinds of live music need suitable music promotion. Promotion involves a wide range of communication activities. For example, major popular music brands rely on the quality of their professional marketing communications to retain customers and refresh their brands. Symphony orchestras, opera companies and jazz ensembles, on the other hand, use niche targeting to sustain the loyalty of their relatively smaller numbers of fans. Marketing communications are designed to build brands, and to recruit and retain customers. They are used to inform live music consumers about upcoming events and to persuade them to try new musical experiences, or recall previous experiences. The most commonly used marketing communication tools to promote live music include direct marketing and public relations. Direct marketing involves two-way communication between marketers and consumers, where direct contact is established through media such as the internet. Many large and established venues have databases, including contact details of customers who previously visited the venue and can be targeted with information about future concerts and other events. Venues rely on those databases to communicate with potential customers about events that might be of interest to them. As long as the database is reliable and contains sufficient amount of information about customers (for example, contact details as well as their preferences and purchase history), it can be a very effective and efficient tool to attract audiences and segment them into smaller target audiences specific to each offered live music product. Often musicians themselves have their own databases containing contact details of their fans and followers, for example through their subscription-based websites and fan clubs. They can also be used to promote live music events and facilitate ticket sales. Social networking websites such as Facebook are now widely used to the same effect, with many local artists promoting their live performances through their social networks online. Equally, it is not uncommon for artists to include references to their Facebook and Twitter identities as they speak to the audience during their performance.

Public relations (PR) is another marketing communication tool often used to promote live music. PR focuses on activities which help to develop and maintain good relationships between musicians, venues and audiences, as well as all other stakeholders of the live music industry. Its popularity is fuelled by having lower costs (which makes it often much cheaper than paid advertising), as well as significant aptitude for creating drama and entertainment, capturing the attention and interest of audiences. The most popular PR tools include press releases (e.g. when a band announces its forthcoming tour), product publicity (e.g. concert reviews), publications (e.g. fanzines), press conferences, media interviews, twitter feeds, special appearances and other public events - as well as instances of bad behaviour. In the end, the choice of the most suitable communication tools and channels depends on music genre, musicians' personalities, venue and audience preferences.

**Conclusion**

As a key 'player' in the marketing of live music, the music promoter fuses the commercial, symbolic and experiential elements of the music business together in ways that are potentially highly rewarding and meaningful for all those involved. We construct the promoter as a marketer who is always situated in a specific cultural context, defined by social, cultural, musical, political, regulatory and commercial circumstances. Good promoters are sensitive to all of these circumstances and to the ways in which they change. As marketers, they need to make markets; as lovers of music, they are keen to play a role in disseminating music to audiences. There are different kinds of promoters, from local to international, from one-person local businesses to international corporations.

Following and adapting Kubacki and O'Reilly (2009), we argue that a live music marketer needs to be a 'situationist', in the sense that s/he take account of a very wide range of factors when formulating the music marketing strategy. These include the roles of the promoter in the relevant musical value chain; the artistic conventions and ideologies which apply there; their audience reach; the musical programming and its 'fit' with the venue; the kind of business model which is viable in their area of work; the influence of government policy, technological developments, the media, social and cultural trends, the economy and so on. Of particular importance to their survival as promoters are their connections in the music business, and their abilities to understand their music consumers and to programme musical performances, create or sustain demand, communicate with audiences, facilitate the experience itself, and manage their business in a sustainable way. However, equally important to the formation of live music markets are music consumers and their practices. A promoter's live music marketing strategy needs to go hand in glove with a cultural-musical strategy which is contextually appropriate yet at the same time distinctive.

In an effort to capture the broader dimensions of live music, therefore, we end by offering the following definition: 'Live music marketing is the set of historically situated social, political, economic, commercial, cultural, technological and musical production, performance, intermediation and consumption practices and discourses which create musical and other value in the live music exchange relationship'.

## Chapter 3
# Musical, Social and Moral Dilemmas: Investigating Audience Motivations to Attend Concerts

Stephanie Pitts[1]

**Who Goes to Concerts – and Why?**

In *Musicking* (1998), the exploration of classical concert life that was one of the inspirations for this book, the ethnomusicologist Christopher Small describes the scene in the foyer of a concert hall, a few moments before a symphony orchestra concert is about to begin:

> Even if we have come alone and know nobody, we can still feel a part of the event as we buy a cup of coffee or an alcoholic drink and look around us as we sip. Amongst those present we might recognize celebrities – a famous violinist, the music critic of a quality newspaper, even perhaps an eminent politician. The latter may be taking cocktails with a group of expensively dressed men and women whom we can assume to be executives, and their wives, of the corporation that is sponsoring tonight's concert. [...] All appear casually at home in this place. We remember our manners and do not stare. (Small, 1998, p. 24)

Now it is entirely possible that the late Christopher Small habitually attended concerts in a different social league to the ones that I go to; or equally possible that times have changed since cocktails were drunk before concerts and executives were assumed to be male and married. Certainly the surface description of this pre-concert scene seems thankfully unfamiliar in the week by week concert life of most regional orchestras and chamber groups. Yet within this scene are some lasting insights on the experience of concert-going that transcend boundaries of musical genre: that even individuals who attend alone do so in relation to the larger social group, that conversation and refreshment are an important part of the

---

[1] The research reported in this chapter was funded by two small grants from the British Academy, a Knowledge Transfer grant from the University of Sheffield, and a Business Link award from Yorkshire Forward. I am grateful to the research assistants and participants in each project, and to the collaborating organisations, for their involvement and interest in the research.

social interactions surrounding live music listening, and that feeling at home in the performance venue contributes to the pleasure of concert attendance, while risking excluding those who stand at the edges of the event. These elements of live music listening apply equally (though in different forms) in the jazz club, the opera house and the pop arena, and are part of the expectations of arts events that shape potential audience members' motivations to attend, and cause them to maintain or withdraw their attendance when other commitments come into competition with their live arts preferences.

An updated attempt at Small's foyer scene might include a hurried office worker eating a sandwich from the concert hall canteen, having come to the concert straight from work; a group of students clutching heavily discounted tickets, who have been persuaded that attendance will help with their musical studies; a retired couple reading their programme and waiting to secure their favourite seats when the doors of the hall are opened; and any number of other keen recorded music listeners, devotees of the composer or the group on the programme tonight, habitual attenders who like to support their local arts organization, or curious first-timers who would feel more readily at home in the cinema or theatre. Their motivations for attending will overlap to an extent, influenced by their previous attendance and musical engagement, the social choices they have made in inviting friends or coming alone, and the level of value they are able or willing to give live music in relation to other financial and practical aspects of daily life. Yet each will have made a distinctive, individual decision to attend, fitting a concert into their everyday consumption of music and other arts, and relating their experience to other social and musical dimensions of their lives.

Less observable, though equally important to an understanding of the contemporary concert hall, are the people who are not here – perhaps put off by an expectation of feeling out of place among the 'expensively dressed [...] executives' (Small, 1998, p. 24) that they, like Small, assume will form the majority of the audience. Research on audience demographics has raised concerns that classical music audiences are generally ageing, predominantly white, middle class, and in the more educated and affluent sectors of the general population (Kolb, 2001). Furthermore, this audience appears to be declining, with each generation participating less as they reach the equivalent age, resulting in a loss of 3.3 million American concert-goers between 2002 and 2008 (League of American Orchestras, 2009, p. 11), and similar patterns in Australia and Britain of a low proportion of potential audience members actively engaging in the arts (Australia Council for the Arts, 2010; Martin, Bunting and Oskala, 2010).

These data on declining audiences have prompted 'audience segmentation' studies, in which the attitudes and arts engagement of a population are categorized into groups towards which arts organizations can direct their marketing efforts (Clopton, Stoddard and Dave, 2006). The Arts Council England's (2011) groupings include the highly engaged 'traditional culture vultures' (4%) and 'urban arts eclectic' (3%), through those who may attend 'dinner and a show' (20%) or are 'mature explorers' (11%), to the 'time-poor dreamers' (4%) and 'older and home-bound' (11%) who may be interested in the arts but limited in their opportunities for participation. The Australia Council for the Arts (2010) labels its categories rather more directly: 'the lovers' (38%) who are highly engaged, 'the flirters' (26%) whose attendance is influenced by friends, 'the un-attached' (19%) who have limited recent or past experience of participation, and 'the outsiders' (17%) who believe that the arts are pretentious, elitist and 'not for them'.

While the English set of labels prioritize behaviour and the Australian ones focus on attitude, both approaches attempt to correlate the relationship between these two aspects of arts engagement – an interest in the art form, and an inclination to actively engage with it. It could be argued that audience motivation rests at the crossover between interest and inclination, capitalizing on people's curiosity, past experience and attitudes to the arts, and overcoming the practical, social and financial barriers to converting interest into attendance.

## Turning Up and Fitting In: Empirical Evidence from Jazz and Classical Music Audiences

The remainder of this chapter will draw upon empirical evidence from audiences in a range of contexts, including new and long-standing attenders at a chamber music festival (Pitts and Spencer, 2008; Dobson and Pitts, 2011), jazz listeners at a festival and in a local jazz club (Burland and Pitts, 2010; 2012), and audience members at an orchestral concert series (Pitts, Dobson, Gee and Spencer, 2013). Each of these case studies has been presented in detail elsewhere, but this is my first opportunity to compare the decision making and range of motivations that are to be found across the various audiences in their different musical contexts. The methods, settings and co-researchers for each project are outlined in Table 3.1:

Table 3.1    Audience studies 2003–2010

| |
|---|
| **2003 Music in the Round (MitR): Audience experience of a chamber music festival**<br>Audience questionnaires distributed throughout the week-long festival (347 responses)<br>Semi-structured interviews with a sample of questionnaire respondents (19 interviews)<br>Diaries completed by 13 members of the audience during the festival |
| **2006 MitR: Audience loyalty in a time of transition (with Chris Spencer)**<br>Audience questionnaires distributed through the Friends of MitR mailing list (78 responses)<br>Semi-structured interviews with a sample of respondents (16 interviews) |
| **2007 Edinburgh Jazz and Blues Festival: Audience experience in a range of venues (with Karen Burland)**<br>Audience questionnaires distributed at a range of gigs and venues (701 responses)<br>Semi-structured telephone interviews with a sample of questionnaire respondents (36 interviews) |

| |
|---|
| **2009 Spin Jazz, Oxford: Audience experience at a jazz club (with Karen Burland)**<br>Online questionnaire advertised through flyers at gigs and on the club's website (91 responses)<br>Semi-structured telephone interviews carried out with a representative sample of those who provided contact details at the end of the questionnaire (15 interviews)<br>Online diaries completed by six respondents, fortnightly for two months |
| **2009 MitR New audiences for classical music: Recruiting listeners aged 21–30 (with Melissa Dobson)**<br>Focus group study, involving six first-time attenders going to two concerts, and participating in group and individual interviews |
| **2010 City of Birmingham Symphony Orchestra (CBSO): Investigating performer and audience loyalty in the symphony hall (with Melissa Dobson, Kate Gee and Chris Spencer)**<br>Online audience questionnaire distributed via mailing lists and through flyers given out at concerts (174 responses)<br>Semi-structured interviews with a sample of audience respondents (20 interviews)<br>Semi-structured interviews with CBSO players (6 interviews) |

This sequence of audience studies evolved to explore differences, initially between audience members and participating amateur musicians (Pitts, 2005a), then between audiences of different musical genres – chamber music, jazz, and orchestral – and in the different settings of an intimate 'in the round' concert venue, large formal halls and above-the-pub jazz clubs. While differences were certainly evident, in the prominence of socializing around the music, for example, or the emphasis placed on performers or repertoire in selecting which concerts to attend, the similarities across the audiences were also striking. Every audience included frequent attenders who were committed specifically to that organization or venue, as well as those with a broader profile of live arts consumption, supported by extensive recorded music listening. Among regular listeners in each context were those who attended more selectively, prioritizing repertoire or performers that they knew or, less often, seeking out rarely heard pieces to supplement their already extensive live listening experience. While audience members often viewed their own experience as distinctive, making reference to their level of knowledge or past attendance habits, they were also reassured to be among like-minded people, expectant of friendly conversation in the interval and being made welcome by venue staff and fellow listeners.

In the questionnaires that I have distributed to audience members over the past ten years, there has often been a slightly cheeky question which asks first 'How would you describe a typical audience member?', with prompts for age, gender, likely occupation and musical interests, and follows this up by asking 'How closely do you fit this pattern?'. While a few respondents have quite reasonably refused to stereotype their fellow audience members, many more have engaged in a moment of self-realization that runs something like this:

> *Age/gender:* 'Mixed but with perhaps quite a lot of "mature" people'
> *Musical interests:* 'People who like to hear good music played superbly'

*Likely occupation:* 'I've no idea but I suspect many are of retirement age'
*Other characteristics:* 'Polite and well behaved'
*Own fit:* 'I have probably described myself'
(CBSO audience member, November 2010)

This response shows respect for fellow listeners, noting their serious attention to 'good music played superbly', while expressing implicit regret at the ageing profile. Being among like-minded people, assumed to share the same values, is an important part of audience experience (Pitts, 2005b) and here provides clues also to audience motivation for attendance. As some other respondents reported from their own experience, the ageing audience is in part a product of the difficulty of getting to concerts straight from work, or fitting attendance around family commitments: while retired audience members are more likely to book a season ticket and prioritize regular attendance, arts organizations are struggling with the increasing tendency of younger age groups to socialize spontaneously, making last minute decisions to go out for the evening only when all other pressures on their time have been accommodated (Kotler and Scheff, 1997, p. 9). The uncomplicated classification of CBSO's repertoire as 'good' music is perhaps also a feature of the educational and social background of an older, professional group, whose respect for and familiarity with the classical canon is more established and open to both reinforcement and extension through concert attendance. Likewise, the tendency to be 'well behaved' suggests an experienced audience, aware of the conventions of concert listening and the effects of their own quiet attention on the listeners around them.

Another respondent reflected on these factors in greater detail:

*Age/gender:* 'There is a range of ages from children to very elderly people. I would say that the 60+ age category is represented more than in the population generally'

*Musical interests:* 'It is clear that many audience members attend regularly and are serious listeners. Some of these doubtless have a high degree of musical knowledge, and from overhearing conversations some are accomplished amateur musicians. A second important group are those who attend infrequently, possibly for the first time, but who have a genuine desire to learn about, or simply listen to, some classical music. A third group are those who attend, not always enthusiastically, with a partner or family member'

*Likely occupation:* 'A significant proportion of the audience are clearly retired. Of those still working I would guess that many are professional or managerial but that may be prejudice. A former concert-going acquaintance of mine was an amateur violinist and earned a living as an HGV driver'

*Other characteristics:* 'Audience members generally are more to the formal and considerate end of the behaviour spectrum'

*Own fit:* 'I am in my early fifties, male, attend concerts alone, and have actively listened to classical music since childhood. I have no formal musical education, and I have developed myself as a listener through radio (mainly BBC Radio 3) and commercial recordings, and some reading. Starting with "mainstream" composers I progressively widened my interests and I have listened to a fair deal of contemporary music, and less well known composers of all eras. Recently I have taken a keen interest in opera, encouraged by the increasing availability of high quality commercial video recordings. My interests are not restricted to "classical" music but that is the majority of my listening and exclusively what I attend concerts for. I enjoy popular (but not "pop") music particularly from the middle part of the 20th century, and I am also very fond of listening to blues when it is done well, and in the right setting' (CBSO audience member, November 2010).

This respondent is keen to illustrate the individuality of concert-going experiences, presenting his own listening preferences as resistant to classification, and offering a reminder that among the highly motivated audience members will be their sometimes reluctant or recently-converted companions (Upright, 2004). In his description of his 'own fit' to the audience, he shows the serendipitous, exploratory nature of musical engagement, as one genre of music leads him into another, and increasingly available recordings supplement his live arts attendance. Quality is paramount, both in recordings and in live music 'done well and in the right setting': this is a discerning, relatively open-minded audience member, making informed selections from the programme offered by CBSO and interweaving other arts consumption among his live concert attendance.

This audience member is unusual in mentioning watching recorded music, arguably an accessible middle ground between attending live arts events and hearing them on recordings, but one not often referred to by other respondents. Although Michael Chanan (2002, p. 373) describes how television could provide viewers not only with broadcast music but also with 'insight into the everyday world of the musician', glimpses of which are highly valued by many audience members in their live attendance, empirical evidence is so far lacking on the extent to which concert-goers make use of such resources, whether on recorded or downloadable visual media. None of the audience respondents made reference to digital streaming, a recent phenomenon that redefines notions of 'liveness' by simultaneously broadcasting a performance from, say, an opera house to a cinema, so linking two audiences in different places to the same performance at the same time. Martin Barker's (2013) research on these hybrid arts events reports low ticket sales and mixed reactions from audience members, but demonstrates the cinema-based audience's critical awareness of the creative layers of the opera and its presentation, through their comments on everything from the camera angles to the emotional connections between characters. Free from the distractions of the opera-house audience, yet with 'a new sense of communality of experience' (p. 29), those in the cinema are able to feel closer to the stage yet more relaxed among the familiar surroundings of a film-going audience. Perhaps more significantly, the new mode of presentation throws open to question the conventions of live music listening, disrupting the behavioural patterns of Christopher Small's (1998) imagined concert hall, and prompting audience members to question why they are there – and not somewhere else – and how their interaction with the live event is meaningful to them and to those around them. This critical distance, while risking alienating an audience who become too much aware of their dissatisfaction with the event, could be a valuable tool in engaging audiences and communicating their perspectives to arts organizations – an idea also demonstrated through post-concert conversations with artists (see Dobson and Sloboda, this volume) and focus-group discussions with researchers (Dobson and Pitts, 2011).

Across the 197 CBSO audience members who answered the survey question described above, the majority reported a close (46%) or partial fit (35%) with their description of a typical audience member, while (11%) felt different from the collective norm, usually through being younger or less musically experienced, and (8%) said they did not know or declined to answer. This demonstrates that, despite occasional reluctance to acknowledge the homogeneity of the group – 'I hate to think of myself as a typical anything' – audience members generally found themselves to be surrounded by people like them or (since these were speculative rather than evidenced observations) were making the assumption that others in the hall shared their motivations, musical experience and enthusiasm for the event. A few went further in acknowledging that these assumed similarities presented their own risks for drawing new audiences into classical music: while some newcomers will quickly feel 'at home' in a group that seems familiar to them, those who are in a minority – whether through ethnicity, age, social background or assumed musical experience – might feel more conspicuous and therefore less engaged. While audience segmentation research goes some way to identifying the preoccupations and priorities of different arts attenders, the complexity of individual experience illustrated here shows that there is more work to be done on understanding and engaging audience members once they have made the first step in attending a live music event.

**Self and Others in Audience Motivation**

As Jennifer Radbourne and her co-authors reflect later in this book (see also Radbourne et al., 2009), understanding of audience motivation through market research has historically focused on the practicalities of attending: how much are people prepared to pay for tickets, how easy do they find it to park near the venue, how satisfied are they with the interval refreshments? These factors are undoubtedly important barriers or incentives to participation, particularly for first-time or infrequent attenders, or those with otherwise low investment in the event who want to minimize the financial risk or potential disappointment of their night out (Harland and Kinder, 1999). However, qualitative research with audiences on their expectations and experiences of concert-going soon reveals a more complex picture, where the practicalities of attendance are weighed up against the musical, social and personal rewards of audience membership (Pitts and Spencer, 2008). Despite these rewards, audience members might still be annoyed by the coughing of their neighbours in a symphony hall (O'Sullivan, 2009), or by jazz listeners who talk or get up to buy a drink at the wrong time (Burland and Pitts, 2012) – their irritation in itself being a manifestation of their commitment to the event, and their consequent frustration with others who seem not to abide by the unwritten, genre-specific rules of live listening. Being an audience member is an emotional risk, as well as a financial one: a performance may be disappointing in relation to a well-loved recording, the acoustics of the hall may be poor, and the seats may be uncomfortable or the view blocked by a tall or wriggling fellow listener. Given that these risks can all be averted by listening instead to a critically acclaimed recording, the appeal of live listening must provide additional benefits that are sought out by audiences across a range of venues and genres.

In studies with jazz audiences, Karen Burland and I found that one clear benefit attributed to live listening was the visual immediacy of seeing performers interacting, with the exchange of gestures and movements helping to draw listeners' attention to the structure of the music, and the close proximity of players and listeners giving a sense of shared participation in a musical event (Pitts and Burland, 2013; Burland and Pitts, 2010, 2012). For improvised jazz, where listeners are being exposed to new musical material, the acknowledgement of a solo or indication of a return to the 'head' helps to provide a sense of cohesion, bringing the audience together within the music, in the same way as a pop chorus or the return of a theme in a classical symphony. Experienced listeners have their knowledge affirmed through this moment of recognition, while those whose attention has wandered are drawn back on track; through the visual clues of performer gesture the temporal uncertainty – 'how long is a piece of music?' – of live performance is reduced, and the performers acknowledge (intentionally or otherwise) the listeners' place in the live event.

Seeing performers was also important to City of Birmingham Symphony Orchestra (CBSO) and Music in the Round (MitR) listeners in creating a sense of musicians' engagement in the event: audience members at these classical events looked for evidence that players were enjoying the performance and appreciating one another's playing, citing instances of smiles between players, apparent warmth towards the conductor, and lively, exuberant playing (Pitts et al., 2013). Attending frequently and becoming familiar with the performers was also helpful, particularly in the 'in the round' Studio Theatre venue of MitR, where audience members reported looking over the shoulders of players at the music on the stand and experiencing a 'feeling of togetherness with the performers' (Pitts, 2005a, p. 104). Introductory talks by players and conductors also created a sense of connection, giving insight into their experiences of the music and offering audience members a chance to assess their personalities and humour, and so generate an assumed familiarity, often likened to friendship or family ethos by frequent attenders. Many arts organizations capitalize on this desire for personal connections with performers through their marketing strategies and publicity: at the time of our research with CBSO, the programmes for concerts included profiles of individual players, which were welcomed by some audience members as helping them 'get to know' the players, while others were more dismissive, feeling that the music should be paramount and such personal trivia left aside. This comparatively new aspect of live classical music is yet another factor to interact with audience members' diverse personalities, preferences and prior musical experience – as well as bringing new demands for performers, some of whom have reported the pressure to talk to audiences to be a distraction from their main task of making music (Tomes, 2012). While seeing performers in live performance certainly distinguishes the experience from recorded music listening, it seems that it brings with it a new set of challenges for concert promoters, performers and audience members to negotiate.

Another distinctive aspect of live music listening is the opportunity to interact with other audience members, though here the research evidence suggests a greater ambivalence in whether the benefits of conversation with like-minded people (Pitts, 2005b) outweigh the frustrations of distracting behaviour from others in the auditorium (O'Sullivan, 2009). While listening in silent appreciation is a relatively recent concert hall convention (Gunn, 1997), there is now a strong implicit expectation that audience members will give their full attention to the music – a demand that can be intimidating for first-time attenders (Dobson and Pitts, 2011), and some way from the truth of how listeners' minds are occupied during a long or unfamiliar piece of music. Eric Clarke (2005) describes how audience listening can encompass shifts in focus from noting the furniture, fashions and surroundings of the concert hall, to being 'aware of nothing at all beyond a visceral engagement with musical events of absorbing immediacy and compulsion' (p. 188): the rhetoric of classical music listening affords cultural prestige to the latter state of mind, and yet this 'is nonetheless just one among many ways of listening' (p. 188).

The challenge for each listener sitting among hundreds (or dozens) of others in the concert hall is to accommodate the listening behaviours of others, both in the minimal interactions of the music's duration, and in the conversation that might be expected in the interval or the queue to leave the hall at the end. One listener in the Music in the Round audience provided a vivid instance of when such conversation might be an intrusion, writing in his diary of a fellow listener 'who apologized for not speaking to me after last night's performance. Said she was so choked up she could not speak. I agreed I didn't want to talk to anyone either' (Pitts, 2005a, p. 100). Here conversation risked disrupting an intense musical experience; at other times it might expose an episode of distracted listening, as for the first-time attenders who described getting 'annoyed with myself, because […] every time I properly listened to [the music] it was really good, but my mind just kept going off anyway' (Dobson and Pitts, 2011, p. 365). New listeners also struggled to find a vocabulary for talking about music, so limiting their potential for integration with more experienced listeners and illustrating Christopher Small's assertion that 'the interval is not a break in the event at all but an essential part of it, providing opportunity for social intercourse with members of one's own reference group, to crystallize one's response to the event by discussion (intervals seem interminable to those with no one to talk to)' (Small, 1987, p. 12). Interaction with other audience members is therefore an essential part of live listening, but by no means a straightforward one, or one that is universally helpful to audience members.

## Keeping Music (A)Live – Musical and Moral Responsibilities

While personal, social and musical motivations were uppermost in audience members' reports of their concert-going choices, another strong theme emerged, particularly among older, experienced listeners – that of the moral or cultural responsibility to attend live arts and so contribute to sustaining their existence. This notion of patronage has a long history in classical music, perhaps highlighting one of the clearest distinctions between pop 'fans' and classical 'aficionados' (Jenson, 1992): the former are broadly driven by the pursuit of individual and group preferences for pleasure and allegiance, while the latter might also articulate a sense of social worthiness or cultural good, largely absent from discourse on popular music. When the Music in the Round audience was faced a few years ago with the retirement of their resident string quartet and the appointment of a new, younger ensemble, some audience members confessed to feeling freed of their responsibilities to the organization, while others expressed a loyalty to the newly arrived players, concerned that 'if [we] don't support them, they will go elsewhere and we will lose the whole thing' (Pitts and Spencer, 2008, p. 234). Audience members, in this case and others, are conscious of providing not just financial support through their ticket purchases, but emotional and cultural support, through their endorsement of the event and their enthusiastic applause.

Audience loyalty is actively fostered by many arts organizations through their 'Friends' schemes, which usually include some element of priority booking, as well as increased access to 'behind the scenes' information through newsletters or opportunities to meet the performers. Typically, the financial incentive to join the scheme will not be its strongest feature, and membership will be promoted as a way of helping the organization and feeling more connected with it – gaining information and engagement rather than substantial discounts on tickets. At CBSO, we found that even people who found the 'Friends' social events rather cliquey or inconveniently-timed, would renew their membership in order to support the education programme or the high standards of the orchestra (Pitts et al., 2013). In this respect, Friends' membership is closer to charitable giving than to canny purchasing, with arts organizations imitating charities in their use of narrative and inclusion to encourage feelings of belonging and continued support (Merchant et al., 2010). For others in the CBSO audience who did enjoy the opportunities to socialize with like-minded Friends and gain additional insight on the performers' lives and experiences, membership enhanced the sense of contributing to the musical event, creating an audience community which existed between events. By fostering memories and connections beyond the transitory sharing of an evening's musical experience, the cycle of engagement continues, and audience membership becomes more embedded in people's lives and musical identities.

In recent years, some writers have expressed concern that live classical music is in decline, and risks becoming a cultural irrelevance that will lapse as older audience members die out, and younger listeners become increasingly sophisticated consumers of recorded music (Johnson, 2002). Other genres, notably folk music and jazz, have gone through similar cycles of ageing consumption in the past (MacKinnon, 1993; Hodgkins, 2009), and subsequently regained a following, though often taking a different form for a new generation of listeners. Niall MacKinnon's survey of folk club audiences in the early 1990s, for example, found that while the 'folk revival' of the 1960s had attracted a following of new, young listeners, this had resulted in an 'age bulge' in folk club membership, as the 1960s cohort were not followed by a second wave of similarly interested younger listeners (MacKinnon, 1993, p. 43). While MacKinnon made gloomy predictions for the future of the folk scene as a result, later commentators have profiled a new resurgence, in this case featuring higher profile performances outside traditional folk club settings, as a new generation of performers headline at festivals, make occasional television appearances and gain nominations for awards more usually associated with popular music (Keegan-Phipps, 2009). Adapting the focus and appeal of a genre risks alienating a core audience, but the buoyant state of folk music is illustrative of the ways in which established practices can co-exist with new manifestations – and that audiences will emerge or diverge to accommodate arts events that seem most connected with their own lives and preferences.

Western classical music remains firmly embedded in contemporary society, not least through its use in films, advertising and public events, but the act of attending concerts and sitting quietly as a live performance unfolds is an increasingly incongruous activity in our data-rich, fast-paced world. For some audience members, this is precisely its appeal; for others – and for the many potential listeners not currently engaged with live arts – the gap between 'everyday life' and concert-going becomes ever wider. The anxiety around this change is not confined to classical music; jazz performers and promoters have also reported concerns about the need to appeal to the widest potential audience, and the consequent 'safety' in programming that can result from this need to create a reliable experience for occasional or unadventurous listeners (Kubacki and Croft, 2005). This discussion is mainly financially driven, as arts organizations struggle with reduced funding as well as the multiple pressures on their audiences' time and resources: the introduction of interactive websites, mobile apps, and informal concert formats might be presented as being about the quality of audience experience, but are often just as much about the survival of the regional theatre company or concert series – a threat which in itself can generate audience loyalty and a commitment to supporting a particular art form. Beyond the pragmatic level, such arguments can also take on a moral tone, expressing concern about the future of a genre and its live performance, with classical music, particularly, viewed as facing a 'legitimation crisis' in contemporary society (Johnson, 2002, p. 3). Empirical research with audiences has a role to play in understanding the extent to which musical, moral and social values are intertwined in audience motivations to invest their time, money and attention in the arts – and more challengingly, how these values appear from the 'outside', to those who do not regularly experience live music.

## Conclusions and Future Challenges

This chapter has shown how the motivations of audience members occupy a continuum from the mundane and practical (ticket price, access, availability), through questions of musical choice (repertoire, familiarity, preference) and social listening habits (attending alone, joining the Friends scheme), through to a broader philosophical and moral sense of responsibility (loyalty to a venue/event, concern for the future of live arts). Broadly speaking, increasing experience of concert-going appears to move listeners further along this continuum, as their investment in the musical aspects of the event and their enjoyment of the social elements of attendance gradually outweigh the practical concerns that might present a more substantial barrier to first-time or infrequent attenders. This deepening relationship is a fragile one, however, which may result in an attachment to a specific group or venue, rather than openness to wider arts consumption, and can be withdrawn if satisfaction with the experience declines, perhaps as a result of changes made by the arts organization. For arts promoters, the balance between retaining their existing audience members and drawing in new ones is a constant challenge: understanding the motivations of regular listeners can contribute to the sensitive development of these strategies, but there is a clear need for further research with lapsed and infrequent attenders, who will have the clearest perspective on how arts attendance can lose its appeal or cease to be a priority.

Empirical research with audiences faces a further challenge in pursuing questions which are intellectually interesting, as well as those that are useful to arts organizations seeking to develop their practice. The two aims are by no means incompatible, but with the latter having a more obvious social benefit, and research in this area depending on the co-operation of arts organizations themselves, it can be easy to be drawn into the realm of market research, albeit with added qualitative depth. Taking audience motivation as an example, while the surface-level findings on inclination to attend, satisfaction with the concert experience, and attitudes to Friends' schemes are both intellectually and practically valuable, of greater academic interest is the way in which live concert-going occupies a place in contemporary society, how it relates to recorded music listening, how it is viewed as a culturally responsible activity, and how audience members develop a vocabulary for talking about their experiences. While sociology of music has a strong tradition of theorizing about concert life (with Adorno, Weber and Hennion prominent in that tradition), attempts to match these theoretical positions with the growing body of empirical evidence from psychology of music are as yet relatively undeveloped.

With these two challenges in mind – research at the fringes of audiences, and the need for intellectual rigour in drawing together empirical evidence – I would assert that audience research is well-placed to investigate some of the central intellectual puzzles in musicology and cultural studies: namely the place of music in contemporary society, and the intellectual and emotional reception of musical works in a live listening context. The growth of research endeavours in this area – many of them represented in this book – suggest that the time is right for these enquiries to be robustly undertaken from multiple, inter-disciplinary perspectives, for the benefit of listeners, performers and researchers in a wide range of musical settings.

Chapter 4
# Safe and Sound: Audience Experience in New Venues for Popular Music Performance

Robert Kronenburg[1]

> I've always disliked this venue [the Royal Dublin Society venue at Simmonscourt] opened in 1975. It might do for a tractor exhibition – which is pretty much what it was built for – but not for concerts…It's an out-dated, truly grim space with absolutely no redeeming features … all this serves to show is how much the country needs a purpose-built, state-of-the-art concert venue capable of hosting at least 10,000 people. (Meagher, 2008, para. 2)

So begins John Meagher's lament for the poor quality venues that hosted the big-name popular music acts in Ireland's capital, in his anticipatory glance towards the future of the new building then being built on the site of the city's Point Theatre. The new venue opened in 2008 is the O2 Arena – a thoroughly modern, multi-use venue with state-of-the-art infrastructure, acoustic environment, and visitor facilities for audiences of up to 14,000. However, there is no doubt that the old Point was a landmark in the Irish popular music scene, being the setting for many notable concerts by nationally and internationally famous acts, live concert recordings, television and film releases, in its thirty-year history. Even before it was renovated, the building had musical significance, as it was where U2 recorded songs for their *Rattle and Hum* album, which also featured in their 1988 film of the same name.

Though the Point was also a flexible space enabling multiple layouts, its significantly smaller 8,500 standing auditorium (6,300 when seated) was not known for either comfort or quality of environment. The rear seats were 20 metres further from the stage than those in the O2, and safety had been an issue with crushing at the front occurring. John Meagher recalls: 'I don't know anybody who had any affection for the place. The sound was never up to much and the sightlines could be abysmal. Factor in horrendously long queues for the toilets (especially for the ladies), even longer queues for the bars and the lack of any worthwhile food outlets and it's little wonder it was seen as bland and soulless'. He concludes with an unqualified welcome for the improvements a brand new (and brand-*ed*) venue would bring: 'The O2's first big test is just around the corner and expectations are

---

[1] The author acknowledges the support provided by a British Academy/Leverhulme Trust Senior Fellowship during the preparation of this chapter.

as high as its new, shiny roof. For those weaned on the grim surrounds of the RDS [Royal Dublin Society] and any number of makeshift marquees, its arrival can only be a good thing' (Meagher, 2008).

However, it is less certain if Meagher's whole-hearted embrace of a new venue, with its undoubted better facilities but also potential removal of thirty years of history and grimy resonance, is perceived as a wholly good thing by the audience who pay to see the acts. A comment on an uploaded amateur film of Nirvana's set at the Point on 21 June 1992 epitomizes the conflicting feelings people have about the venues of the past: 'The Point was a kip but it was our kip, this footage is just great. Imagine what it was like to be there, memories that they will never forget' (*kip* is Irish slang for a poor standard dwelling or hostelry) (Roscanuck83, 2012). The pop music gig is a unique and visceral event, which at its most resonant can be a consummate experience involving all the senses. There is a real feeling for the concert-goer of it being for one night only, in that place, at that time, and of being something that can never be replicated – despite the fact that the band will often be playing the same numbers with the same light show on subsequent nights of the tour.

This perception of the uniqueness of the concert experience is accurate – music performance is essentially live and, therefore, any number of factors can impact on audience experience, from the performer specifically introducing variety into the set (such as Elvis Costello's *Revolver* tours 2011–13, in which a wheel was spun to select which songs are played) to who you sit next to (friend, stranger, or someone annoying). However, nostalgic memories about places and events that merge recollections of an individual's personal situation at the time with the impartial qualitative appreciation of the music and the venue are an obfuscating factor in the analysis of audience experience – the memories of someone attending their first gig in a brand new building today may well be as powerful in fifty years' time.

Is the intensity of experience and the longevity in the memory of live music's impact at the same level when generated in a safe and comfortable environment, rather than in a performance space, inferior in these terms? Or maybe it does not matter where the music is played – if it is good enough perhaps all environmental problems can be transcended? Venue developers are concerned with these issues as they want to ensure that people will continue to patronize the premises in which they have invested, but also because performers will refuse to play somewhere that has a poor atmosphere, especially if audience numbers are reduced.

**Venue Typologies**

In my book *Live Architecture: Venues, Stages and Arenas for Popular Music* (2012, p. 5), I proposed a typology for the places of performance based on whether they make use of adopted, adapted, dedicated or mobile strategies. Buildings and spaces at all points on the scale of audience capacity can be found within each of these types – from a busker setting up to play on a street corner (adopted) to an external stage at a major pop festival (mobile), from a bar room entertainer singing to backing tracks via the house public address system (adapted) to a major branded arena in a capital city (dedicated). These typological building differences affect the audiences in terms of both their expectation of what the events will be like and their experience of the events as they happen. For example, there is an expectation that a performance by a four piece rock band in a small bar will be relatively informal with minimal stage lighting, while the same size combo appearing in a stadium will require a major audio and visual show. The audience experience of the performance in the small bar might be more intimate and personal than that in the stadium, though the larger event may compensate with a more dramatic and sophisticated show. Anticipation, gratification and disappointment all play their part in defining the actual experience and establishing subsequent memories.

The route to creation of popular music performance spaces is very diverse. The addition of a stage and/or a simple amplification system and some lights transforms the back room of a public house or a café into a venue, with little thought given to the performer (or their audience) save that they be heard and seen. Informal settings in a building or exterior space can be created temporarily by the performers with equipment they bring themselves, but a venue's continued success requires organizational interventions in setting the character and ambience of the room, the arrangement of seating/standing in relation to the performance, the quality of décor and lighting, and the acoustic environment. Many successful venues have been created and operated without any professional design involvement at all – and even in more sophisticated larger places, a good venue manager's experience and appreciation of what is best for his or her place is invaluable.

Adopted venues sometimes cling to their original ambience with minimal intervention because by chance or design they are well suited to the type of music that is played there – shortcomings are tolerated as they reinforce the special sense of place. For example, the former basement restaurant that has been the home for the 100 Club in Oxford Road, London, for more than seventy years has changed little except for upgrades in amplification (which the club does not even own, the sound company being paid each time it is used), a change in the stage position to accommodate space for a bar in 1964, and the addition of a further bar in 1967 (Jeff Horton, owner of the 100 Club: conversation with the author 25 June 2010). Many adapted venues have developed and changed as years have gone by, responding to change as necessary by alteration and amendment of the original building fabric, sometimes until it is completely unrecognizable from its original use. However, others have emerged as an inventive re-imagining of a building asset in a good location or of architectural significance seeking a new use – this circumstance occurred not once but twice in the history of the Point Theatre which was converted from the original Victorian train depot in 1988, and then into the O2 Arena in 2008. The most famous historic venues (those that have a national or international reputation for the acts or events that they are associated with) are adopted or adapted buildings that have coped with this gradual accretion of change over years and decades, occasionally pausing for a complete refurbishment that brings in new technology, but leaves the building fabric and the performance space largely recognizable. In these venues, an important part of the audience experience is that of authenticity, of being in the place where something important happened, although the physical space and its environment may well have been changed over the years (and occasionally completely rebuilt such as the Cavern Club, Liverpool, and The Joint, Las Vegas, discussed later).

Dedicated buildings are not a recent phenomenon. In the late 1840s, variety entertainment, during which alcohol could be consumed, was licensed by local magistrates in Britain, and this gave rise to purpose-built concert rooms being built attached to public houses. From the 1850s these developed into the much larger music halls (Earl, 2005, pp. 15–16). Nightclubs and dance halls of the first half of the twentieth century are also a part of this history. However, the grandest phase of popular music performance space building is one that has occurred in the last two decades with the creation of dedicated arenas with capacities of 10–25,000. The design of popular entertainment arenas stems from the use of sports venues for music performance using mobile equipment instigated at The Beatles Shea Stadium shows in 1965 and 1966. Indoor sports arenas previously used for basketball and boxing began to be used regularly for popular music events, and larger shows took place at outdoor stadiums. Arena and stadium rock became a genre in its own right, the venues converted overnight with temporary floors and the band's touring show equipment.

This new arena development phase began while their main role was still perceived as sports venues – for example, the Manchester Evening News (MEN) Arena (at that time the NYNEX Arena, named after its cable communications business sponsor) was built in 1995 as part of the city's unsuccessful bid for the 2000 summer Olympics, though it was used for the Commonwealth Games in 2002. Buildings such as the MEN were also designed to be flexible enough to host popular entertainment such as ice shows and conferences; however, their most common use has developed into popular music events – their large paying audiences making it viable for touring artists to mount sophisticated mobile stage shows. The MEN was named International Venue of the Year in the 2002 *Pollstar* Awards and nominated in the same category every year between 2003 and 2009. It sold more tickets than any other venue in the world in every year between 2003 and 2007 including Madison Square Garden, New York and Wembley Arena, London. Though undoubtedly successful in commercial terms, this first phase of hybrid buildings can often be criticized for their poor acoustics and atmosphere, bearing the traits of their primarily sports event design focus. A 2010 article extolling the merits of the MEN in the *Manchester Evening News* (the local newspaper that acquired its naming rights) generated comments by members of its audience that its facilities were now dated:

> The Arena may have put Manchester on top of the world, but eventually acts will look to play elsewhere if they don't clean up the MEN Arena soon! ... You go to newly opened venues ... and you can see the difference ... those venues offer

an exceptional customer experience whereas the MEN [is just] a concrete shell of a place with poor acoustics if your *[sic]* not right up near the stage (Larry. Cool, 2010).

As live music has come to dominate attendance at these venues comprising 60% of all attendees (6.59 million in the UK and Ireland in 2010), the latest phase in their development has seen their designs improved to provide better acoustics, sight lines, catering facilities, loading facilities and sound separation from neighbours to avoid noise restrictions and time curfews (*Music Week*, 2011).

The description of any music venue can be defined in terms of the physical space it occupies, the number of people who can be present during a performance, the catering and ancillary provision that the audience requires, and the technical and operational supporting facilities that the performer and venue staff utilize. However, what cannot so easily be described is the ambience and character of a venue that makes it a great place to see and hear a great performance. In a business that operates in such a highly commercial environment, it might be thought that venues that have successfully created this atmosphere will simply continue to be successful, but popular music is also a business in which change is a constant – music scenes develop, morph, or renew, leading to new trends in which inevitably, old ones are left behind (Bennett and Peterson, 2004, p. 6). Add to this the vagaries of potential mismanagement, occasional disregard for conventional operating methods, pressures of licensing and national and local regulations, urban renewal and impoverishment, and it is not surprising that venues open, close, move and rebrand as frequently as they do. The story of successful venues invariably includes the ability to cope with and manage response and adaptation to change in a realistic and pragmatic manner. The physical changes that are introduced into existing venues as alterations, or as design objectives in the creation of new venues are driven by three basic forces: legislation and licensing; commercial income and competition; and advances in performance technology.

**Legislation and Licensing**

National legislation, local regulations and licensing are powerful drivers in music venue design and operation. They play a crucial role in shaping the physical form of new buildings in terms of space, access, lighting and security, which design professionals need to take into account when planning a building and its internal environments. They also impact significantly on the maintenance and improvements expenditure that existing venues must budget for in order to continue operating. Although audiences are rarely directly aware of the impact that legal controls have on their experience, their influence is profound, maintaining their safety and comfort, but also the fundamental viability of venues to begin or continue operating.

In the UK, the Building Regulations control many aspects of new construction and works to existing properties where significant changes take place. They are constantly updated by central government to take account of developing technology and changing issues such as, for instance, the changes in universal access arrangements that were a result of the Disabled Discrimination Act 1995. Regulatory areas that particularly affect popular music venues include structural safety (Part A); behaviour of the building fabric and means of escape in case of fire (Part B); sound resistance (Part E); ventilation (Part F); hygiene and sanitary appliances (Part G); drainage and waste disposal (Part H); stairways (Part K); access (Part M); and electrical installations (Part P), although most aspects of the building regulations will apply to any sizable building. Although mandated by central government, the building regulations are managed by local authorities, and incorporated in the normal construction process undertaken by building design professionals at the design stage. This includes submission of plans for approval followed by inspections on site to ensure the approved plans are being adhered to. The building regulations system is operated throughout the developed world, usually on this basis of a mix of national and local standards that are administered via local authorities. Some regulations are international, particularly in the EU, which has standards of construction, manufacture and operation that are observed by all member states.

Adherence to regulations is mandatory and often costly, and can be decisive in determining if a building project's lifetime costing is viable. The lifetime cost includes the initial construction investment but also the estimated costs in operating the facility over its projected life including energy use, cleaning, and building maintenance. Higher initial construction cost in, for example, energy saving design features, may therefore lead to a lower overall lifetime cost. For example, when designing the Liverpool Echo Arena, an 11,000 capacity performance space completed in 2008, architects Wilkinson Eyre, together with engineers Faber Maunsell (now AECOM, an acronym for Architecture, Engineering, Consulting, Operations and Maintenance), established a sustainability management system that would ensure that the building not only met current building regulations but also would maintain energy efficiency throughout its working life. This meant integrating heat recovery, 'free' cooling systems, on-site wind turbines, and rainwater collection into a coordinated strategy that led to it being rated the 'greenest' building of its type in Europe (Kronenburg, 2012, pp. 129–132).

Though initial construction and lifetime costs for new projects can usually be accurately determined prior to committing to build, retrospective work bringing older existing venues up to contemporary standards is harder to predict, making the business difficult to sustain, and in the most extreme cases causing the venue to close. The Point venue in Cardiff was established in a former church in 2003 that had been serving as a community centre and theatre since 1992. The building was completely renovated, maintaining much of the listed historic interior and exterior. However, new apartments built near to the venue in 2008 led to increased noise complaints from residents. Although soundproofing work was carried out, the venue closed in February 2009 because the £65,000 cost of the work had forced the venue into liquidation (*New Musical Express*, 2009; Rostron, 2010). Changes required in order to meet the conditions of a licence may work in the same way as retrospectively applied building regulations, causing added expense or simply making a venue unviable in the location it has occupied, perhaps for many years. For example, new signage, emergency lighting, and fire extinguishers might be relatively easy to incorporate, but if soundproofing or the means of access are unacceptable there is little that can be done without considerable expense.

**Commercial Income and Competition**

Venue owners and managers have to balance running costs against the income they can generate from the various aspects of the business they run. Naturally they are concerned to maximize that income and in doing so make changes that will either increase it directly (by introducing retail opportunities in food, drink, shopping) or indirectly (by extending business hours, activities, locations). These changes include making alterations that keep the venue in vogue with audiences and performers (décor, sound and video systems, stage and floor lighting) or improvements in the venue's environment (air-conditioning, layout, facilities). External improvements might include signage, improving access for audience vehicle parking and loading access for bar and catering supplies and band equipment. Although the venue operators determine these changes they are often consistent with the desires of the audience and performers – in fact the most effective changes are market led, the venue's requirement to make additional income coinciding with a response to audience desires. For example, the famous London jazz venue Ronnie Scott's has continuously evolved in response to commercial needs while retaining its original ambience as a classic music and supper club. Founded in 1959 in a former tea-bar and taxi drivers' rest room in Gerrard Street, Soho, it relocated to bigger premises in Frith Street in 1965. This building has been regularly remodelled over the years adding a second performance space, kitchens, bars, dressing rooms and a shop – the latest changes occurring in 2005 after new owner Sally Greene commissioned a complete refurbishment of the decoration, lighting and sound systems while still retaining its authentic historic character (Paul Pace, music bookings coordinator, Ronnie Scott's Jazz Club: conversation with the author 13 July 2010).

Those promoters who operate separately from the venue management may well have similar priorities; however, this is not always the case. Their commercial ambitions are to drive the visibility and profitability of the acts they are promoting and these may not coincide with helping venues generate the income they need for the ever-increasing overheads of staffing, energy costs, building maintenance, licence applications, lease or rent, rates, and so on. Local promoters that put on a string of popular local bands with a ready-made audience, eager to make good use of the bar and catering, work well for venues even if the room rental is relatively small. Larger promoters, however, may bypass local venues for their more popular acts, but still hire them to promote a new band for which audiences are small. The venue is therefore unable to balance its expenses via bar and catering sales. Even historically important long-running venues such as London's 100 Club have been put under financial pressure to close by actions such as this, coupled with unrealistic rate increases demanded by local authorities (Jeff Horton, owner of the 100 Club: conversation with the author 25 June 2010). Audiences do not always sympathize with the commercial pressures that venues have to operate under, and may initially be antagonistic towards revenue generating initiatives (increased entry fees, more costly drinks or food) even though without their introduction the venue cannot continue to operate. However, they can also show tremendous loyalty to venues they cherish such as the threatened 100 Club, which stimulated online petitions, fund-raising events, and a Facebook page with over 19,000 members, before being saved in February 2011 by corporate sponsorship from the shoe brand Converse.

**Performance Technology**

Given the variety of adopted, adapted, dedicated and mobile buildings in use for music events, it is not surprising that there are dramatic differences in performance technology between venues and stages. Before the development of electronic amplification, enclosed historic venues provided a space limited in size by the constructional technology of the time. Enclosed performance spaces from classical times until the end of the nineteenth century could be no wider than 27 metres due to the structural limitations of contemporary timber spans, and if a larger audience was envisaged, the hall was stretched to become long and narrow. At the beginning of the twentieth century, large steel trusses were introduced that enabled the span to be increased and the shape and volume of spaces changed to allow a larger audience to be seated closer to the stage. However, these early halls were often criticized for the less reverberant acoustic environment they produced. The science of natural acoustics is now an essential part of designing any performance space with the proposed space digitally modelled to determine the sound it will produce prior to construction. In the most up-to-date halls reverberation times can be altered to accommodate different types of performance, either by physically changing the room's surface or via electronic means (Jaffe, 2010, pp. 11–19).

Unamplified musical performance still takes place in small venues and on the street; however, even so-called 'unplugged' performances using acoustic instruments now frequently make use of electronic amplification. The potential and limitations of artificial amplification were made clear at the first large-scale popular music performances. The noise made by the crowd drowned out that made by the musicians, and the small-scale 'back-line' amplification connected into stadium public address systems produced highly reverberant sound of poor quality. However, by the time of the famous Woodstock festival (officially titled the Woodstock Music and Art Fair) held in New York State, USA, in 1969, amplification had already developed dramatically. Bill Hanley (who was also chief sound engineer for the Newport Jazz and Folk festivals from 1957 and Bill Graham's important New York rock venue The Fillmore East between 1968 and 71) designed dedicated electronics and microphones, and 16 loudspeaker arrays built on specially made towers. Though intended for 150–200,000 people, more than 400,000 turned up – despite this, Michael Lang, the Woodstock promoter stated: 'Everyone could hear, nothing blew up, and it all hung together perfectly' (*Front of House*, 2006). The improved sound and light shows that were beginning to accompany performances and the popular films that were being made of such events, made clear the benefits of adding simultaneous transmission of visuals of the artist and other images associated with the music. Audiences could now hear and see the artists more clearly enabling a far superior engagement with the performer, a benefit for both sets of participants in the live show. Audience expectations similarly increased in anticipation of a better quality experience and other venue operators and promoters soon felt the pressure to follow leading exponents in improving visual and acoustic capabilities.

Performance technology developments are implemented essentially in two areas: permanent installations in clubs and auditoria; and mobile installations used by artists travelling from venue to venue. The introduction of increasingly sophisticated permanent installations has taken place primarily in small to medium-sized venues, while arenas and stadiums cater for the large touring acts who develop sophisticated audio-visual shows which they bring with them. The smallest bar and club venues may still have 'piped' music from a relatively small amplifier and speaker set-up or a juke box, relying on the artist to bring their own equipment when live music is performed. However, even the smallest venues now often provide stage lighting and some form of public address system (PA) for microphones and semi-acoustic instruments. Most medium-sized venues have now found it essential to retrofit more sophisticated equipment; a professional standard PA, specified for the particular space, together with an engineer to set up and monitor the performance; a lighting system that is remote controlled and programmable, either automatically depending on performance volumes or digitally designed in advance for recall during the set. Specific models of equipment are chosen for their familiarity among musicians and their road crew, so that travelling artists can integrate their own instrument set-up with the permanent installation quickly and reliably, including wiring their own control desks into the amplification power and speaker set-up if required. Advance information for agents and promoters making choices about which venues to book is important so most now list their technical facilities on their websites. The promoters' insistence on the best technology in venues arises from the need to keep up with the competition – they must provide the best show possible to draw regular full audiences and ensure that their acts' performances are not compromised. Venue managers have to comply with these demands if they wish to retain the most popular acts at their venues.

Venues of over 1000-seat capacity are becoming more likely to also incorporate a live performance video feed and projection system, allowing those audience members at the back to follow the visual nuances once restricted to the lucky few at the front. Mobile equipment is not second-rate compared to static set-ups. Incredibly reliable and custom-designed for the industry, artists can rent or buy any element ranging from a simple guitar combo amplifier to a full touring stage with megawatts of power and LED (light emitting diode) live action screens. The shape and design of these mobile stages, though constructed primarily from standard reusable components, are commissioned and designed to create a powerful image unique to the artist (Kronenburg, 2010, pp. 310–2).

Although audiences are at the receiving end of this improvement in performance technology, it is primarily the artists and promoters who have driven its development. Musicians who create increasingly sophisticated sounds in the recording studio have subsequently had the desire to reliably reproduce these sounds on stage. For example, in the early 1970s Pink Floyd had trouble performing on stage the new material they were rehearsing that would eventually become the *Dark Side of the Moon* album. In 1972 after a show was brought to a halt at The Dome in Brighton, Roger Waters announced 'Due to severe mechanical and electric horror we can't do any more of that bit, so we'll do something else …' (Blake, 2007, p. 175). During 1973 Pink Floyd went on to play the album live in its entirety, with its extensive use of loops, synthesizers and acoustic instruments, and by 2006, Waters would include it as just a part of his *The Dark Side of the Moon Live* world concert tour, performed without a glitch night after night. As electronic and synthesized instruments have developed, eventually turning into mass-market products, the technology has become so ubiquitous that any artist can reproduce almost any sound, in any venue. Improved technology helps provide the confidence that musicians need to create a good performance, which derives in part from working with reliable equipment that provides quality sound and feedback regarding what is being heard by the audience.

The increased sophistication of performance technology is not just there to enable more complex shows – the flexibility of contemporary technology also benefits the simplest performance. For example, Adele's 'no bells, no whistles, just a piano, and her voice' performance of 'Someone Like You' at the 2011 Brit Awards, O2 Greenwich Arena, London, before a live audience of 20,000 people and a television audience of millions, was only made possible by such technology (McCormick, 2011). It took advantage of a key benefit of improved performance technology – the relative ease with which live transmissions or recordings can be made, either straight from the performance desks or via an external recording truck linked into these sophisticated stage systems. Adele's Brit Awards performance is credited with boosting her song from outside the top 40 to number one, and with helping her album *21* to retain its top place, making her the first living artist to have two top five hits in both the singles and album charts in one week since The Beatles in 1964.

## Audience Safety and Comfort

As will have become apparent in the preceding sections, the people furthest from the decision-making process in the implementation of changes in venue design and operation are the audiences. They have no control over providing what musicians need to optimize their performance and often little knowledge of the technical issues faced by the artists and their support teams; no influence over which venues are chosen by promoters or why; no influence over the decisions building managers make in operating the venues they visit; and no direct power over the decisions made by legislators and local government to manage their safety and quality of environment. However, the popular music industry is constantly striving to meet the needs and desires of audiences, delivering a product that they will want to own and experience – even if it can be asserted that a good portion of what it does produce is done cynically with its own commercial gain in mind. This leads to the question at the heart of this topic: are the changes that have taken place in venue design and operation something that has improved the quality and interactivity of audience experience or something that has diluted that experience to the level of meaningless commercial entertainment?

It is clear that in terms of safety and comfort, new venues and those that have undergone extensive refurbishment are safer and more comfortable. Designers are obligated to follow strict rules inspired by real world experience to control crucial aspects of people movement and protection from dangerous events such as fire. Careful restriction and organization of spaces where people stand and sit are intended to prevent problems in crowd control, and specification standards control the standard of building construction and fittings including overhead gantries, balconies, stairways and railings. Improvements to cooling, ventilation and sanitation also alleviate potential health dangers where large numbers of people are gathered together. Problems still occur, but when they do they are investigated and the lessons learnt are fed back into the drafting of revised or new regulations. It is hard to argue against the implementation of such rules when lives are at stake – but in achieving this level of safety has the quality of audience experience been lessened?

Comfort is perhaps not always synonymous with what constitutes a great experience at a popular music performance: for some audience members the discomfort of becoming hot, sweaty and battered in the 'mosh pit' is an essential feature that also adds something to the atmosphere for those situated further back. Older venues, while nevertheless meeting regulations by updating safety features, may still not provide comfort, which for the reason above some may deem optional. However, they might also not provide the best view or sound, so that a portion of the audience will have a compromised experience. In an older venue, most would agree that this is just something that comes with the territory, a downside outweighed by the venue's character and atmosphere. This is so much the case that even when rebuilding a historic venue its faults may also be recreated. For example, when reconstructing the Cavern in Liverpool in 1984 an identical series of low brick vaults was rebuilt using many of the original bricks of the older building, creating a dark, acoustically reflective, tunnel-like space hardly conducive to providing the best experience for the audience or performer – but correct in its recreation of a seminal venue in popular music history (David Backhouse, architect of Cavern Walks: conversation with the author, 7 December 2010.).

There is no reason why exciting performance conditions cannot be provided safely, and, indeed, designers of contemporary venues strive to do just that. The provision of safety in popular music venues is not something that intrinsically impedes an authentic audience experience, whatever those nostalgic for the quirks of older venues may feel. The excitement of live music should after all come from the qualities of the performance and the sharing of that with like-minded fans – not from experiencing it in a dangerous environment. Because of greater flexibility in modern venues (which designers have recognized is the key to hosting a variety of acts and attracting their different audiences), audience experience can encompass everything from the crowd pressing together directly in front of the band, to the individual sipping a cocktail in a private box. Rather than excitement, which should remain part of experiencing live music, the emotion that should be removed from concert-goers is fear of being hurt in an unsafe environment. In addition, it enables all who wish to experience the music to be able to do so, rather than restricting it to those sufficiently brave and physically able.

Related to the issue of comfort is the provision of support facilities for the audience. This is an area where venues can derive a large part of their income – providing alcoholic and non-alcoholic drinks as standard, but also food and sometimes shopping. Some forms of popular music performance have always had this as a crucial part of their activity, for example jazz clubs and musical theatre/cabaret. However, this is a key area in which development has taken place in new venues, aiming to provide the concert-goer with a complete experience, defining the venue as a 'destination' with other events and entertainment opportunities taking place around the core concert performance (John Barrow, Populous, senior principal and project architect for the O2 Greenwich: conversation with the author, 7 June 2010.).

The ultimate example of this is the O2 Arena at Greenwich, London, completed in 2007. Around the main 20,000 capacity arena are situated a smaller 2,350 capacity facility, IndigO2, and an outside piazza for external events, a multiplex cinema, a popular music museum 'experience', and a street of shops, restaurants and bars. Nearby there are hotels, and space for a planned conference centre and casino. Though few venues will have a range of facilities this varied, all new ones incorporate dining areas, franchised fast-food provision, and bars designed physically (size) and technically (fast-flow beer pumps) to serve large numbers of people quickly.

Clearly it is in the interest of venue managers to increase their revenue, but how does the provision of these facilities impact on the audience experience? Indulging in catering can make the concert event a much more expensive one, as prices are generally high in such a controlled environment. More critical is how

Figure 4.1    Entertainment Avenue, the retail street at the O2 Greenwich, London (©Robert Kronenburg)

the experience during the performance may be affected – it could be the audience are more relaxed having arrived early and enjoyed the pre-concert 'build-up', or, perhaps, more restless as people regularly leave their seats during the performance to stock up on refreshments. The relationship between alcohol consumption and live music performance is outside the scope of this chapter; however, recent venue management trends now seek to maximize income by enabling (or even encouraging) audiences to continue spending throughout the performance, not just during the breaks. Bars remain open throughout the performance, new large venues now locate them in the auditorium as well as the foyer, and drinking containers are made of materials that do not pose a safety risk. However, in many ways these embedded commercial opportunities for audience crowds are not an innovation but merely a bringing together under one roof of something that has always occurred. Older venues that are situated in urban areas are also surrounded by eating and drinking opportunities, operating close by to take advantage of the large numbers of people who regularly congregate there (although these independent businesses may result in more competitive costs).

Improved specification in performance technology has mitigated the stress and anxiety associated with the way people experience live music, enabling a much greater likelihood of this being positive, with more individuals able to engage fully with the show. Sound quality is not only better overall, but there are more sophisticated mixes in which particular instruments and voices can be emphasized during different parts of the show, or tailored to different parts of the auditorium. Lighting and video not only allow the artist to be seen more clearly, they enhance the visual experience, creating specific moods and complementing the performance; this enables more complex and sophisticated ideas to be communicated via non-performance footage and ancillary props or devices. Small venues may not need (or want) such sophisticated audio-visual systems, and consequently large venues have seen most change.

**Conclusion**

Audience experience has certainly been affected by the changes documented in this chapter, but the evidence for the extent and nature of this change is somewhat lacking. Industry surveys of viewing figures give the bald facts about how many people are attending popular music events, but these indicate numbers rather than experience, and although numbers might well be affected by customer satisfaction, they are undoubtedly also influenced by other variables such as changing disposable incomes and the state of the economy. The National Arenas Association (NAA) annual report 2010 indicated a 19% downturn in attendance numbers across their 17 member venues compared to 2009, though that was still an increase on 2008 (*Music Week*, 2011). At least until the economic downturn in 2008, industry confidence was high with considerable investment in new buildings, often on a large scale as global companies such as AEG (Anschutz Entertainment Group) and Live Nation have become more involved. Top artists too now perceive live concerts as an integral part of their income stream rather than simply a way to promote their recorded music – successful tours replacing the income lost from declining CD sales. The dramatic increase in the number of festivals, in which popular music is the focus of an event that is part lifestyle experience, part holiday, also indicates that new ways of experiencing live music are an integral part of how this market is developing, with over 670 events in 2010, with the top 200 contributing a turnover of £450 million in ticket sales, travel, accommodation and food (Warman, 2010).

Media reviews of live music provide indications of how innovations in audience experience are occurring, but also how they are received. In one regard music critics provide a useful 'educated' viewpoint as they go to more gigs than most other individuals (often at the same venue), and they are articulate in

Figure 4.2    Phoenix on stage at The Joint by Vogue, Las Vegas
              (©Robert Kronenburg)

delivering their verdict when the venue, rather than the artist, lets the event down. However, music critics, like all of us, have their own biases, history and affections/ dislikes, and so their opinions cannot universally be taken as without prejudice. The comments of concert-goers are perhaps the most impartial, with no ulterior motive except making their own opinion heard, against the balance of fellow fans' comments to graduate the response. Objectivity can sometimes be overwhelmed on fan forums by partisanship to their favourite artists and nostalgia; however, comments on the ever-increasing amateur video clips of gigs posted on wiki sites such as YouTube, Vimeo and DailyMotion (such as the Nirvana gig at the Point) often provide interesting insights beyond the 'I was there' type, displaying affection and disappointment for a venue and how it affected their experience of the event (see Lucy Bennett and Paul Long's chapters later in this book).

It is of course the aim of newly-built or refurbished venues to be successful, to draw consistently full audiences, and have artists happy to return for further performances. It is also required of them that they are safe and economically viable. Developers and their design teams are challenged to create the physical and technical criteria to achieve these aims, while still building venues that will be the home of memorable events that audiences will remember with equally powerful resonance as those of the past. Many historic venues were (and still are in some cases) clearly challenged in the areas of audience comfort and acoustic/

visual experience; however, they have a unique charisma integral to their place in the history of popular music. They persist because of this history and the local, national or international status they have rightly achieved – and also because good gigs still happen there. It would, however, be ridiculous to build into new venues compromised viewing areas or a less satisfactory sound system, in the vain hope this would replicate the authenticity of the older ones. It is therefore equally ridiculous to state that a new venue, designed with higher performance support standards therefore has less character because of these characteristics.

In a new building like The Joint by Rogue (see Figure 4.2), the 4,000 capacity venue which opened in Las Vegas, USA, in 2009 (to replace the older one of the same name on the same site), there are no obscured sight lines and the sophisticated line array PA system controlled by a computer based sound equalization programme ensures quality sound at every point in the venue, delivered by a bewildering number of different speakers tuned to the immediate spaces they serve (Kronenburg, 2012, p. 120).

The venue affords great flexibility for the promoters who can confidently book all kinds of artists knowing they will feel they are in the right place, from Paul McCartney to Drake, from Santana to Avenged Sevenfold. The upper of its three levels can be curtained off to improve acoustics for smaller shows, its floor level can be laid out for all standing or seating, or seating can be placed on the stage for an in-the-round show. Storage below the stage on quick moving pallets provides easy access to the extra equipment. The Joint's interior design maintains some continuity with the grungy building it replaced, incorporating its recycled wooden floor, and slightly kitsch guitar fret board and cymbal décor. Safety has been achieved together with variety in audience experience, at the same time providing equal engagement and enjoyment opportunities for all regardless of their physical status. Audiences benefit not only from its inclusivity in terms of physical access but in the variety of viewing options that provide a large range of ticket prices.

New venues like The Joint do not have the history that seems to seep into the walls of old, continuously operating venues such as the 100 Club, but it is not unreasonable to argue that these places are building their own history, in this case starting with the opening night when local Las Vegas band, but now global stars, The Killers, provided the entertainment, in which: 'They rocked the place… just tore it up before a pulsating crowd of 4,000 mostly standing fans who more than knocked the sawdust off the just-finished music hall' (Katsilometes, 2009).

# SECTION 2
# During the Event:
# Listening and Connecting

Chapter 5
# Interlude – Audience Members as Researchers

Stephanie Pitts and Karen Burland

In this book so far we have heard much about the people who go to hear live music – why they go, what they experience there, and how their concert attendance relates to other aspects of their listening and leisure use. Authors writing in different disciplines refer to these people in different ways, as fans, consumers, concert-goers, even customers, leading us as editors to wonder whether these differences are important. We have preserved the terminology of each chapter, following Iona Opie's (1993) suggestion of using the language that makes sense to its users: when Opie asked the children she was researching with how they referred to each other, they said simply 'people', and so her perceptive account of children's playground games acquired its evocative title, *The People in the Playground*.

The names for the people in the audience, however, have different connotations according to musical genre and context. Popular music listeners tend to be more comfortable with the notion of being a 'fan' than their classical music counterparts (Jenson, 1992; Cavicchi, 1998), wearing their fandom as a badge of musical identity and loyalty to a specific performer, in a way that is more exuberant than the quiet devotion of a regular chamber music listener. The sedate behaviour of a classical music 'aficionado' or 'music lover' might seem outwardly different – since singing along is discouraged at the opera, but welcomed in a pop star's arena tour – but within the conventions of the venue and genre, both audiences are expressing their enthusiasm and comment to a similar degree. Audience members, in their own minds at least, are therefore much more than consumers or customers; though for arts promoters and market researchers charged with ensuring the financial stability of their musical venture, a more commodity-based view of the event is appropriate (if usually hidden from the audience).

The chapters in the next section show how audience members take on an additional role, as commentators on the event, or co-researchers in understanding its meaning and effects. Sometimes this is self-initiated, as in the texting and tweeting undertaken by Tori Amos fans in Lucy Bennett's chapter: here the fans at the gig feel a responsibility to the larger community of 'virtual fans', and their present experience is filtered through the commentary that they provide to fan forums and social media sites. Bennett herself adopts the label 'aca-fan' to denote her dual engagement as a listener and a researcher: her enthusiasm for the music and membership of the audience is part of her research perspective. While less explicit in their positioning, other audience researchers also note the value of 'being there', not just for their participants, but for themselves as interpreters of the event and of the data that they collect there (Radbourne, Johanson and Glow, this volume).

When not actively adopting the role of co-researchers, audience members are nonetheless seeking out and reporting an understanding of their experience in each of the chapters in this section. Gaining real-time responses from listeners without disrupting their experience is a challenge tackled by Kate Stevens and her co-authors, who have developed software to facilitate the tracing of emotional engagement 'in the heat of the moment'. This 'continuous audience response technology' is in its infancy, and part of Stevens et al.'s research is an investigation of the impact of the hand-held devices on audience members' enjoyment of the event. In comparison to Bennett's tweeters and texters, they seemed relatively undisturbed by the request to record their experiences in real time: as was the case for Burland and Windsor's improvisation listeners, there may even be benefits in the heightened attention of knowing that your response to an event is being elicited and reported for a particular purpose.

These novel methods of real-time or immediate response, particularly where they involve discussion with other audience members, contribute to the creation of a community of listeners by providing rare access to the listening experience of fellow attenders. Sidsel Karlsen offers another demonstration of how these communities evolve in festival settings, through the intensity of repeated attendance at a significant location – an experience which environmental psychologists describe as 'place attachment', whereby loyalty to a venue builds up enriched memories and reduces awareness of the foibles of uncomfortable seating or other irritations (Pitts and Spencer, 2008).

For researchers and listeners alike, audience research can yield moments of 'intensified participation' (Radbourne, Johanson and Glow, this volume), when the interests of both parties coincide and the mutual desire for understanding brings rich insight on the listening experience. Equally well, if the questions are obvious or the methods of asking them intrusive, audience research has the potential to ruin an event of significance to its participants. The responsibilities of research in this area are keenly felt in the chapters that follow, and the understanding of the audiences in a range of musical and other artistic settings is insightful as a result.

Chapter 6

# The Value of 'Being There': How the Live Experience Measures Quality for the Audience

Jennifer Radbourne, Katya Johanson and Hilary Glow

Imagine yourself seated in the concert hall, the lights have dimmed and the chatter of anticipation is silenced. From this moment until you stand to leave, the extrinsic and pragmatic issues associated with your decision to attend – the difficulty of getting here and finding a car park, the cost of your ticket, how you found out about the performance and how helpful that information was, and the professionalism with which your needs were met by staff – all of these factors should ideally be forgotten. What exists for you in these few short hours is simply the performance, your fellow audience members, and your own responses to both of these. If the concert is successful, these hours offer a rare opportunity for sustained absorption.

These few hours in the concert represent the great investment of artistic development, practice and skill on the part of the producers, and the investment of time and money on the part of the audience. Yet paradoxically, what exactly the audience member makes of these hours is one of the least well-understood aspects of the performance. As we describe below, most measures of the quality of the performance have focused not on the audience member's experience in the concert but rather on either the extrinsic aspects of the production – most of which are principally of relevance before or after the performance – or on expert assessments of artistic quality. This tendency to neglect the audience's experience of quality is currently being addressed. In an era in which music companies are increasingly risk-averse in their efforts to prevent audience decline (Burland and Pitts, 2012), understanding more about the qualities that the audience seeks and gains from their experience in a music performance offers music companies and their stakeholders opportunities to build audiences around informed artistic goals.

This chapter is concerned with what the audience sees, hears and experiences during a performance, based on focus groups and surveys conducted immediately after a performance with the audiences of five music companies performing a range of musical genres and in a range of venues. The focus of the chapter is entirely on the audience's experience of the live performance because, the chapter argues, the very elements of 'being there' contribute to the qualities identified as important to the audience. The chapter examines how the live audience experience of a music performance contributes to the value of the performance. It examines audience-reported responses to the nature of their experience at a performance, and then analyses these reports in the context of research on the specific qualities of the live performing arts experience.

## Conventional Measures of Quality in the Performing Arts

For many years it was accepted that quality in the performing arts was the rationale used for government subsidy and sponsor investment, and resulted in increased attendance and audience satisfaction for performing arts companies. To this end, arts companies established or were given performance indicators to measure their quality so that governments, sponsors, donors and ticket buyers could evaluate the 'quality' of a company or a particular production. Companies and funding agencies collected, compared and then used data as economic and social indicators of the value of the arts. While economist Myerscough in his 1998 study *The Economic Importance of the Arts in Britain* described the intangible nature of the arts product and the 'waste' of empty seats at a performance as problematic in measuring outputs (cited in Evans, 1997, p. 442), economic measures of inputs (costs, resources, subsidies), throughput (number of people affected by the activity, target groups' attendance, number of performances) and outputs (venue capacity against attendance, income against production costs) were the most common labels of quality measurement.

Some data sets included a qualitative assessment of audience satisfaction as an 'outcome indicator' designed to answer the question 'What impact did the concert have?' This was an attempt to determine if the audience experience had resulted in increased self-confidence and well-being of the defined group of users (Evans, 1997), or a more general change in the community or society. Generally, however, indicators of quality were confined to measuring satisfaction with service which assesses the difference between the consumer's expectation and experience of attending the venue and performance. Performing arts venues often relied on simple measures of audience satisfaction such as the number of complimentary or complaint letters received, and how many staff could recognize a patron by name. None of the indicators related to the experience the audience had during the performance. The use of indicators increasingly became the subject of critical scrutiny. In a political economy dominated by concern for commercial performance, Evans (1997, p. 443) suggested that more meaningful performance measures are not those driven by economy and efficiency measures. He stated that performance indicators 'are not […] a measure of quality, artistic excellence or a full measure of how far policy objectives are being met'.

## Research on Audience Measures of Performing Arts Quality

In the late 1990s other researchers began to turn their attention to audience indicators of quality and value in the arts, which often identified these qualities as relating to personal fulfilment. Research by Tzokas and Saren (1999) argued that customers decide whether or not to become involved in an arts performance based on their own set of values. These values are extrinsic or intrinsic consumption values and include achieving shared experiences with peers, social recognition, self-fulfilment, aesthetic appreciation, a sense of belonging, emotional satisfaction and understanding of quality (Radbourne, 2002, p. 60). Botti examined the extrinsic and intrinsic rewards of arts consumption, claiming that the intrinsic rewards of such consumption carry more subjectivity and uniqueness for their target audience:

> The audience of an opera [...] give their own meaning to the work they are witnessing, based on the emotions it sparks. In the case of the performing arts [...] there is a 'dual mediation' since the way the artist performs the piece influences the audiences' interpretation of it. (Botti, 2000 p. 19)

What bestows value on the music from the audience's point of view depends very much on their emotional reaction to it: 'the emotional experience that is elicited when the individual's personal feelings come in contact with the meanings the artist has chosen to transfer through his/her work' (p. 19). Rossel (2011, p. 88) argued that empirical studies of audiences for music should 'expect to find two modes of consumption: one more analytical and intellectual, and the other focused on pleasurable aesthetic emotions' (p. 88). This emphasis on the emotional aspect of a performance has been neglected by conventional measures of artistic quality. The consistency with which it appears as a factor in audience accounts of their experiences, however, suggests that research on audiences must attempt to evaluate the audiences' emotional response to the performance and the performers. While governments have values (and rewards) around operational performance and efficiencies, consumers and audiences have their personal values. These values are the benchmarks against which individual audience members attribute quality.

For the link to be made from emotional response and satisfaction of intrinsic needs to a measure of value and quality, the quantitative and qualitative observations provided by cultural economists make an important contribution. Ake Andersson and David Andersson (2006) presented detailed research on the economics of the arts and entertainment experience. Their discourse on quality includes both the quality of composition and the quality of production. They describe the musical composition process as a plan based on what has occurred at earlier stages (technical training and practice), arriving at 'equilibrium' where no change would improve the performance. Such consistency highlights the training, technical skill and performance achievement of the musician. Quality is thus defined as 'consistency with the rules of composition' (p. 25), and is usually the context evaluated by experts and critics. However, their second analysis describes the dimension beyond the objective technical and professional skill of the artist, to the subjective dimension judged by the buyer, consumer or audience member. Quality measurement, they determine, is in the hands of the audience.

Audiences increasingly seek a kind of authenticity from the experience of the musical performance, where authenticity delivers on audience perceptions and expectations. Recent research has begun to investigate the emotional or cultural impact of the arts on audiences with the aim of identifying intrinsic dimensions (Pitts, 2005b; McCarthy et al., 2004), although not with a view to using such knowledge to evaluate artistic quality. Holden (2004) claims that 'responses to culture are personal and individual' (p. 18), while Brown and Novak (2007) determine that the quality of an artistic performance resides in the individual audience member's definition of quality, based on their intrinsic experience of a performance. Rossel's study of audiences at classical music concerts concluded that the conventional notion of a passive, concentrating audience 'only describes a part of how a musical performance is actually appreciated' (Rossel, 2011, p. 94). Intent on identifying various ways that audiences engaged with the concert, the study found that there are far more diverse ways of listening than only with concentrated attention or by consciously analysing the music heard:

> Many listeners in our survey were also emotionally moved, or used music as an escape from more worldly concerns, or even felt an urge to dance and sing – an impulse quite rarely acted upon at classical concerts in contemporary Western societies! These findings challenge the sociology and psychology of music to develop a theory to explain such diversity in music listening. (Rossel, 2011, p. 94)

New research (Barker, 2013; Chesher, 2007; Bennett, in this volume and 2012) examines the use of media to capture and transmit the performance, and of social media to give the audience and performers opportunities to interact. Such research notes that new media technologies increasingly replicate the perceived attractions of liveness for remote audiences by, for example, offering a limited number of 'tickets' to a performance and limiting the period in which a performance can be accessed (Duffett, 2003). Paradoxically, these efforts to achieve the perceived benefits of liveness deliberately reject the benefits associated with internet-based media, which include universal and long-lasting access to the material transmitted. Duffett (2003) argues that such efforts are contributing to a redefinition of the meaning of liveness. Rather than referring to a concert in which both performers and audience members are physically present, 'live' is increasingly used to identify the way in which a performance was recorded or transmitted and 'the distinction between an event and its recording appears to have been erased' (Duffett, 2003, p. 311).

These efforts aside, a quality that contributes to the great expansion of the audience and its opportunities for engagement is social media's capacity to transcend the temporal restrictions of a performance: audience members can participate in a performance and the excitement and discussion that surround it at their own convenience. In keeping with this chapter's focus on the audience's experience *during* a performance, the audiences we study here were physically present at the performances. As Reason points out, the fact that 'experience is a phenomenon created by the non-live does not negate the potential impact of audience perceptions of the live nor suggest what that experience of liveness might be' (Reason, 2004). The study described below represents one among a growing number of efforts to investigate what the audience experiences during a live performance.

## Five Australian Music Companies and their Audiences

Studies from 2006 to 2011 of audiences at the music performances of five Australian companies were designed to identify how audience members define the quality of their experience during the performance. All of the companies are relatively small. They include an experimental Queensland orchestra called Deep Blue (2006), the Queensland Orchestra (2007), a Melbourne season of Musica Viva (2008), and two small innovative music companies: the Australian Arts Orchestra (2010) and the Victorian Opera (2011).

The companies and concerts selected present a range of different musical genres, venues and audiences. At the time of the study, the experimental orchestra Deep Blue had developed a new repertoire specifically in response to expressed audience needs and desires, presenting an eclectic selection of existing works and new compositions with projected visual images, player involvement and audience involvement, no conductor, no music stands, and a shared performance and audience space. The Queensland Orchestra performances included one classical and one popular orchestral concert. The two Musica Viva performances were held in two very different venues and with two different programmes. The first was a concert by a Melbourne-based piano trio, the Benaud Trio, performing in a small, informal jazz bar. The second was a concert by the touring Choir of Westminster Abbey, performed at Melbourne's largest concert hall. The Victorian Opera is a state professional opera company with a focus on presenting new works and an unconventional repertoire across the state, often in collaboration with partners. The final company, the Australian Arts Orchestra, is a national ensemble of improvising musicians focused on using music to socially connect people.

Our research team conducted focus groups and surveys with audiences of each of these companies. Participants included both regular attenders of the work of that company, as well as people who had not previously attended performances by that company. In all cases, the audience enjoyed the interaction between the performers and themselves, positively describing the live enthusiasm, and the benefits of being among other audience members. At the Deep Blue performance, audiences enjoyed the absence of physical barriers between themselves and the performers, and the fact that the concert stretched the boundaries of their relationship with music. At the Queensland Orchestra performance, the musicians/

performers were considered the best element of the performance. Irrespective of the different audience demographics, it was important for people to connect and engage with the performing artists. This was reiterated at the Musica Viva performances where, despite the very different nature of the concerts, participants described the excellence of the performance and expressed their appreciation of performer–audience interaction and communication between audience members or a sense of common experience. The Australian Art Orchestra performance involved the orchestra accompanying Australian 'Indie' singers Paul Kelly and Vika and Linda Bull. It attracted many audience members who were familiar with the singers' work from Melbourne's lively pub scene. Participants commented that they expected a high quality performance from these singers, and were pleased to find that it was enhanced by the involvement of the orchestra.

The research undertaken involved two phases: 2006 to 2007, and 2008 to 2011. The research focus in the first phase was on performance innovation and capturing the audience response to this. Focus group questions allowed for a free-ranging discussion about when and where this audience usually experiences music, their feelings during the performance, their view of the role of the audience, and if they would come again to such a performance.

The first-phase studies provided foundational data on the audience experience, their attribution of quality and their value of the live experience. The findings facilitated expansion to other music genres and spaces, and with other demographic and cultural environments, in the second phase. In 2008 new focus group and survey questions were designed to specifically test expectations of audiences, the participation experience, and the value of the live performance. Some of the questions were similar to the earlier research, for example, asking audiences to identify what they liked most and least about the performance, their view on the role of the audience, and would they re-attend. The additional focus group questions were:

At what point in the concert were you most engaged with the music or musicians and how did you express that? Is there another way you would like to express this? How does the experience of a live performance differ from seeing a film or TV version of this concert, or listening to a CD of the music? What makes the live arts experience authentic? The findings from both phases are summarized here.

*Deep Blue (2006)*

The Deep Blue project demonstrated a shift from the traditional orchestral performance. It involved many new product components (repertoire, technology, visuals, venue, staging, musicians, instruments) challenging audience understandings of orchestral music. The test orchestra performed in a range of styles using specified acoustic, amplified and digital instruments, including synthesizers, samplers, laptops and strings. Surround sound systems and multi-screen live and pre-recorded visual images were added to the performance. The repertoire included a combination of new works, 'Elegy' composed by Robert Davidson, 'Raising up

Water' composed by Phil Williams, 'Chill' composed by Yanto Browning, and 'Mars' from 'The Planets' by Holst, arranged by Robert Davidson.

In total about 40 people attended the initial test performance of the four works. Twenty-six audience members completed the survey. The greatest number of people in the audience preferred classical music, with a number of other styles identified such as funk, blues, folk and electronica. They commonly listened to music at home, in their car and in concert halls, and they nominated the musicians/performers as the best part of the performance. While respondents nominated the style of music as what was least liked, they described the performance as 'experimental and innovative', 'an awesome production and great musicianship', 'fun and a new look', 'exciting and moving', 'a contemporary orchestra', 'music that would be good in a movie', 'different but enjoyable', 'an amazing collaboration of drama, lighting, costume, sound production', 'a break away from traditional ways of experiencing a performance', and 'refreshing, innovative, explorative but where boundaries can still be extended'.

Seventeen respondents (65%) said they would not buy a CD of this performance, although all but one respondent declared they would come again to a performance like this. They identified the role of the audience in a musical performance as an 'emotional listener' and 77 per cent of respondents either agreed or strongly agreed that 'a musical performance evokes an emotional response in the audience'. Sixty-five per cent agreed or strongly agreed that 'the context (venue, ambience, behaviour, of audience) contributes to the meaning of a music performance', and that 'interaction between the audience and performers results in audience enjoyment'. Thirty per cent of respondents disagreed that 'pre-performance information is important to enjoyment of a musical performance'.

Subsequent concerts by this orchestra were sold out. The performance was presented during the annual state music festival and in a partnership with the Queensland Performing Arts Centre in 2008. Over 600 people attended the Deep Blue shows in the festival and 220 completed the survey. Responses were overwhelmingly favourable, with 96 per cent of the respondents stating they would re-attend. An interview with the co-producer stated that expectations of audience size and reaction were surpassed and that the Deep Blue project has significant market potential.

*The Queensland Orchestra (2007)*

Two Queensland Orchestra concerts were evaluated by surveys and focus groups in 2007. The first was part of the Maestro Series and included Brahms' Violin Concerto in D major, Ligeti's *Concert Romanesc* and Respighi's *Pines of Rome* symphonic poem. The venue was the Concert Hall at the Queensland Performing Arts Centre.

The audience demonstrated their enjoyment of the concert by their enthusiastic applause at the end. Consistent with the conventions of twentieth-century Western classical music performances, the musicians were formally dressed and did not appear to acknowledge the audience during the performance, being completely focused on their music scores and instruments. However, the conductor did informally acknowledge the applause of some audience members who 'incorrectly' applauded between movements.

This audience reported that they mostly listened to music in their own home and car, as well as in the concert hall. Ninety-five per cent preferred classical music to other music styles. When asked what they liked best about the performance, 71 per cent indicated the musicians or performers. They were enthusiastic in the words they would choose to describe the concert to others, using 'wonderful', 'spectacular', 'exciting', 'moving' and 'amazing'. The violinist was mentioned a few times as being a 'great soloist'. Sixty-seven per cent of respondents stated that they would not buy a CD/DVD of the performance, and 97.7 per cent agreed that they would come again to a performance like this. When asked to describe their role as audience, the highest response (74%) was for the 'emotional listener' and that 'musical performances evoke an emotional response in the audience'.

In contrast to the highly conventional first performance, the second Queensland Orchestra concert performance for this study had a science-fiction theme, including Superman, ET and Star Trek. The programme included acrobats and a compere who spoke in the style of the narrator from *Star Trek*, and contained a re-enactment of some scenes from other science-fiction movies. Non-traditional classical orchestral instruments were integrated into the performance, such as a bass guitar, electronics and sticks waved to create different harmonics.

Audiences reported that they like to hear music in the concert hall (95%), closely followed by 'in the car' and 'in their own home' (both 91%). Ninety-five per cent nominated classical music as their preferred style of music. As with all the other concerts analysed, the musicians/performers were rated highest as the most liked element of the performance.

This concert was designed to use theatrical elements to enhance the musical enjoyment of the performance, and 33.3 per cent of people stated that they liked this least about the performance. Despite this feeling, responses were very positive, with many people describing the performance as 'fun, a great night out, exciting, different, entertaining, spectacular'. A few people commented that the spoken elements were too long and distracted from the music. Only 47 per cent of respondents said that they would buy a CD/DVD. Ninety-one per cent of respondents said they would come again to a performance like this, reflecting that a great part of the enjoyment of performance is that it is 'live'. As with all the other concerts surveyed, the perception of the role of the audience as 'emotional listener' received the highest score with 77 per cent. Audiences strongly agreed that 'a musical performance evokes an emotional response' and that 'interaction between audience and performers results in audience enjoyment'.

## Musica Viva (2008)

The first Musica Viva performance was the Bernard Trio of pianists, performed at a Melbourne jazz bar. Two focus groups were conducted: one with regular Musica Viva attendees and one with audience members who had not previously attended a Musica Viva performance. Participants described the music as 'buoyant', 'fantastic' and 'wonderful' and clearly these descriptions resulted from the intimacy of the venue and the close proximity of the performers, as described below. Where the participants identified limitations of their experience, it appeared that the intimacy of the performance was not matched by engagement of performer and audience member. For example, one participant said 'I guess there wasn't a lot of interaction […] there wasn't a lot of connection between the performers and the audience; or maybe it would have been good to get some more eye contact, and maybe try to draw the audience in a bit more'.

The second Musica Viva performance was a performance by the touring Choir of Westminster Abbey in a formal setting: Melbourne's then-largest concert hall. Focus group responses to the performance were somewhat divided between respondents who clearly saw the choir as rooted in a cultural and spiritual context – that of the English church – and were resigned to if not disappointed with the performance in a concert hall, and those for whom such a context was not relevant. Spiritual or religious references were common in the responses of the former group of participants, who remarked that the concert was 'uplifting' and 'I felt like I was in heaven'. The music was described as 'exhilarating', with 'exquisite voices'. Participants commented that they would highly recommend the performance to their friends and families.

## Australian Art Orchestra and Victorian Opera (2010–2011)

The final concerts in this research were with two small innovative groups in Victoria, the Australian Art Orchestra and the Victorian Opera. Researchers conducted a focus group and a survey. The focus groups revealed that audiences do not generally seek pre-show information but want to leave the performance with new learnings and understandings about themselves or particular social issues. They acknowledged the benefits of the emotional experience of the performance using phrases such as 'fantastic, I was really blown away', 'those two (singers) together, there was a peak there, an absolute peak where they just got in to a groove where it was a kind of a perfect amalgam of rock and jazz […] something very, very special', 'it was terrific', 'the hairs go up on your arms', 'you think how great they are', 'it's in the zone, it's transcendent, you know' and 'it's magical in a way because it's just that wall of sound: a voice and all the musicians' (Australian Art Orchestra), and 'they're adventurous, they're fresh, they're intimate', 'exciting in its production and very modern and colourful', 'imaginative and very exciting', 'wonderful voice', 'stunningly cast' and 'you're involved and emotionally engaged'. The audiences for these performances expected the company to present quality performances, particularly to meet their expectations of entertainment, believability and transformation. For them, the live performance precipitates a heightened experience. Ticket price is not the driver of the decision to attend, but is expected to equal the value of quality, entertainment and intrinsic benefit.

For the Australian Art Orchestra, most respondents agreed that they attended as many performances as possible in the venue. They liked the singer, liked the company and this type of performing arts, have looked forward to attending and would go more often if possible. They were not interested in attending with others. Most used social media. They felt that it was important to have notes on the programme, that the performance matched the promotion, that audiences knew how to behave, and they wanted to discuss the performance with others. They felt that it was very important (75%) that the musicians have technical skill, and they wanted to be challenged by the performance. One hundred per cent of respondents learned something new and their enjoyment was enhanced because they understood the meaning of the performance. Although they had no previous knowledge of the show, they felt the quality was worth the cost, and matched the reputation of the performers. Most respondents felt that other members of the audience shared their experience but this did not increase their understanding of audiences.

Despite the diversity in type and content of the concerts and the diversity of the audience, all audiences in these studies acknowledged that their role is to be an emotional listener. This role, selected from a list of options, shows the audiences place their personal emotions, which are derived from their intrinsic values and rewards, as their predominant means of engagement. They then used this role, or these intrinsic values, to define quality in three ways:

- Their appreciation and engagement with the performers/musicians was rated the highest of all components in the performance.
- They used emotional and spiritual words and phrases (exciting, fantastic, wonderful, imaginative, emotionally engaging, amazing, refreshing, innovative, awesome) to describe the live performance experience.
- Over 90 per cent of audience members stated that they would re-attend, or recommend to friends to attend this concert.

This reinforces that the audience experience in all these musical concerts is inextricably bound to their personal measure of quality, and to 'live' performance.

**The Value of 'Being There'**

The focus group questions prompted respondents to reflect on the nature of their experience as audience members and to consider a variety of elements which enhanced or detracted from it. Participants were asked to reflect on their responses to the performance, such as when they most felt engaged in the performance, what prompted this engagement, what emotions were elicited and how they expressed this emotion. In particular, respondents noted that the live nature of the experience was qualitatively different to the experience of being an audience for the non-live (electronically recorded and transmitted) arts, noting in particular the nature of the live experience as a shared, communal audience experience. The importance of being among other audience members was a recurring quality identified by the participants of this and other studies (Radbourne, Glow, Johanson and White, 2009). In this context, it is no surprise that social media have contributed to people's willingness to engage with electronically transmitted performances (Bennett, 2012), because it offers a greater opportunity for a sense of being part of an audience that was not so achievable in the era of broadcast radio and television.

Auslander (2008) argues that the notion of liveness began with and is inevitably dependent upon its opposite: the recording. Before there was recording, there could be no notion of the live, and while there is no inherent superiority of one over the other, the aim of making such a distinction is often to identify the qualities that distinguish liveness from its opposite. Moreover, as new technologies develop, they challenge existing notions of liveness, causing that notion to be repeatedly redefined (Auslander, 2002). Barker (2013) identified a number of elements unique to the experience of liveness, including: physical co-presence with performers and performance; simultaneity with the performance; direct engagement and absence of intervening (technological) mediation; a sense of interaction with performers; a sense of interaction with others in the audience; and a feeling of intensified participation through sensing any of the above. The data gathered in the course of the present study confirmed many of Barker's categories of engagement in audience responses to live music concerts, and also suggests, as Auslander contends, that the audience seeks from the live experience those qualities that are not available through electronically broadcast music.

A participant at the 2011 Australian Art Orchestra focus group was particularly eloquent in articulating the experience of live music: 'When you go to a live performance, it's happening, it's in the zone, it's transcendent. You feel like you're a part of something special: you've actually been present; you've borne witness to something'.

One of the key themes to emerge from the present research related to liveness as a form of 'intensified participation' (as identified by Barker, 2013, p. 20): liveness was seen to be a critical factor in determining the quality of the audience member's experience as a listener or attender. One respondent noted: 'I think when you are actually here in person you are more focussed and probably more attentive and more involved ... than listening to it at home'. Another participant noted that the liveness of the experience allowed for 'dedicated' listening: 'I think you're actually dedicated to listening to the performance, whereas at home you could get distracted by everyday things'.

In addition to the idea of dedicated attention or focused listening, respondents noted that seeing what they were hearing – what Barker refers to as the 'physical co-presence with performers and performance' (p. 20) – was also a key factor: 'I don't think there is anything quite like hearing the real thing, you can almost sort of feel … you can see the strings move as they are being hit and you just wouldn't get that from a CD'. A Musica Viva respondent noted that 'I connected more with the leader (of the choir) when he turned around and said a few things – I suddenly became interested in him'. It was interesting that one participant identified the expectation that the performer should engage with the audience as an Australian – or at least a non-European – expectation: 'I like the dynamics of one of the performers taking a break and coming to the microphone and just talking about the music [ … ] I don't care if they don't do it in Europe. We're Australians and that is the way we enjoy our presentations'.

A further theme relates to the sense of connection with the performers and the other audience members: 'A live performance is about the people more than just the music … and you've got to be there'. Another respondent noted that in addition to the aural pleasures of attending live music performance, there is 'the body language [of the performers] and seeing the expression and being part of the collective audience'. This was also the case for a Musica Viva research participant who declared that 'I like to sit at the front, how close you are to the performers. I liked the energy you could see in the performance'. Another participant also identified the 'intimacy' of Musica Viva's performances as one of the key attractions and the motivations for her subscription: 'And I am very fortunate in that I have a seat close to the front and the intimacy is enhanced'. Yet another participant in the same focus group said that her opinion of where she was placed changed over the course of the performance: 'at first I didn't like the fact that I was near the front, I was uncomfortable with the amount of noise. As it progressed I actually started to really like the fact that I was close to it and you could really see detail and what was going on, and the facial expressions that I think you might have missed if you were sitting further back'.

The research presented here relates to the audience's direct engagement with the performance and the absence of intervening mediation. One respondent noted: 'I think on television you see the show through the eyes of the cameraman who tells you what to watch; when you see live theatre you choose what you will watch'. Another affirmed this point by comparing the live performance, which is 'like watching a tightrope walker' to watching mediatized images which have been 'airbrushed', a statement which underlines the excitement and the sense of authenticity that can come with the live experience. Reflecting again on research into the use of social media in performances, it is clearly significant that social media can be employed and disseminated directly by audience members, in contrast to the professionally produced media that our participants referred to, because it means that those watching or listening to a performance remotely are not subject to the same 'airbrushing', or in fact, 'ear-brushing'.

## Conclusion

The aim of this study was to identify what the audience experiences and values about their presence among other audience members in a live music performance, with a view to contributing to increasing efforts to understand the audience's experience and to place this experience in measurements of the quality of a performance. Participants in a range of concerts by five different music companies consistently identified the value of the experience as including: the existence of and shared experience with other audience members; the proximity of the performers; and the opportunity to be thoroughly immersed in a performance. One respondent emphasized this last theme:

> Somehow when you're in the theatre with the cast and in the moment you're part of it, you're involved and you're emotionally engaged. When it's something on television you can choose to be involved, you can get up and stretch your knees, make a cup of tea and lose interest.

For the participants, these qualities are no doubt shaped by a sense of a distinction between the live performance and the transmitted or recorded performance. As Duffett (2003) notes, the notion of the live performance is changing as new media technologies develop and increasingly reproduce the perceived qualities of the live experience. The introduction to this chapter identified the fact that the relatively brief period of the performance itself represents the fulcrum of work by the music company and the expectation of the audience, and yet the experience that the audience has is still little understood. A potentially beneficial research endeavour would be to examine whether and how the production of a live performance and audience assessments of the qualities of the live experience are both changing in an effort to maintain the distinction, and therefore the practice, of the live music event.

Taken together with the summary of responses relating to emotional engagement during the performance, the audience live experience is a critical driver of the value and quality of the musical performance. As an article in the *Australian* newspaper reported, too many marketing campaigns 'are based on the assumption of repeat business, that a 60-something who buys a ticket to a Tchaikovsky symphony will want to hear another Tchaikovsky symphony the next time' (Westwood, 2013). Rather than simply gathering information about audience preferences, arts organizations that cultivate an understanding of the impact of their productions on the audience's social, intellectual and emotional lives are in a better position to increase the value of those productions.

Chapter 7
# In the Heat of the Moment: Audience Real-time Response to Music and Dance Performance

Catherine J. Stevens, Roger T. Dean, Kim Vincs, and Emery Schubert[1]

> that mysterious intimacy between audience and performer […] I wanted to challenge the implicit ritualism of performance, acknowledge its boundaries and subvert them. But how? (Jones, 1995, p. 164)

Social interaction and class display are supposedly important components of the concert experience, as well as other factors such as watching the performer(s), other audience members and the environment. But music listening during the concert has an expected salience. However, measuring this multifaceted experience has been difficult for researchers. Traditional, retrospective and single moment reporting of audience experiences are now being augmented by responses made as the performance unfolds. Encouragingly, new techniques for tracking responses continuously have developed beyond infancy, with various techniques available for moment-by-moment self-reports of variables such as engagement, 'when something happens', arousal and valence.

## Introduction

There are at least four reasons for investigating audience response to music and dance. First, if we take as a given that cognition is situated (Barsalou,

---

[1] The research reported here was supported by grants from the Australian Research Council (LP0562687, LE0347784, LE0668448, DP0987101, FT120100053). The study was conducted as part of *SEAM 2010* – Somatic Embodiment, Agency & Mediation in Digital Mediated Environments, and made possible by Garth Paine and Margie Medlin. For the opportunity, we are extremely grateful to Garth, Margie, choreographer Gideon Obarzanek, dancers Sara Black and Harriet Ritchie, Chris Mercer, Nick Roux, Rachael Azzopardi and Chunky Move, Timothy Jones and staff of Seymour, Sydney, Critical Path, Bertha Bermúdez, Frédéric Bevilacqua, Scott deLahunta, and Emio Greco | PC; for technical and research assistance we thank Jon Drummond, Paul Osborne, Staci Vicary, and Johnson Chen. We would like to acknowledge Stephen Tropiano, the Editor of the *Journal of Film and Video*, who obtained the high-quality photographs shown in Figure 7.6.

2008; Hutchins, 1995), that is, dependent on the immediate environment of the respondent, then studying the audience within an event presents an ideal opportunity to describe and document the perceptual, cognitive, social, and environmental contexts of the creative arts. For example, Corbett (1995, p. 233) has argued that jazz and particularly free improvisation, 'requires a [...] kind of listening in which the listener is active, a *participant-observer* of sorts'. Empirical evidence on jazz in a festival setting supports this in showing that such audiences show strong 'individual taste' that leads to 'loyalty' to performers and genres, rather than festival or occasion (Burland and Pitts, 2010). Cognition, including that of a performance audience, may necessarily also be culturally situated and the site of contested agendas, as in the case of Australian Aboriginal dance (Henry, 2000). Second, if cognition is embodied, that is, inseparable from the bodily functions of the respondent, then studying the multifaceted nature of response to a live performance – the interplay of visual, auditory, somatic, olfactory, tactile, kinaesthetic senses in a social setting – will be informative. A valuable review about embodied and social cognition aspects of dance has been provided recently (Sevdalis and Keller, 2011). Third, in the contexts of practice-led research (Barrett and Bolt, 2007; Reason, 2012) and particularly of research-led practice (Smith and Dean, 2009) it may be of interest for artists to have the means to gather information and co-relate artistic intention and audience reception (e.g., Brand, Sloboda, Saul, and Hathaway, 2012; Dobson and Sloboda, this volume; Reynolds, 2012; Weale, 2006; Whatley, 2012). Fourth, methods for the collection and analysis of continuous data will be beneficial to programmes of audience development and engagement (e.g., James, 2000; Pitts, 2005b; Walker-Kuhne, 2005), and interactivity and participation in our present and future mobile technologies and ubiquitous computing (Rieser, 2011; Sgouros, 2000, 2003; Tepper and Ivey, 2008).

This chapter begins with brief discussion of historical precedents to measuring audience response continuously. We then report a descriptive case study of audience response to a live dance work, provide a time series analysis of the performance features and responses, and discuss directions for future research.

## A Brief History of Continuous Audience Response Technologies

The computer based tools used for collecting responses from audience members 'in the heat of the moment' – that is, while they are in the midst of the concert/performance experience – can be traced back at least as far as the 1940s. Much of the technology was invented because of the desire from industry to monitor and improve their marketing, and later for educational applications which allowed for private but instant responses in a group setting – such as pressing a button, rather than raising one's hand in a class voting situation (Kay and LeSage, 2009). Millard (1992) refers to this application of audience response as 'electronic hand-raising'. Indeed such software is also seen in 'worm' readings on live television debates and in market research where, for example, competing political candidates are evaluated in real time live ratings for approval or disapproval (Davis et al. 2011). Of particular relevance to the measurement of audience response in live performance, several technologies were developed to measure reactions to films, TV and radio programmes using electronic hand-sets. A range of devices appeared, with audience members operating devices with push buttons, dials and sliders in response to predetermined questions (for a review, see Millard, 1992). These devices were precursors to the 'off-line' (single user) tools used for explicitly rating aesthetic responses, pioneered in the 1970s and 1980s with Nielsen's tension tongs (Nielsen, 1987), Clynes's sentograph (1989) and Madsen's Continuous Response Digital Interface or CRDI (Madsen and Fredrickson, 1993). It was not long before the next generation of such devices would be used to investigate audience responses to live performances.

## Applications to Live Performance and Usability of Portable Continuous Recording Devices

In recent years, ready access to affordable hand-held computers and wireless technology has enabled the recording of audience reactions in naturalistic and group settings. For example, McAdams et al. (2004) custom built a pair of sliders that audience members used during live performance of a piece for piano, chamber orchestra and computer processed sound by Roger Reynolds. Mobile computing and social network sites such as Twitter are also being used for audience research (e.g. Deller, 2011). Stevens, Schubert, Haszard Morris et al. (2009) developed a hand-held portable device on which responses were made via a stylus pointer as a dance work unfolded. Ratings along one or two dimensions were sampled twice per second.

In laboratory-based studies, continuous single dimension ratings include engagement, tension (Fredrickson, 2000; Krumhansl, 1998; Madsen and Fredrickson, 1993; Schubert, Vincs and Stevens, 2013; Vines et al. 2006) or aesthetic quality (Madsen, 1998). Two-dimensional scales have been used based on two-dimensional emotion spaces such as that of Schubert (1999) (2DES) with perceived emotion mapped onto the dimensions of arousal and valence (after Russell, 1980; Wundt, 1874/1905) projected at 90 degrees in the space. Other studies where arousal and/or valence have been rated continuously include Dean, Bailes and Schubert (2011), Egermann, Pearce, Wiggins and McAdams (2013), Ferguson et al. (2010), and Nagel et al. (2007). Such laboratory-developed techniques produce time series of self-reported ratings and have become common approaches for gaining insight into the moment-to-moment experience of a live performance from the perspective of the audience member. Continuous data can be interpreted with reference to other time series including the musical soundscape, a structural description of the work, or the kinematics of the performer (e.g., Stevens, Schubert, Haszard Morris et al. 2009).

While portable data recording devices for a theatre or gallery are now in use, from a human factors perspective it is important to scrutinize the ergonomics of such devices. A usability study was conducted on the portable Audience Response Facility (pARF) (Stevens, Schubert, Haszard Morris et al. 2009). The pARF records one- or two-dimensional data sampled twice per second. Questionnaire data can also be obtained. The pARF was developed on personal digital assistants (PDAs) but could be implemented just as easily using iPad or smartphone technology. We opted for a small hand-held device over a laptop computer so as to be portable and as inconspicuous as possible. Audience members use a stylus as input to the PDA. Touchscreens on tablet devices (iPads, Kindles) or other devices could now be used to optimize compatibility between the dimension being recorded and the nature of the response. For example, a touchpad where the finger position on a screen is recorded, a device with graded, haptic resistance to measure tension, a joystick that returns to a central reference position, or a device with accelerometers such as the Wii remote.

In a usability study, the first, third, and fourth authors asked: is the pARF user-friendly? Is training in its use helpful? What attentional resources are required to use the PDA during a performance? Would audience members prefer to complete a pen and paper questionnaire *after* a performance or use a continuous recording device *during* the performance?

Average, pooled usability ratings from a sample of 37 participants watching a live 10 minute contemporary dance piece at Deakin University in Australia are shown in Table 7.1. Ratings indicate that evaluation of the pARF was generally favourable. On a five-point scale with 5 referring to *Totally Agree*, and 1 to *Totally Disagree*, the mean ratings concerning ease of use and clarity of instructions were both greater than 4 (i.e. positive). Ratings of enjoyment tended toward the *Agree* range of the scale. Participants indicated that they would not prefer to use a pen and paper questionnaire to rate engagement *after* a performance rather than use the pARF *during* a performance. Perceived cognitive load imposed by using the pARF during a live performance is reflected in items regarding distraction and ease of use. A mean rating of 3.41 ($SD=0.87$) for the former refers to a mid-range *Slightly Distracting* rating of the statement 'I found the PDA distracted me from the performance' with a rating of 3 referring to neither disagreeing nor agreeing with the statement. Ease of use received a mean rating of 4.16 ($SD=0.55$) suggesting that, on the whole, audience members found the pARF easy to use. These results are quite similar to previous reports: for example, McAdams et al. (2004) report of their audience response study on Reynolds' *Angel of Death* that "several listeners indicated spontaneously in the questionnaires that the focused task enhanced the quality of the listening experience, because it drew them into the piece more". On the other hand, Egermann et al. (2013), studying audience responses to acoustic flute music, found modest 'negative impact' of a similar real-time response procedure (using iPods) on listening, as well as modest distraction due to other audience members.

Table 7.1    Mean usability ratings for the pARF where the maximum rating of 5 refers to "totally agree", 3 to "neither disagree nor agree" and 1 to "totally disagree".

| Item | Mean | SD | t |
| --- | --- | --- | --- |
| I enjoyed using the PDA. | 3.65 | 0.63 | 6.28 |
| I found the PDA easy to use. | 4.16 | 0.55 | 12.83 |
| I found using the PDA distracted me from the performance. | 3.41 | 0.87 | 2.87 |
| It was easy to rate my "engagement" continuously using the PDA. | 3.43 | 0.90 | 2.91 |
| I would prefer to use pen and paper to rate engagement *after* the performance than use the PDA to rate engagement continuously *during* the performance. | 2.16 | 0.93 | -5.49 |
| The instructions about using the PDA were clear. | 4.49 | 0.51 | 17.77 |

In Table 7.1, where $t$ is greater than $|1.688|$ then the ratings are significantly different from the midpoint 3, 'neither disagree nor agree', [based on $t$-crit(36)=1.688 at $p$=0.05]. All $t$-tests were significant at $p$=0.05. The question 'I would prefer to use pen and paper to rate engagement after the performance than use the PDA to rate engagement continuously during the performance' was rated as significantly lower than the midpoint of the scale, 3 (hence negative $t$-value). That concerning whether the PDA distracted from the performance also indicated a mild effect.

Tools for collecting continuous data can supplement qualitative data gained from answers to open-ended questions and questionnaires or Likert (rating) scales that summarize responses across a work. Survey and open-ended methods are administered easily and are information rich. However, they are also retrospective, rely on observer memory, and provide less of an account of moment-to-moment changes in response that may occur over the course of the performance. For illustrative purposes, in the next section we describe continuous measures of response to a live dance work.

## Case Study: Audience Response to Chunky Move's *Glow*

*Participants, Procedure, Materials, and Equipment*

In October 2010 in Sydney, Australia, the first author was involved in an arts-research symposium – SEAM 2010 Agency and Action – and had the opportunity to conduct a live, theatre-based audience response study. An experimental aspect of the study used a pre-performance installation of a 15-minute version of the *Double Skin/Double Mind* (DSDM) interactive DVD that had been developed by choreographers Emio Greco | PC in the Netherlands and a team of collaborators (Ziegler et al., 2007). The goal of the DSDM experiment during SEAM 2010 was to investigate the effect of a movement-based pre-performance experience on response to a subsequent dance work. The data reported here do not refer to the pre-performance installation or its effects but to a set of continuous data recorded from a sample of audience members as they watched a live performance of Chunky Move's *Glow*.

The sample consisted of 10 audience members (age $M=38.7$ years). Of the 10 participants, 6 had no training or experience in dance and 4 had extensive training or experience in dance ($M=11.25$ years). Prior to entering the theatre, participants who had volunteered to be part of the study read an information sheet and signed a consent form in line with the Human Research Ethics Committee at the University of Western Sydney (HREC7835). They completed a Background Information Questionnaire to collect demographic data. Participants were then given a PDA and briefly trained in its use. They recorded their self-report ratings of emotion continuously as the performance took place. Sitting together and near to the rest of the audience, the 10 participants watched a performance of Chunky Move's *Glow* at the Seymour Centre in Sydney, Australia.

*Glow* is a 25-minute illuminating choreographic essay by Artistic Director Gideon Obarzanek and interactive software creator Frieder Weiss. Beneath the glow of a sophisticated video tracking system, a lone organic being mutates in and out of human form into unfamiliar, sensual and grotesque creature states. Using interactive video technologies a digital landscape is generated in real time in response to the dancer's movement. The body's gestures are extended by, and in turn manipulate, the video world that surrounds it (http://chunkymove.com.au/Our-Works/Current-Productions/Glow.aspx).

Continuous responses from the 10 audience members were collected on the pARF, which recorded two dimensions of emotion as the performance took place. Participants used a stylus to draw on a two-dimensional space, 200 by 200 pixels, sampled at a rate of 2 Hz (Figure 7.1). The x-axis represented the valence (positive–negative) scale of emotion and the y-axis the arousal (aroused–sleepy) scale of emotion (Russell, 1980; Russell, Weiss and Mendelsohn, 1989). The axes crossed at the midpoint (100, 100). If the stylus was removed from the PDA the rating stayed where the last sample was collected until the stylus was returned to the display. The trace of the stylus location remained on the display for 10 samples even if the stylus was removed (see Figure 7.1).

The control application/web server/database server (Acer TravelMate 8000) was equipped with a 1.8 GHz Pentium® M processor with 1GB of memory, running Microsoft Windows Server 2003. The client device was a HP iPAQ Pocket PC h5500, with Intel PXA255 processor and 128MB memory, running on Microsoft Pocket PC version 4.20.0. A digital camera (Sony HandyCam HCR-30E) recorded both the server clock and the live performance for later reference.

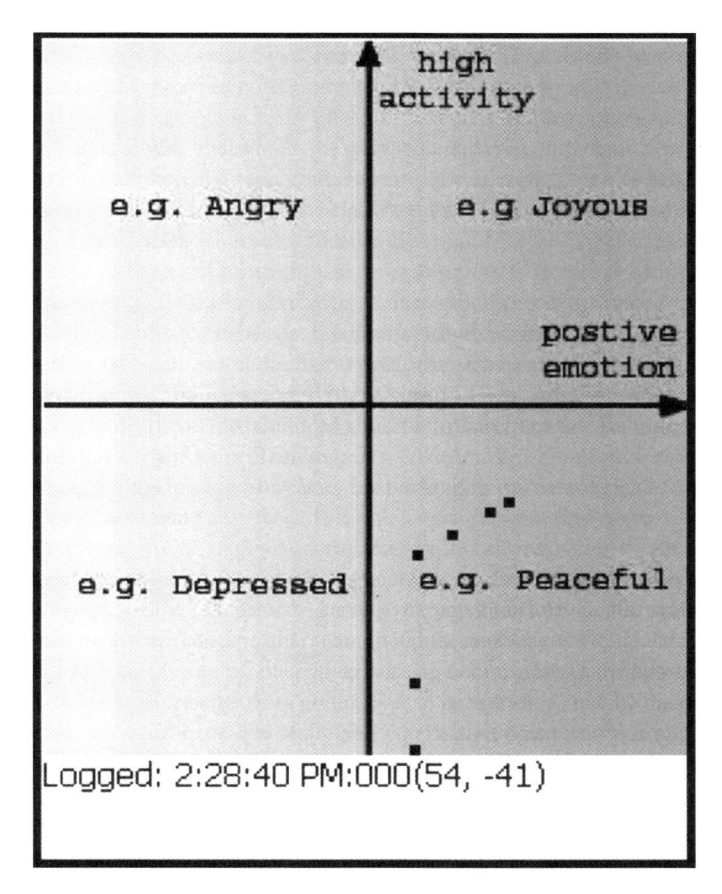

Figure 7.1  Two-dimensional representation of emotion on the portable Audience Response Facility (pARF). [Source: *Int. J. Human-Computer Studies, 67*, 800–813, © 2009, Elsevier, re-used with permission.]

*Average Continuous Ratings of Emotion*

In Figures 7.2 and 7.3 we see the group average raw (no preprocessing) time series data for the dimensions arousal and valence, respectively; group standard deviation (or variability of the ratings between respondents) is also shown. The darker line on each graph reflects the moment-by-moment mean response from participants. The figure also shows the main sections of the dance work.

Seven sections of *Glow* were delineated based on the nature of the movement material and the digital projections (highlights of *Glow* can be seen online at: http://chunkymove.com.au/Our-Works/Current-Productions/Glow.aspx). Section 1 introduces the solo dancer and builds to a climax in movement and sound.

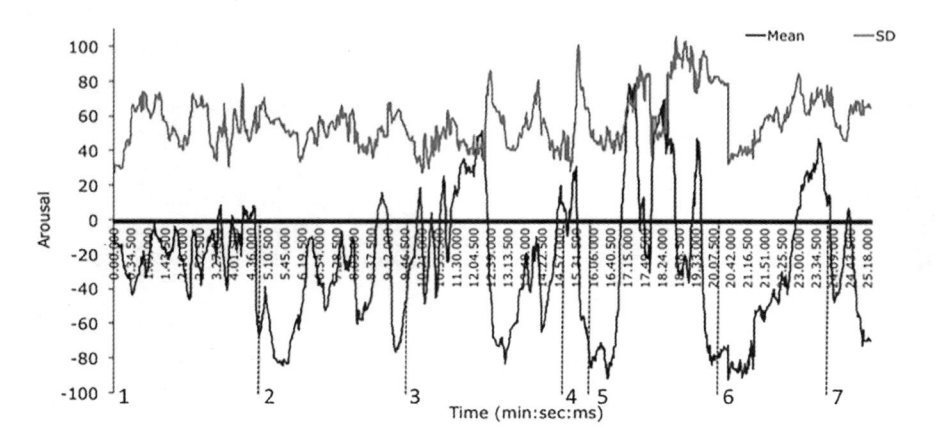

Figure 7.2    Mean arousal response and standard deviation across the 25-minute performance from 10 audience members

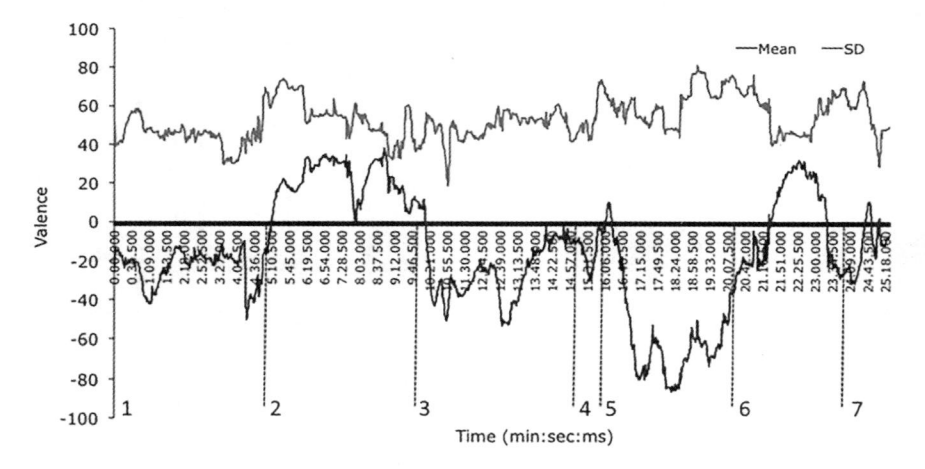

Figure 7.3    Mean valence response and standard deviation across the 25-minute performance from 10 audience members

Section 2 involves more lyrical movement and organic projections generated in real time in response to movement of the dancer. Section 3 includes new straight-line projections emanating from, and boxing in, the dancer. Section 4 is a short section with dark malleable projections enclosing the writhing, prostrate dancer. Section 5, nightmarish in feel, combines a number of different kinds of projections with the dancer contorting, convulsing and screaming. The glowing projections are black and the seeming shadows become autonomous and threatening to the dancer. Section 6 contrasts the previous section with more gentle, subtle movements. It builds to a resolution that climaxes as expanding white light, and concludes in Section 7.

In Figures 7.2 and 7.3 above, the rating scale for arousal consisted of 201 points (pixels), traversing -100 to +100. The seven sections of the work are marked with a dashed line and section number indicating the commencement of that section. Figure 7.2 highlights that relatively positive peaks in arousal/activity occurred in Sections 3, 5, and the latter half of 6. Figure 7.3 shows that there are two sections of the work that elicited positive valence, Sections 2 and 6. The "nightmare", Section 5, elicited negative valence ratings. The time series of audience response data will now be considered in light of the dance events and soundscape as 'independent variables'.

*Dance Structure and Soundscape as Predictor Variables of Audience Response*

The continuous audience perceptions of arousal and valence expressed by the dance were modelled by the second author in relation to acoustic and dance parameters by conventional techniques of linear multivariate time series analysis (autoregressive analysis with external predictors, ARX, and vector autoregression, VAR), as we have detailed previously for the analysis of responses to music (Dean and Bailes, 2010; Bailes et al. 2012). We used both STATA and R as appropriate. These are statistics packages that help to automate some of the complex computations involved when interpreting time dependent data. The continuous responses from 10 viewers (2Hz sampling rate) were averaged for these initial analyses. Arousal was statistically stationary (that is showing constant statistical features throughout) and thus suitable for the analysis, but valence required differencing to achieve stationarity. Differencing simply constructs a new time series based on the difference between successive values of the original time series. Thus differenced continuous predictor (and modelled) variables were used whenever valence was included in the analysis. They are referenced as dvariable (e.g. dvalence, where d indicates differencing). Models were selected by the relatively parsimonious BIC (Bayesian Information Criterion), meaning that the models are reliable, efficient and explain some of the variation in responses.

The predictor variables considered initially were thus 'section' (the dance sections, consisting of seven large-scale segments: a categorical, that is discontinuous, variable); and the continuous acoustic variables 'intensity' and 'spectral flatness' (an index related to timbre or tone colour). These acoustic parameters were measured on the performance video recording using Praat software, which provides specialist options for analysing audio signals. We also annotated the dance and segments in more detail, and defined shorter segments each characterized by a particular feature. We required a minimum segment duration of 10 seconds (20 data points), for reasons of statistical plausibility. Twenty-four features were defined for the dance movements, and several were recurrent. Apart from 14 seconds at the beginning before the dancer appeared, these dance segments encompassed the whole of the performance.

We considered the features of each response series taken as a whole. Arousal and valence were both autoregressive of order 5/6, as would be expected (Dean et al., 2011). This means that 5/6 immediately previous responses contribute to the prediction of the next response. In preliminary analysis (bivariate ARX analyses), the overall feature section was a significant predictor of arousal but not dvalence. Of the acoustic variables, only spectral flatness was predictive of arousal. Neither were significant predictors of dvalence.

Next we assessed whether there were Granger-causal relations between the responses in VAR. Granger-causality is an indication of statistical predictive correlations which might suggest causal relationships. For example, acoustic variables and/or dance structure might statistically drive arousal ratings. Considering arousal with the acoustic variables and with dance section, only the influence of spectral flatness was Granger-causal of arousal. In the equivalent analysis for the moment-by-moment change in valence (dvalence), there were no significant predictors. Given our hardware/software combination, we could not run VAR in STATA with all 24 dance features as endogenous predictors together with the acoustic variables as exogenous predictors; they were run in 2 batches of 12, and all but one were not significant predictors of the overall time series for arousal or valence. This is perhaps not surprising given that each feature type, even the most recurrent, occupies only a small portion of the total dance. Furthermore these variables only have two levels (on/off), unlike the nuanced acoustic predictors.

The segment variable 'static', describing periods with the dancer essentially motionless, was a significant predictor in the best models of dvalence (parallel with previous data emphasizing the importance of movement in arousal responses to dance: Calvo-Merino et al., 2008; Ferguson et al., 2010; Jola, Pollick and Grosbras, 2011; Reason and Reynolds, 2010). But these remained very poor models. When both darousal and dvalence were included as endogenous variables, there was no Granger-causality between them (in other words, they were separate responses). Good models of arousal (for example, with $R^2$ values in VAR > 0.4) could be obtained even with stringent model selection by BIC, but the $R^2$ values for valence were always small, with $R^2 < 0.07$.

Using the changepoint analysis (Changepoint package in R), detecting segments in either the valence, or the arousal univariate time series on the basis of segment differences in mean and variance, only partial alignment of the arousal and valence segments with the main sections was observed. Generally only 2 of the 7 sections coincided with changepoint-defined segments (even where coincidence was taken to be within 20 seconds). This suggests that the perception and affect elicited by the dance is rather more complex than simply predicted by the sections (see also Stevens, Schubert, Wang et al., 2009), just as it is also only slightly influenced by the acoustic parameters. Multivariate segmentation might resolve the sections more clearly, and this caused us to develop some less discontinuous measures which summarize the dance elements of the performance.

For this purpose, a dance- and choreography- practice and pedagogy expert, author three, defined four variables, each with a 1–5 Likert-like scale, which characterize the dance movements in the piece. The variables were based loosely on the elements of Laban Movement Analysis, specifically two effort qualities (time and flow) and two spatial parameters (body shaping and use of spatial pathways) (Bartenieff and Lewis, 1980). This selection was made in response to the specific choreographic approach of the work, albeit at a very generalized level, and was intended to emphasize the spatial configurations that were key to the interactive effects and the changes in movement speed and tone that characterized specific sections of the dance. Author three then made an assessment of the value of the variable at every point in the piece. In general these values change about once every 8 seconds, and commonly several change at the same time, giving only moderately more nuance to our descriptions of the dance portion of the work than discussed so far. Our 'variable' designations and author three's characterizations are as follows: 'Extension': Spatiality- dancer's body extension where 1 = small, contained and 5 = large, expansive; 'Speed': Dancer body movement tempo where 1 = slow, leisurely and 5 = fast, accelerating; 'Tone': Dancer movement tone where 1 = yielding and 5 = muscular; 'Spatial Movement': Dancer movement through space where 1 = stationary and 5 = travelling fast/far. The value 0 corresponds to the condition in which the dancer was not visible. These ordinal continuous variables were used in the next analyses. The goal was to ask whether the influence of musical intensity and timbral profiles might be strongly counterbalanced by that of relatively continuous dance parameters which may be their rough counterparts in that domain, and together constitute a fairly global description of the dance. For a further exploratory analysis, taking account of the continued relative sparseness of these dance descriptor data, we also combined the values of the four measures into one which we termed 'change' by simply summing them, to probe the possibility of an effect related to the amount of change in any combination of these variables, i.e., an effect related to change regardless of the variable in which it occurred.

The four measured variables did not provide improvement for arousal modelling singly or all four together in VAR, nor alter the required predictor terms in the best model: besides autoregression, spectral flatness was still required. The situation was exactly the same for the newly constructed 'change' dance variable. In analyses of valence, the individual dance variables were ineffective, and while dchange (the difference time series of the 'change' variable) was effective, it was not as powerful (and could not replace or add to) the predictive capacity of the section 'static' variable described earlier. These additional analyses support the conclusion that perception and affect in response to the dance is much more subtle than our analyses yet define, particularly with respect to perceived valence. In particular, it seems that we need stronger continuous variables which describe features of the dance and movement (and possibly the lighting) at least as fully as the simple global acoustic variables intensity and spectral flatness describe the audio.

Finally, we considered separately two of the major and very distinct sections of the piece, 2 (which is very calm: 302–587 seconds of the piece elapsed) and 5 (which is the peak of energy, and in some ways may be disturbing: 965–1217 seconds elapsed). Neither of these was fully delineated by the changepoint segmentation analysis. But it is noticeable that Section 5 contains within it a subsection defined by the crossing over of arousal and valence values, with strong mirroring between arousal and valence; and this can be detected by changepoint analysis. Thus we assessed whether and in what ways the time series properties of the perception of Sections 2 and 5 differed. Figures 7.4 and 7.5 show the dramatic difference in the arousal and valence responses to these two segments: Section 2 having low (mainly negative) arousal and moderately positive valence, Section 5 the converse. Particularly in the first there is mirroring of arousal by valence. This suggests that in VAR analyses of these sections individually, there might be significant predictor relationships between the perceptual responses, in addition to the modest influence of spectral flatness noted for the overall time series. Consistent with this, in the best model of section 2, dvalence was Granger-causal of darousal (coefficient negative, as expected) but not vice versa. dintensity was a predictor of arousal (dspectral flatness was not informative). The $R^2$ values for the models of section 2 darousal and dvalence were respectively 0.46 and 0.002, so only the former was indicative of a substantial predictive contribution. That is, the model accounted for a reasonable amount of variance for Section 2 darousal (but not dvalence). For section 5, there was no mutual influence between the perceptual variables, while intensity had some influence on arousal ($R^2$ for the darousal model was 0.21, and that for valence was again low, 0.02). It was also found that in part of section 5 between the arousal/valence crossover points there was again influence of arousal on valence (coefficient negative as expected for a mirroring process). Given our currently poor understanding of valence perception, it is reasonable to predict that these statistical influences of arousal on valence may have counterparts in causality.

We reconsidered those relevant amongst the 24 dance segment annotations in relation to Sections 2 and 5. None were influential in 5, but in 2 the segments labelled 'static' (as noted for the piece as a whole), 'floor' and 'fast' impacted significantly on darousal, and 'static' also on dvalence (improving the $R^2$ values to 0.48 and 0.03 respectively), again supporting the importance of motion parameters as predictors.

Perhaps the most interesting aspects of the dance perception revealed by these analyses are the difficulty of modelling valence, the distinctiveness of some of the sections in perceptual terms, and in comparison with listening to music, the relatively slight influence of acoustic intensity. Timbral properties (concerning the tone colour of the sound) were of comparable (modest) predictive power here to those observed with music. It was difficult to attribute perceptual change to most of the dance segment-types, though the motion-free segments seemed to be influential, reflecting the contrast between extensive and slight motion. It may be that defining continuous dance movement parameters (where a real-time perception of the parameter is made as a piece is viewed) is a more powerful approach to assessing the impact of dance structural segmentation on perception. This would be akin to acoustic intensity or spectral flatness for musical sound and may provide

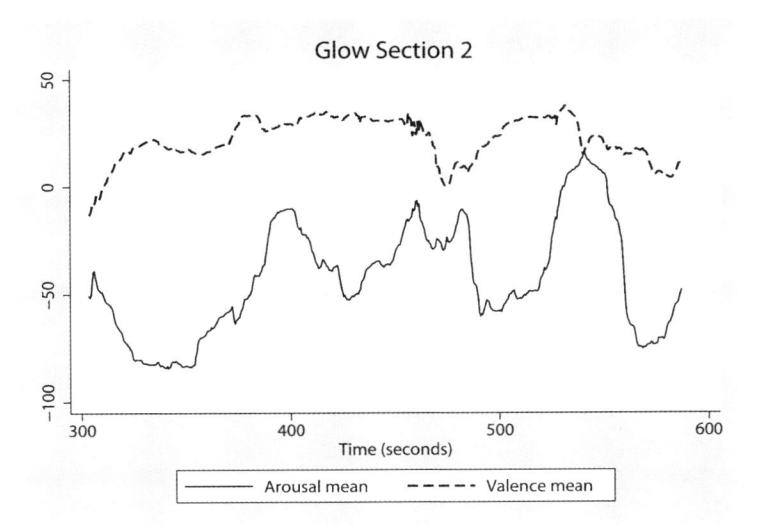

Figure 7.4   Mean arousal and mean valence continuous ratings recorded in Section 2 of *Glow*

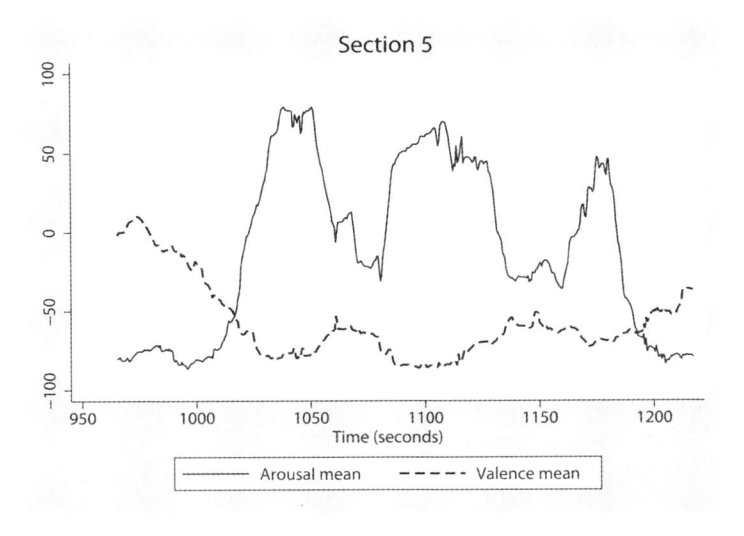

Figure 7.5   Mean arousal and mean valence ratings recorded in Section 5 of *Glow*

highly informative parameters in models of the kind we describe. The assembly of these continuous data into distinct segments may be a means of constituting gesture analyses, or in the musical analogy, motive (melody) analyses. We have also as yet not investigated the substantial lighting sequencing in the piece, nor specifically the computer-mediated continuous imagery; however they mostly occur congruently and simultaneously with the changes in the dance parameters. Previous studies have suggested that in purely sonic contexts, computer-generated acoustic segments can have a unique power (see, for example, McAdams et al., 2004), and there are similar suggestions for computer-mediated dance imagery in other works (Brooks, 2008).

**Discussion**

In this chapter we have described some of the methods and tools that have been used to record and analyse self-reported continuous responses of the live performance experience. The methods require the participant to make (usually) simple ratings throughout the performance, and therefore even in the heat of the moment, when something special happens. The analyses of these data suggest that we are able to answer questions about what actually happens to the listener at different points in time during a performance. From these investigations we draw the following conclusions: the audience member can identify, and is able to report, a range of feelings and observations about the music/dance experiences s/he is observing, and these experiences change over time. The comparison of these experiences with musical and dance features suggests that there is at least a modest relationship between the physical artistic production on stage, and the way it is reported and interpreted by the audience members. We presented two general techniques for analysing such data, from descriptive observations to statistical time series analysis, to help find relationships between audience members, and between audience and performers/performance. Furthermore, the tool we have used in our case study to collect the data – the pARF, a hand-held, stylus-interface system – is easy and enjoyable for the participant to use, though slightly distracting, and this is likely to also apply to other devices used for continuous response data collection in response to live performance.

Further research will develop our ability to understand quantitatively the moment-by-moment responses to a live performance. There are several time series models that have been successfully developed in predicting emotional responses to music, such as the fluctuations in acoustic intensity predicting emotional arousal response (Dean et al., 2011; Schubert, 2004). In our current analysis we have, to some extent, replicated this finding, since even with a visual dimension present (a dance performance), the changing intensity level of the music still predicted arousal ratings in at least some sections of the performance.

Questions to be answered are concerned with assumptions that underlie continuous self-reporting while a live performance unfolds. Although the usability data indicated that participants were able to complete the continuous response task successfully, more implicit measures may be needed to ascertain unconscious effects and demand characteristics (possible responses made by the participant as a result of guessing the hypothesis or hoping to please the experimenter).

Furthermore, part of the uniqueness of the live experience is that it is usually a social one, with more than one person in the audience. It is far from clear what impacts this has. There are questions concerning the audience–performer interactions, as well as the intra-audience interactions. On the one hand many performers take a positive view, as for example rock-guitarist Steve Howe (of the band 'Yes'): 'the audience do contribute an awful lot [...] You start [...] directing yourself at the audience' (in Bailey, 1992, pp. 44–5). And Berliner (1994, pp. 449–484) provides many anecdotal comments from jazz musicians to the effect that their work is positively influenced by the audience, though tempered by discussions of commercialization and its sometimes negative impact. From within classical Western music, English pianist and chamber musician Susan Tomes comments that 'In a concert, your consciousness embraces all the listeners as well as your colleagues. You catch them, they see you and you catch their eyes' (Tomes, 2004, p. 144). There is some evidence such eye gaze may enhance audience responses (Antonietti et al., 2009). On the other hand, both Indian musician Viram Jasani and flamenco guitarist Paco Pena express reservations (in Bailey, 1992). Jasani states that 'a musician [...] will try to put on his best performance before an audience, but he feels restricted. He's very careful' (p. 45), while Pena observes that 'If you have a large audience [...] it doesn't seem to give it a chance to be what it really is. Playing before an audience is always a compromise' (p. 46). Several elite figure skaters participating in a study concerning performance 'flow' (a state of absorption by the performer in their performance) also noted that a lack of audience response might negatively impact their realization of flow (Jackson, 1992). Such hesitations were taken to an extreme by renowned Canadian pianist Glenn Gould, who made influential live performances in the 1950s, including some in the Soviet Union, but refused to perform outside the recording studio after 1964. One possible factor on this decision is the extensively documented evidence of amplification of performers' anxiety in public compared with private, even with student performers (e.g. LeBlanc et al., 1997).

The issues of intra-audience interactions are probably less extreme, but nonetheless real. The most common comment on such interactions probably concerns distraction due to others; but there is also evidence that jazz audiences may 'value the opportunity to be amongst like-minded jazz enthusiasts' (Burland and Pitts, 2010); and concerts can also be a vehicle for shared audience political or sexual-orientation agendas (e.g. Morris, 2001). Furthermore, audiences may collectively infuse the live performance experience with emotional synergy through a contagious, 'rippling' effect of the kind Barsade (2002) refers to in a study of group behaviour in a business setting.

But it could be that making ratings on electronic devices draws too much attention away from the typical in-concert audience activity (ecological validity),

84   COUGHING & CLAPPING: INVESTIGATING AUDIENCE EXPERIENCE

Figure 7.6    Photographs of a 'test' audience watching a film at two points in time. The second photograph was reportedly taken during the funniest scene of the film. (Rose, 1954: a: Figure 2, p. 2 and; b: Figure 3, p. 5,). Copyright Journal of Film & Video, reproduced with permission.

making it little more informative than the continuous response studies (e.g., Dean, Bailes and Schubert, 2011; Madsen, 1998) that gather responses to a pre-recorded stimulus with the participant watching a computer screen/listening on speakers, in isolation (for example).

Future research will need to experiment with and expand the kinds of details that are measured. We have focused on self-report measures alone. However, there are many other possibilities, such as collecting physiological data (e.g., heart rate, skin conductance), brain scans (fMRI, MEG) and observational data continuously. Recording a range of indicators of audience response to a live performance will shed light on the interplay between sensory modes such as vision, audition, kinaesthesis, and changes in physiological arousal. To conclude this review, we will briefly speculate on one area, which is the continuous observation of facial and bodily expressions, one of the 'observational' approaches, and a subset of physiological approaches.

**Future Directions**

A recent study by Chan, Livingstone and Russo (2013), which tracked participants' facial muscles while watching a film of a singer expressing different emotions, produced evidence of spontaneous matching (mimicry) of facial muscles to the expressions of the singer. This study may suggest that it is possible to track the audience response to a live performance by observing facial (and bodily) activity. Audience members code facial expressions and bodily gestures in an audience setting that serves to signal emotional states, and communicate information to other audience members (see, for example, Lees and Stevens, 2002; Egermann, et al. 2011; Decety and Meyer, 2008; Jakobs et al., 2001). A hypothesis that audiences will automatically mimic emotions displayed in a performance, within the social context of the audience setting and live performers, presents the basis of a theoretical explanation that is testable, and suggests an alternate approach for future audience response research in live performance settings. This depends on the assumption that the key displayed emotions of a multi-dimensional performance are visible facially – an assumption open to empirical investigation.

Analysis of audience movement and facial expressions might overcome some of the limitations that current techniques for continuous monitoring of audience response exhibit. Another level of criticism of some facial/body monitoring approaches is that they, too, can be 'invasive' if measured via direct muscle activity monitoring. Moreover, non-invasive, observational coding protocols, such as Ekman's Facial Action Coding System (Ekman and Rosenberg, 1997), are time consuming. One innovative, relatively low-technology solution to tracking audience reactions by 'observation' is the analysis of applause and type of laughing in a recording of live music, which has been reported by Huron (2004) in recordings of music composed by 'PDQ Bach' – Peter Schickele. However, this depends on complex assumptions about the relations between humour and expression. We have seen gradual improvements in automatic analysis of facial expressions (Fasel and Luettin, 2003) and of the relation between movement and emotion (Camurri, Lagerlöf and Volpe, 2003; Demeijer, 1989; Sogon and Izard, 1987) meaning that little more than a high definition video of the audience will be sufficient to allow this kind of examination of audience reaction, when appropriate.

Ironically, motion and facial expression analysis approaches have origins in the invention of photography in the mid nineteenth century, where images of the audience were taken and then analysed. Take, for example, Rose's (1954) discussion of the use of 'test' audiences to report on the efficacy of a film that is in the final stages of editing. Figure 7.6 is a reproduction of two photographs from this 'experiment' and shows two instantaneous responses made by the test audience watching the film, which was clearly a comedy. Although the analysis presented resembles an early, primitive version of an audience response questionnaire (audience members completed a questionnaire, and they were allocated specific seats so that the questionnaire and photographs could be compared), the analysis of the audience facial expressions were at best general, speculative and non-systematic (this was not the main concern of Rose's exposition). However, the principle is one that lends itself to expansion into modern audience analysis of facial and bodily expressions. For example, Rose did observe that an audience member might look at an intra-audience companion in their vicinity at a key moment (compare 7.6a and 7.6b), foreshadowing some of the literature on contagion in sport and public speaking (Behnke et al., 1994; Freedman and Perlick, 1979; Hocking, 1982), and some more recent research in film viewing though under more controlled and smaller scale conditions than the historically interesting Rose study (Jakobs, 2001). The Jakobs study involved analysis of the viewer's facial expressions made during the watching of film clips. This is an example of how non-invasive (i.e. observational) video analysis may also be used to provide an additional dimension of data (e.g., Castellano et al. 2008). It will probably be important to obtain psychophysiological indicators which vary continuously, as well as the discontinuous, audible parameters such as laughs, sighs, applause, shouts, whistles, wriggling, fidgeting, coughs, murmurs and whispers, given the limitations of sparse data revealed by our analyses in this chapter.

**Conclusions and Limitations**

Audience response devices have developed considerably, particularly in recent years with the advent of easy to use, wireless mobile technology. We now have a growing literature documenting quantitatively moment-to-moment reactions, thoughts, behaviours, emotions and other ratings of audience members while present in a live event. We have been able to identify some relationships that are difficult to determine with retrospective accounts and more qualitative approaches, such as the finding in the case study of continuous responses to a dance work. In that piece, consistent with previous literature, we found that emotional arousal is related to the auditory channel (usually the music), and, in particular, to loudness or signal intensity. Relationships with other parameters of sound, and indeed with dynamic visual and spatial dimensions, require further investigation (see, for example, Calvo-Merino, 2008), although with regard to movement the literature provides several interesting predictions (e.g., Bachorik et al., 2009; Boone and Cunningham, 1998; Detenber and Reeves, 1996; Ferguson et al., 2010). The methods discussed may be used to investigate artistic intention and audience reception and/or have application to audience development.

Despite major advances both in technology and techniques, tracking continuous response to live performance has several limitations and beckons interesting psychological and philosophical dilemmas that will engage the research community into the future. Most significant is the possible anomaly of the social aspects of being at a live concert being usurped by the solitary activity or responding to a self-report device. In this respect, one may argue that there is no point having the complication of equipment to collect data in the live setting, as the results may be the same if the responses were collected from an audience membership of one, and/or in response to a played-back recording of the live work. This can be investigated by manipulating audience size and live/recorded conditions. Furthermore, methods of measurement that minimize intrusion on the cognitive processes of each audience member are nascent. Physiological measures may be viewed by some as invasive, and as being limited in the ability of the research to investigate the range of behavioural activities of the live experience. However, with technological and methodological advances, measurement of facial and bodily changes hold promise of a new generation of quantitative understanding of audience responses to live performance.

Chapter 8
# Texting and Tweeting at Live Music Concerts: Flow, Fandom and Connecting with other Audiences through Mobile Phone Technology

Lucy Bennett[1]

**Introduction**

> Everybody was holding up their hands, and here and there I could see guys holding up their cell phones, playing the music for someone else. (Strauss, 1998, para. 1)

In recent years, the use of mobile internet and social media platforms such as Twitter, Facebook and SMS text messaging has changed the live music experience for some popular music fans and audiences quite considerably, developing even further than the raised mobile phones first observed in 1998 by Neil Strauss. Within music fandom, live concerts have been determined as constituting a 'powerful meeting' place where individuals come together to 'enact the meaning of fandom' (Cavicchi 1998, p. 37). The arrival of these social tools has permitted a powerful interjection into the behaviour within this meeting place, by not only allowing music fans to find and connect with each other, but also to tweet and text concert setlists, photos and other information as they happen, thereby allowing non-attendees around the world to feel part of the event. This chapter will examine the process of texting and tweeting and mobile phone use by live popular music concert attendees as they attempt to connect with, and inform, a non-physically present audience. Through empirical research, in the form of a questionnaire conducted with fans of prolific touring artist Tori Amos, the impact of this practice on the physically present audience will be explored, in an effort to understand and unravel the consequences of this process on their live music experience. I will examine the responses of those engaged in this activity during concerts, and how non-users perceive it, in order to ascertain how technological tools and subsequent

---

[1] The author would like to thank Iñaki Garcia-Blanco for his valuable comments and suggestions during the conducting of this research and Rachel King for her support and help with the survey dissemination.

connections with non-physically present individuals can change an audience's engagement within the live listening process.

Another important consideration of the study will be to ascertain what fans at live music concerts perceive is gained or lost by the incorporation of these emerging social platforms into their live music experience. For example, mobile phones are now increasingly held in the air during concerts, replacing the tradition of using cigarette lighters (Strauss, 1998; Lingel and Naaman, 2012) and being 'constantly present' (Chesher, 2007, p. 217) within the audience. I will question how this may disrupt the concept of 'flow' (Csikszentmihalyi, 1990 [2008]) and how the engagement of a live music audience is viewed as being affected and impacted by the new tools. I argue that there is a tension for some fans between wanting to engage in acts of service to the fan community through texting and tweeting to the non-physically present audience, and committing to what is perceived as their own undisrupted engagement in the live concert experience.

The rise of mobile phones and internet has, in recent years, begun shaping and changing the live music concert experience for many audience members in attendance (Strauss, 1998; Bruno, 2011; Rose, 2009). The ability to preserve and share moments of the show as they happen – to take photos and upload them instantly, to capture videos of certain songs and moments and upload them via YouTube, to text friends that may be in the audience, or phone them during the show (Watkins, 2007) – is now being offered and utilized through smart phones and mobile internet. In addition, and as I have outlined elsewhere (Bennett, 2012), some individuals within, and communities of, popular music fandom have pleasurably embraced these activities, utilizing the tools to keep non-physically present members informed and granting them the ability to follow the developments of the concert as it happens, 'live', in front of their computers. However, in this chapter, I want to examine how this process not only impacts on participating and non-participating fan concert attendees, but how they articulate and negotiate this technological activity in terms of their engagement with the concerts.

A useful concept with which to understand and approach audience engagement is Mihaly Csikszentmihalyi's (1990 [2008]) notion of 'flow', which describes 'the state in which people are so involved in an activity that nothing else seems to matter; the experience itself is so enjoyable that people will do it even at great cost, for the sheer sake of doing it' (p. 4). In this work, Csikszentmihalyi explores 'flow' with regard to musical performance, concerts and listening, asserting that 'the very conditions of live performance help focus attention on the music and therefore make it more likely that flow will result at a concert than when one is listening to reproduced sound' (p. 110). He describes 'flow' in musical listening involving 'deepen[ing] concentration by dousing the lights, by sitting in a favorite chair, or by following some other ritual that will focus attention' (p. 110). Although work has been conducted on musical performance and 'flow' (Byrne, MacDonald and Carlton, 2003; Sheridan and Byrne, 2002) there remains little investigation into the concept with regard to musical audience engagement, especially concerning the use of technological devices. Thus, this study intends to consider how music fans perceive that 'flow', this focused attention, may be heightened or disrupted by connecting with the non-physically present audience through mobile internet.

**Live Music Concerts, Technology and Engagement: A Tori Amos Fan Study**

In order to question and explore how fans perceived these forms of technology in connection to their engagement, or 'flow', when they are physically present at live music concerts, I selected the fan community of American singer-songwriter Tori Amos as a case study that may offer rich insight into how these practices are being adopted and regarded. Tori Amos is a prolific touring artist who changes her setlist from show to show (Farrugia and Gobatto, 2010; Amos and Powers, 2005), includes improvisational songs and has a large fanbase with many attending multiple shows each tour and others who archive and discuss these performances at length online. Each concert has a texter or tweeter assigned by the fan community, who relays the information on the songs being performed, as they happen 'live', to fans gathered online on Amos's fan forums, Facebook and Twitter. Photographs are often tweeted, as are soundcheck setlists, if fans hear them from outside the venue, resulting in further discussion and speculation as to which of these songs would be performed during the actual show. As a singer and pianist, Amos either performs solo, with a three piece band, or with full orchestra, depending on the tour. Her solo and orchestral concerts lend themselves to an audience that remain quiet and focused throughout songs – playing the majority of the time at venues that have a seated audience. In contrast to this, her concerts with the band sometimes occur at standing venues and provoke a more active and physical response from fans in attendance. Irrespective of the setting, her concerts have been described as 'intimate' and 'intense' (Jeckell, 2005, p. 17), due to the strong connection and focus from Tori and her audience.

Tori Amos does not engage in social media other than having a Twitter account which very occasionally features messages seemingly from her – the majority of the tweets are from her management. However, she maintains a strong connection with fans at live concerts and the meet and greets that precede them – playing requests nightly and looking directly at people in the crowd throughout the show. As an 'aca' or scholar fan (Hills, 2002, p. 2) and regular attendee of her concerts since 1994, I have witnessed the changes in technology and the different demands and tensions this has placed on her fans in attendance at the shows – a process explored more systematically through this study. Thus, my position as an 'aca'/scholar fan delivers further insight to the investigation, increasing my ability to comment on the newness of fan behaviour relating to technology at live concerts, and its impact on this particular fan community.

## Approaches to Fan Research

In order to unravel and examine the responses from Tori Amos fans towards the use of mobile internet and texting during live concerts, I designed an anonymous online survey that would address these issues and during October and November 2012 posted an invitation to participate on Unforumzed (her unofficial fan forums), Twitter and a Tori Amos live concert tour group on Facebook. The survey was both quantitative and qualitative and received 56 responses, with 44 of these offering to take part in follow-up interviews and questions. From the respondents, 45 per cent identified themselves as male, 55 per cent as female, with no one identifying themselves as other. The survey reached a fairly widespread audience in terms of age: three per cent were aged 18 and under, with 32 per cent being aged between 19 and 29, and 61 per cent between 30 and 44. Four per cent were also aged between 45 and 65. Respondents came from 17 different countries, with the USA and UK dominating.

However, the limitations of an online fan study of this nature should be considered. The sample size equates to the impact of technology on specific online Tori Amos fans being testified within this study, but the number of followers who were not reached through this study, or are not online, are not accounted for. In this sense, the findings of the study do not claim to represent all Tori Amos or live music fans, much less all music audiences, but rather a proportion of online Tori Amos fans that use her fan forums, Twitter and Facebook and were motivated to respond to the survey. Given the newness of the fan behaviour being explored here, the relatively small sample was judged sufficient to make some preliminary investigations into uses of mobile technology during live music performances, and to identify questions and theories that can be developed in future studies.

## Changing Engagement? Fandom, Live Music and Technology

The dominant theme from the survey responses centred on engagement within live Tori Amos concerts, and how use of mobile technology during these events is perceived to heighten or disrupt this focus on the musical performance. As I will demonstrate, there is a tension for some fans between wanting to engage in important acts of service to the fan community through texting and tweeting to the non-physically present audience, and committing to what is perceived as their own undisrupted engagement in 'flow' and the live concert experience. In other words, the fans surveyed appeared to articulate a precise and sharp distinction between the two activities, with fans having to actively choose between both acts.

When asked if they had texted or tweeted the setlist and other information to an online audience during Tori Amos concerts, 13 of the respondents claimed they had in the past, or intended to in the future, whereas 43 of the respondents asserted that they would not engage in this activity. Reasons for engaging in this practice were overwhelmingly encased in a consideration for non-attendees who were following the updates in front of their computers or smart phones:

> I've done it for Tori Amos concerts just when they were in Dublin, mostly because there's a big online community who are always eager to know what songs she plays, as she plays a different set every concert.

> I have tweeted (and texted, before Twitter came along!) setlists as well as other information of interest that has taken place during live concerts. I have done this for various artists but primarily for the live concerts of Tori Amos due to the interest and demand of her large, dedicated cult fan base who are attracted to her widely-varying setlists night by night and her penchant for playing audience requests and rarities. I have tweeted from a variety of different venues from royal concert halls, theatres and clubs as well as outdoor festivals.

Others similarly expressed this motivation, underlining the pleasure they experienced when being in the position of following the setlist live at home, and subsequently being inspired to commit the same act in return for the fan community:

> The last two Tori shows I saw ('11 and '09), I texted a friend from the forums so he could post the songs to the thread. And when he went to a show, he texted me. I figured since someone always tweets/texts, when it was my time to go to a show, I could take a turn. I enjoy other people's live setlists so I had to give back.

> Yes, I have done this many times because when I am not at a show I like to see what's being played in real time.

Two other respondents had engaged in this activity in the past, yet declared they would not continue texting and tweeting due to a desire to be more 'present' within the concerts:

> I have for a couple concerts, because when I'm not in concert attendance it's fun to live vicariously through others updating in real time. I don't think I will continue this in the future, I have begun to abandon photo taking and texting/tweeting during concerts that have a real significance to me … I want to be more present during certain concerts (Tori Amos concerts for sure).

> I don't anymore because it is too distracting for me. I can't remain present or in the moment.

For these fans, use of mobile internet was perceived as disrupting their engagement with the concert, acting as a barrier and rendering them as non-present in the moment and event. In other words, the preservation and sharing of moments of the concert through technology appeared to reduce their connection and pleasure at the event, rather than enhance it.

Other respondents who did not partake in the activity of texting and tweeting also articulated the practice as being a disruption to engagement with the live event, using terms such as 'immerse', 'focus' and 'connected' to describe the important sensations that were perceived as being breached:

> No. I believe doing so violates the sanctity of the concert-going experience. If one is too busy fiddling with devices during a show, it is impossible to engage and be emotionally present.

> No, I don't text or tweet – when I'm at a concert I just want to focus on the artist and lose myself in the music. Personally I would find using my phone every song a distracting and annoying thing to do.

> No, I don't do this, because it would keep me from being connected with the music and the emotions. To me, a Tori Amos concert is an emotional experience. I want to feel the music and feel the emotions that her music creates for me and absorb them.

Others professed to logging the setlist through other means that did not involve their use of a mobile phone during the show. Instead, for these fans, a paper and pen was sufficient for them to note down during the concert the songs played:

> No, I write them down on a note pad, and then type them up online after. I do not do it during as it would be too distracting for me.

> I don't tweet or text the show. I am really trying to be present in the moment, and not be distracted by technology. I used to write them down by hand.

However, it is interesting that the use of writing, rather than texting, during a concert is not perceived as disrupting engagement with the event in the same manner as texting or tweeting.

When asked if their own texting or tweeting or that of fellow attendees had ever disrupted or improved their engagement with a concert, 21 respondents declared that it had never disrupted them, while another 21 reported that it had disrupted them, with three other respondents claiming that tweeting and texting in particular had never impacted on their engagement with a show, but taking photos or filming in their iPads by fellow fans severely had. One respondent described a moment where one fan was taking photographs with a loud beep that disturbed her so much

> I briskly crossed the [a]isle to her side and whisper-yelled STOP THAT. She jumped out of her skin, and complied. So comparatively, silent texting barely registers.

Overall, only one respondent directly claimed that it could be viewed as improving their engagement with a Tori Amos concert, which could be an indication of the activity being largely viewed as performed out of a duty to the rest of the Tori Amos fan community, rather than for personal gratification of the audience members.

In answers from participants who had never been disturbed or disrupted, there was a sense from some that their focus on the concert and performance was so strong that it could not be broken by being exposed to this act from other audience members:

> It hasn't because, well, because I've only been to the one concert and as far as I could tell no-one was doing it! Having said that though, my focus was all on Tori!

> During a show I only have eyes and ears for the artist. I've never been disrupted by someone while they were texting. I don't follow the tweets and text if I'm actually present.

Of those who did, or thought they would, feel disrupted by texting and tweeting, the glow of the mobile phone handset was a recurring theme, being mentioned by nine respondents:

> It hasn't [disrupted me] but I can imagine that if someone right next to me were to be doing it it would, because it's usually dark in the venues and a distracting bright light next to me would be annoying. I think that Tori's music is suited to dark and quiet and seating, rather than at most other pop/rock concerts where screaming and phones and talking and jumping/walking around can actually add to the atmosphere.

In this sense, the bright glow of the mobile phone handset is viewed as a pollutant that contests the 'dark and quiet', traditional setting of seated music concerts that Tori Amos events lend themselves well to. An essence of 'flow', the 'dousing [of] the lights ... that will focus attention' (Csikszentmihalyi, 1990 [2008], p. 110) is thus also viewed as being breached. Similarly, of those who felt disrupted and had engaged in this act of tweeting and texting during shows, there appeared an acknowledgement that it was impacting on their engagement with the show:

> I definitely don't feel as connected to the moment when I'm texting/tweeting. I try to pause and take in the music and the performance before sending an update.

> It does disrupt the flow of the show for me. Both the actual texting and the buzzing in my pocket that I have a response. I feel the anxiety to respond and

keep other fans in the loop. For a headliner or band I really enjoy I'll keep my phone in my pocket on silence.

Another respondent also expressed the same feelings towards missing certain elements of the show in their efforts to keep the non-physically present online fans informed:

> Sometimes, when you feel there is a dependency on you to tweet or text the setlist, you can become so engaged in doing so that you may not get to experience every subtle nuance of the show. You may miss a quick joke that is delivered by the artist on stage or a quick look or just a single note of a song and you will never get to experience that moment again. On the other side of the coin, by texting and tweeting, you are effectively creating a 'log' of the setlist in the sent items folder of your phone, so after the show, you can go back through and solidify your memories because you have them in written form, so in that sense, being a texter or tweeter can improve your own personal experience because you are thinking of the show in a more technical way instead of just soaking up the experience.

For this individual, the small and subtle moments of the performance that can be missed when using a mobile phone are the key drawbacks of the practice. However, an important aspect of this fan's response is the consideration of the idea that this use of technology can improve an audience member's experience in the form of 'solidifying memories' that may otherwise become lost or un-clarified over time. In other words, the act then produces something the fan can return to in the future, something 'solid' that can be used to remember the live experience in which they participated.

In terms of the technological act itself and its placement within the wider Tori Amos fan community, I asked participants to describe how vital they perceived this process to be within Tori Amos fandom. Despite the majority of respondents earlier indicating that they would not engage in the practice, a recurring theme was a sense that the technological practice by physically present fans offered a sense of inclusion to those who could not be there:

> As a frequently non-present fan, I think it's very important. We get a huge sense of community when we are taking part in a show we're not actually in. It's also interesting how we feel happy when an unusual song gets played. The good thing is that we know/hope there'll be a video or bootleg later so we can listen to it as well, and then we can (almost) share the experience of those who were there.

> Since I can only go to one show per tour tops, I love getting setlists in real time for the other shows I don't go to. Sometimes I will even play the same songs in my iTunes to see if I can get the vibe of the show by hearing those songs in that order.

> It's quite important, it enables the online community not able to physically enjoy the concert to somehow participate in it. It promotes group experience of the concert. I see it as quite a social thing to do.

While these fans reflect on the shared experience that the practice promotes, others also articulated how the process importantly worked to strengthen, solidify and maintain a sense of community among the fans:

> I think it is very important, (as someone who has not had the opportunity to attend concerts), it plays a very important role in keeping the Tori community together, I for one loved sitting in front of my computer waiting for that next tweet and all the facts and figures that follow from other fans, whether at the concert or also watching the set list live-tweeted, someone has always got some contribution to make.

> I think it makes the fanbase more solid, cooperative and it works as a feedback to the shows. It keeps people's excitement high during all the tour, a thing that never happened to me with other bands who always stick to the same setlist night after night, or who's not really good live. I really enjoy participating in the setlist frenzy, you actually feel the tour is happening, somewhere.

In the above responses, fans who were unable to attend multiple concerts on Tori Amos tours in particular expressed their value of the texting and tweeting process. In this sense, Cavicchi's notion of concerts being a 'powerful meeting of the various forces and people and ideas involved in [fans'] participation in musical life' (1998, p. 37) is further invoked, with the boundaries of these events being contested to include non-physically present fans who, together with the attendees that include them through technological acts, are able to repeatedly 'enact the meaning of fandom' (p. 37) where they may have been unable to before. As one respondent stated:

> It's very important. It feels that Toriphiles are committed not only to Tori but to each other too.

Another respondent also articulated the powerful impact of this process, expanding the energy of the live performance beyond the boundaries of the room:

> If you think about it ... energy is everywhere ... in all of us and to be in the moment, all at once ... sonically in the mind ... be it in the room or online ... I really think it has the potential to make everything as a whole more powerful ... charges the entire thing ... makes the energy level as a whole really expansive, [and] the fact that everyone who can pay attention ... [is] paying attention. Longing and hoping actually can [make them] vicariously enjoy and put out good energy into the universe (how's that for a really deep thought).

It could be argued that the perception of physically and non-physically present fans being together 'in the moment', despite their separated locations, rests at the crux of this texting and tweeting activity. The pursuance of this inclusivity could be interpreted as the driving force for engaging with this technological practice for some of these Tori Amos fan respondents, despite any conflicts or disagreements that may occur within the fandom. Another fan respondent viewed the value of the practice resting not only in its power of communal inclusion, but also in its preservation of important historical moments within the fan community that may otherwise not be chronicled:

> I think it's very important. I often go to a lot of small gigs by up and coming artists who do not yet have a long-term loyal fan base. Sometimes, these artists don't even have a setlist on stage so there is no way of actually CHRONICLING what these songs are and when and where they are being played. There are even some recent Tori shows that don't have complete and accurate setlists and this is a terrible shame for an artist who has such a long term, loyal fan base who are interested in the statistics of her concerts. By tweeting or texting a live occurrence, we are helping to record moments in history that may never be repeated and this fascinates me, especially when I know how much pleasure the non-present fans gain from this.

Thus, it appears, for the fan respondents to this survey, that while the practice of engaging in technological acts during a live concert can, on occasions, disrupt and disturb the engagement, or commitment to 'flow' for fans physically attending a live concert, the act delivers a great amount of pleasure to non-physically attending fans and works to solidify and foster further a communal and inclusive spirit within the community.

## Conclusion

This study illuminates how mobile internet and phones are impacting on popular music fandom and the physically present audience at live Tori Amos concerts. This case study demonstrates how some fans are experiencing a powerful tension between wanting to engage in acts of service to the fan community through texting and tweeting to the non-physically present audience members, to preserve and share elements of the show, and committing to what is perceived as their own undisrupted 'flow' (Csikszentmihalyi, 1990 [2008]) or engagement in the live concert experience. I show how these technological acts during live concerts are now perceived by some fans as a vital element with which to solidify feelings of communality and inclusivity amongst the fan community.

These findings lead to two key considerations. Firstly, for some music fans, there now appear to be two audiences, or groups of individuals, to consider and engage with at the same time during a concert: the audience members physically located around them at the show and the fans who are following it 'live' remotely through their computers or smart phones. As mobile internet technology develops further and may offer more tools for the inclusion of this non-present audience, absent fans may have an even stronger presence that works to stretch this tension even further.

Secondly, how engagement is approached by other music fans may also be called into question and complicated further. Younger fan cultures have grown up with mobile phones (Carah, 2010); Schlager (2005) observed at a teen music concert that the mobile phone 'appeared at the ear or in the palm of virtually everyone present' (p. 4) as audience members were texting across the arena, calling, taking photos and emailing. However, in the same audience will often be those who attend concerts by acts in different music genres and by artists who do not change their setlist between shows, and their responses to these activities may be remarkably different. For example, within some music fandoms and their respective live concerts, and in particular those that are encouraged by the artist themselves (Baym, 2011; Schlager, 2005), being engaged may involve raising mobile phones in the air during songs, taking photographs, shooting video and texting or tweeting to those who are not physically present.

Finally, future research could attempt to keep pace with these changing technologies by conducting other exploratory studies of live music audiences, either through ethnographic research during the shows, or by analysing data on social media platforms. In this sense, the impetus should be an examination of how fans not only use the platforms and technologies, but how they articulate and understand these practices. For, as technology develops even further, we may find that, for some individuals, their notions and understandings of engagement as an audience member or fan in attendance at a live music concert also develop and shift accordingly.

# Chapter 9
# Moving the Gong: Exploring the Contexts of Improvisation and Composition

Karen Burland and Luke Windsor
(with Christophe de Bézenac, Matthew Bourne, Petter Frost Fadnes
and Nick Katuszonek)

'It's the auditory and visual experience from the audience that I'm actually working with ... that's the material I'm manipulating'

The contexts of improvisation and composition afford and constrain creative performance in interesting, and previously under-researched ways. Using the practice of musical improvisation as a starting point, this chapter aims to explore the impact of the audience (as well as other factors, such as instruments, fellow performers and playing contexts) on a musical event as it unfolds, through qualitative analysis of a formal discussion between practitioners and music psychologists preceded by a musical performance. For the purposes of this analysis, we refer to performance context as more than just the physical space in which the music is being created; rather this term refers to all of the sensory information available during a performance – the acoustics, the physical and emotional atmosphere, the instruments, the musical material (where it exists), the contributions of fellow musicians, the audience (who they are, their expectations, their response and attentiveness), the time of day and the situating of the performance. These aspects are important to all types of musical performance, but their significance becomes arguably more pronounced in improvised music, where typical musical constraints (e.g., the score) do not exist, or exist only in limited form. While many of the chapters in this book focus on audience experiences of live performances, this chapter aims to explore the direct role of the audience in the *creation* of the musical performance from the perspective of the performers.

The theoretical context we adopt is drawn from ecological psychology, considered broadly as the study of behaviour as a mutual outcome of interactions between organisms and environments. This context is best represented in mainstream psychology in the field of visual perception where the work of Gibson (1950; 1966; 1979) presented a challenge to traditional explanations of seeing and the role of structured information in the guidance of action. However, as Heft (2001) has attempted to argue, such an approach presents a wider and more fundamental challenge to cognitive psychology. Heft reintegrates Gibson's work within a pragmatic tradition of radical empiricism, in particular bringing together the work of Gibson (ecological psychology) and Barker (e.g., 1968), whose work on behaviour settings (e.g., Barker and Schoggen, 1973) or 'ecological science' redresses the lack of attention to rich cultural and social environments in ecological psychology.

The first contribution of an ecobehavioural approach is the concept of *affordances* (see e.g., Gibson, 1977; 1979; Heft, 2001, pp. 123–135; Windsor and de Bézenac, 2012):

> The mutual relation between organism and environment is encapsulated in the affordance in the following way. Affordances are dependent upon the structure of the organism. This structure has been referred to as the organism's effectivities; its size, shape, muscular structure, movement capacities, needs and sensitivities that make action in the environment possible (see Shaw and Turvey, 1981). A rock which afforded throwing to an adult might be too massive to do so for an infant who does not have the appropriate size and muscular strength, and a pen would only afford writing to a human who has appropriate abilities. As affordances are a function of the relationship (or fitness) between an organism and its environment, they are not static, but change due to reciprocal changes in organisms and their environmental niches. For example, a dried river-bed no longer supports life for fish but may afford a crossing for a colony of ants. Likewise, as a child grows and becomes stronger, a rock that may have previously been unliftable may now afford throwing. This mutuality between an organism and the events and objects that surround it is central to ecological psychology. Hence, the concept of the affordance implies that whether we wish to study perception or action, the relationship between environment and organism is paramount, challenging mind/body and subject/object distinctions common in much modern philosophical and psychological thought. (Windsor and de Bézenac, 2012, p. 104)

In this context we focus on the settings for music-making and how these afford particular courses of action for the performers. A corollary of this approach is to consider the *constraints* a setting may furnish. The application to music of Gibson's most controversial (see e.g., Fodor and Pylyshyn, 1981; Sanders, 1997) but productive of concepts in this context is fairly unusual. However, work such as that by Windsor (2000; 2011), Reybrouck (2005), Clarke (2005), Krueger (2011), Menin and Schiavio (2012) and Windsor and de Bézenac (2012) has begun to use the concept of the affordance to better understand, for example, the role of the body in musical performance and listening, or the ways in which instruments constrain and afford musical outcomes.

The second theoretical contribution that this ecobehavioural approach can make to the understanding of creative practice is in its acknowledgement of and empirical focus on *behaviour settings* as higher order ecological units that both constrain and afford musical behaviour. Behaviour settings contain *topographical features* (such as the layout of a symphony orchestra, or the presence of a balcony in a concert hall), and *climatological properties* (such as the humidity and temperature of a concert hall or club). Cutting across and interacting with these are *sociocultural practices* (such as those described by Small (e.g., 1998) in relation to Western concert practice), and the objects, tools (instruments), people (co-performers, audiences) that are available within these settings (see Heft, 2001; Davidson and Good, 2002; Windsor and de Bézenac, 2012). In addition, the environment of a performer also contains the products of human cultural behaviour and their agreed significance (Windsor, 2004).

To summarize, we propose that the behaviour of musicians is afforded by relationships with their behaviour settings, and it is important for a psychology of performance to investigate these settings, the information they furnish and the use we make of them in performance: both behaviour and setting need to be examined in tandem.

**Participants and Research Method**

The starting point for this chapter comes from an invited panel entitled 'On the margins of idiomatic jazz: creativity in improvisation, performance and composition', which took place at the Centre for Musical Performance as Creative Practice (CMPCP) Performance Studies Network Conference at Oxford University in 2011, and its associated performance the previous night. The panel consisted of Luke Windsor and Karen Burland, who led the discussion with five musical improvisers – Christophe de Bézenac (saxophone) and Metropolis (Petter Frost Fadnes (saxophone), Matthew Bourne (piano), Colin Sutton (bass), and Nick Katuszonek (kit)). The performers have worked together in different ways previously, in ways that were helpful to the reflective nature of the research: de Bézenac and Bourne play regularly together as a duo, and de Bézenac, Bourne and Frost Fadnes completed doctorates in performance supervized by Luke Windsor. Some of the performers were less familiar with each other, since there were two performance groupings reflected in the membership, while all have an interest in the boundaries between free improvisation and composition.

In some sense these performers represent an opportunity sample, and any grouping of improvisers might have been appropriate. However, their shared interests allowed for the possibility of a richer discussion across the continuum between improvisation and composition than otherwise might have been afforded by, for example, a group of free improvisers or a group of idiomatic jazz musicians. The high levels of general and musical education possessed by the group may or may not be entirely representative of improvisers (or musicians) but is indicative of a sophisticated level of both technical and philosophical engagement. The web of relationships between the players (and indeed the researchers) allowed for a number of interesting interpersonal dynamics to emerge from both the performance and subsequent discussion.

Figure 9.1    View of the performing space from the balcony

**The Performance**

On 16 July 2011, Metropolis (Petter Frost Fadnes, Matthew Bourne, Colin Sutton and Nick Katuszonek) and Christophe de Bézenac played a late-night set at the CMPCP Performance Studies Network Conference; the following day they were joined by Karen Burland and Luke Windsor for the invited panel discussion. The performance took place in Robinson College Hall, Oxford, and was preceded by a formal dinner. Figure 9.1 shows the performing space during rehearsal taken from a balcony: during the performance about half of the audience watched from this vantage point, half from the floor of the hall on the seats as set out at long tables for the dinner. There was a high audience turnover, with many appearing and disappearing to and from the adjoining bar. The acoustic was extremely reverberant, and there was no stage lighting, making the venue unusual for this style of music.

The performance began with a duo (Bourne and de Bézenac); this was followed by a section in which the other musicians of Metropolis took over (starting with Katuszonek and Sutton, then Fadnes and Bourne), with de Bézenac returning and the full group continuing in varied configurations for the remainder. The performance lasted for approximately 90 minutes.

## The Invited Panel

Following a brief introduction by Luke Windsor, the panel introduced themselves and provided some biographical information to contextualize their experiences as improvisers. Karen Burland led the discussion, which began by considering the previous evening's performance before moving on to a broader discussion of the contexts of musical improvisation. The aim of the panel was to explore the aspects described above, focusing in particular on the behaviour settings of improvised music. The final 30 minutes of the discussion solicited input from the audience, which yielded further insights beyond the specific contexts and experiences of Metropolis and de Bézenac. The discussion was transcribed verbatim and analysed using thematic analysis (Braun and Clarke, 2006) to reveal five main themes which can be considered as *behaviour settings* which influence improvised performances: other musicians, instruments, musical material, the performance context and the audience.

This chapter complements others in the volume by offering insight into the impact of performance contexts (including the performance space, the audience and other musicians) on the performers and the overall performance experience – perhaps particularly pertinent to an improvisational context. As discussed elsewhere in this volume, albeit with different terminology, behaviour settings have an impact on audience experiences in live performances (i.e. the venue, other audience members, perceived atmosphere – see chapters by Pitts, Kronenberg, Karlsen), and this chapter offers an insight into the experience from the other side of the stage – suggesting that performers, and performances, depend upon the range of behaviour settings described above.

## Topographical Features/Climatological Properties

Given the unusual nature of the performance venue and context, it is perhaps appropriate to begin our discussion by considering the impact of the physical space on the musicians, before considering the impact of sociocultural practices related to other musicians and the audience. As stated in the description of the gig above, the acoustics of the performance venue were extremely reverberant and therefore challenging for the musicians.

> The room plays a massive part and the more dense the texture the more difficult it is, you know, it's good for a room to tie you together in certain ways, but it can go overboard. (CdB)

However, in the same way that the musicians perceived 'musical' challenges as inspirations, so too a venue's acoustics shape the performance:

> Initially I think 'right, I have to adjust the way that I play' which automatically puts me in a position where I've kind of not been before, and I have to think about whether I can still play the tunes and improvise and still get the message across, so I'm kind of dealing with a whole different set of circumstances really, just think about how I still get the energy and the message that I want to get across, but still kind of keep it under control ... it's good in a way, it might not feel like that when you soundcheck in the afternoon, you think 'shit, what am I going to do?!' but looking back it's good, 'cause you realise you have to adapt and it forces you to kind of face up ... it might push you into new areas that you might never have been in before (NK).

The challenge of working in an unfamiliar and unflattering venue highlights the ways in which topographical features shape performances. While the planned performance may not be possible in such a setting, the implication in the quote above is that such contexts may actually enhance the performance: the acoustics in a venue can affect the ways in which a performer adapts the performance – in terms of communicating 'the message' to the audience – while also maintaining some sense of control. Concern for the audience's experience is at the heart of the performance choices made by the musicians, and responding to particular topographical features brings that concern to the surface and, in some instances, provides new inspiration for the music. This also indicates an intricate web of interactions between different behaviour settings; other musicians offer affordances for a given musical performance, but such interactions take place within a physical environment which also affords and constrains particular behaviours.

One example of this emerged within the audience Q&A at the end of the roundtable session – providing an insight into the impact of the performers' choices on the audience. As already described, the musicians began the gig with a duo (Matt and Christophe), incorporating the dinner gong which happened to be present in the room as well. Earlier in the discussion the musicians highlighted that it was the nature of the room's acoustics that had led to the decision to start as a duo. In addition, the choice to use the gong demonstrates a concern with exploring sound to engage an audience:

> It was interesting having the gong there too ... it could be anything, for me it doesn't necessarily have to be a piano, I mean you can make music out of some glasses, it's not different ... I think that's why we kind of work well together ... because the instruments that we play and practice on so much can still be ... you can still find amazingly fresh things within them, and certainly for the piano, especially with a grand piano, there's so many things, harmonics, between, and obviously using other objects to get sound from them is really interesting (MB).

The gig started with Matt playing the gong, a choice that drew the audience's attention to the unconventional performance space, immediately engaging the audience and drawing them into a creative process that relied entirely upon the precise performance context at that moment in time. This choice was particularly successful, according to one audience member:

> I really liked the way you started, the duet started playing the room ... with that very percussive approach right at the beginning, dealing with the reverberation and so on ... I think it was really helpful to start the gig like that, just feeling your way into the space.

By recognising the affordances of the specific performance space, the performers were able to enhance the audience experience; the musicians and audience alike were affected by the specific performance context (i.e. 11pm, unconventional performance space within a grand Cambridge dining hall) and the choice to work with the affordances of such factors helped the audience to engage more immediately with the performance.

In addition to the physical space, its particular climatological features also impact on a performance:

> There are people who rely less on their intuition and rely more on, you know, on the things that they've learnt to carry it off, you know, they battle against all these natural circumstances rather than giving themselves over to it, and I think in a lot of ways ... some people end up missing out on all the surprises and fun and enjoyment you can get from giving over to it. You know, maybe the room's really hot, and at first it might really piss you off, but then again you might get really into it, and just starting thinking, well I'm slightly hot, so I might as well work as hard as I can and just sweat! (MB)

Matt suggests here that challenging performance settings can potentially detract from the performance. However, he implies that 'giving ... over to it' can actually enhance the performance, affording new musical opportunities and experiences that might otherwise be missed. While Matt is talking specifically about the room temperature in the quote above, all musicians agreed, and provided evidence throughout the discussion, that 'giving over to it' – whether 'it' is a difficult acoustic, physical performance space, or performance time – affords a wide variety of musical opportunities. It is possible that this may be particular to contemporary and open improvisation, but we suggest that such perspectives inevitably have an impact regardless of musical style – they are simply brought to the fore in a discussion about music which does not rely solely on a written score.

**Sociocultural Practices: Other Musicians**

The relationships and interactions between musicians are important within any performance context, but arguably these are magnified within an improvisational context. Unlike more traditional musical performances, musical improvisation does not rely wholly on fixed notation; in addition to the performance space, the audience and the instruments themselves (which will be considered below), other musicians can offer inspiration – both in terms of performance intention (i.e. when planning a performance or rehearsing) and in the live performance.

*Like-minded, but Different*

For the musicians in the current study, a shared vision among co-performers was important when deciding to work together initially, as well as for developing material:

> It was very much a bit of rebellion against the system to start with ... it was just finding people with similar interests really. (NK)

> It's the people that are willing to actually stay together for long enough to ... figure something out ... and there's also the intention to [use] everyone's various backgrounds, but to try to find something new or some common goal within a particular context ... it can't just be the typical jazz thing in terms of 'we're getting this music together for a particular event', there has to be a reason for getting the music together ... it's in and of itself a valuable thing, and not everybody thinks that way. (CdB)

The implication is that working within an improvisational context relies upon establishing a sense of value-based cohesion which allows the musical material to be the primary focus, allowing an eventual performance which is meaningful and rich, cohesive yet individualistic. Value is placed on a musician's individuality, their (often) diverse musical backgrounds and on finding a way to explore those differences within any performance. Indeed, conflict is perceived positively by these musicians:

> We've just kind of accepted that we're different and that ... makes it what it is, and we've ... gone at it so much that the ... disparate elements... form that one sound, if you like. And that's certainly the case in the way that we operate, I mean, each of us... operates differently. (NK)

> The worst music I hear is music where you can hear all the musicians agreeing, or seemingly agreeing, and ... playing together as one big happy family ... we're not trying to be, and we're not afraid to just ... go 'OK, you can hear we're clearly not agreeing in this' but it ... gives it tension, so for us to agree would be completely against what we ... do. (PFF)

Aside from the 'rebellion against the system' (NK) providing a foundation for the music in its broadest sense, differences between performers afford the exploration and development of musical material that is entirely dependent upon that particular moment in time and the performers' individual experiences of that shared context. The tension arising from the 'disparate elements' is ultimately the unifying feature of this particular group of musicians; conflict affords musical opportunities. In a similar way, the musicians spoke about the inspiration derived from introducing new players into the group:

> [Bringing new players into a group] broadens it up straight away ... getting another saxophone player in ... you get torn and you start anew, you hear new sounds and you think 'OK, we could try that' ... it's like having conversations, suddenly, you know, you get new impulses, new ideas. (PFF)

There is a tension here between musicians working together long enough to find some common ground (see Christophe's comments above) and taking inspiration from a new player with whom they have shared less performing experience. Both situations offer musical affordances of different kinds in the context of improvised music, yet both are described by the participants as inspirational and as having a direct impact on the musical material. The spontaneous nature of improvised music is thus shaped in part by the affordances of other musicians, although this only works when there is a certain amount of trust between the musicians.

> Walking on stage in a room like that, you know, at 11 o'clock, in a sense the situation is against you, but we know each other well and I trust them that whatever happens we'll ... be able to pull through ... obviously you want to be pushed and you want to ... be on edge in the sense of when you're playing together and move into interesting areas, but at the same time you want the trust there that if I stop, other people are doing different things and you know, if I do this thing, and react to it. (PFF)

There is a clear sense of shared responsibility between the musicians to ensure the quality of the performance regardless of the specific performance context (in this case, the late timing of the gig); the experience of the audience is implicated in the quote above, but co-performers are trusted to challenge, enhance and support the individual performer and the performance more generally.

**Sociocultural Practices: The Audience**

While the emphasis so far has been on the performer perspective, the other integral participant in any performance is the audience. Christopher Small (1998) describes the separation between performers and the audience, suggesting that the latter have no impact on the musicians on stage. Recent research suggests that this is far from the truth in a variety of contexts such as chamber music (Pitts, 2005b), jazz (Hytönen-Ng, 2013) and popular musics (Karlsen, this volume), although there are few examples of such studies. The improvisers in this study also acknowledged the role of the audience, emphasizing its influence on their experiences of any given performances, as well as on their musical choices.

*Relevance and Communication*

There was agreement among the panel that the audience has a direct impact on live performances, describing them as 'completely linked'. The audience is both a source of information which may guide the performance, and a focused target for the musicians' actions. Communicating with the audience was of primary concern and all musicians spoke of their awareness of the audience – its experience of the performance, its visible or audible reactions – and its impact on the performance. The behaviour settings described above would be incomplete without the presence of an audience, particularly in relation to the musical score:

> I think it's about what you, as a performer, what's the process that you want to go through to, in a sense, communicate something meaningful, so in that sense the audience and the performance are completely linked … .I mean if we stand there and read and have like ten page scores, and maybe play music that sounds relatively similar to what we're doing, but it would make us fundamentally unhappy as performers, we wouldn't necessarily be able to communicate a sense of excitement, a sense of edge, all the things you expect as audience. (PFF)

The combination of behaviour settings described so far directly impacts on the performers' experiences of a performance, which in turn has consequences for the experience of the audience. Within the broader context of other musicians and the performance space, the musical score is potentially limiting for the live performance. Indeed, the beginning of the gig as described above would not have been possible had the performance been reliant on that ten page score. However, it would be misleading for us to suggest that improvised music is most successful when it is completely free; the musicians all acknowledged how the presence of some notation affords a range of musical opportunities:

> I think that just by having the tunes there themselves, it just opens it up and makes it even more free, I know that's a bit of a contradiction but just turning up and playing free is kind of limiting in a way … for me it kind of comes with all that baggage and that's the kind of sound world and you can do things to get away, but having the tunes there as well, and having that as almost like a departure point for improvisation … it just kind of opens up a new area. (NK)

> It's very easy to get stuck in various ruts … if you're sort of exploring a texture … well for me anyway, I'm sort of falling back into certain licks or tricks, whereas … I think if you've got a piece of music in front of you … it can help to stop that sort of, you know, reliance on … sort of autopilot in playing, so you can look at the score and think 'OK, I'm going to take that, that needs to

be there' and play around with it, and then all of a sudden you're into these new areas without even … having to work particularly hard at that, and you'll just sort of become … immersed in the music. (MB)

While the audience are not mentioned explicitly in the two quotes above, the musicians are aware that the performance may suffer if the innovation and inspiration afforded by the interleaved behaviour settings are absent; the musical material contributes to these settings and also affords opportunities for creative and engaging performances.

On a different level, an audience's reactions during a performance can also shape it. At the most fundamental level, the audience has a direct influence on a performance, with Christophe stating that 'it's the auditory and visual experience from the audience that I'm actually working with … that's the material I'm manipulating'. The audience becomes an integral part of a live performance, complementing the affordances of the other behaviour settings described above. Continuing the theme of 'giving over to it', working with, and responding to, the atmosphere created by the audience affords additional opportunities:

It … depends on how much you're willing to embrace the atmosphere in a situation where you're playing, and that includes the audience and … for me at least, the audience is really, really, really important, because even though, there's this very strange quality, there's a certain energy being given off by our audience, and there are certain things you can pick up on and certain things you can't, that, that unavoidably, I think it depends on how much you, you've got your ego switched on, but, but sometimes you think, well, 'I'm doing this, and this is fine, I don't need your reaction, I don't need to feed off it', and then sometimes, it depends on your own psychology, but you're like 'just give me something!' and I think sometimes it, … in France especially, if you're playing on your own, the audience is so quiet that if there's something that you might do that's particularly frenetic or whatever and usually you might hear some fidgeting and someone going [whispery mumble] it, it's all these things that you can hear and absorb, and for you they can, those disturbances, they can come to mean certain things, you think 'oh this is going well, I'm getting a reaction'. Not that you do it to get a reaction, but, you know, there's certain signifiers and, um, for me those things are really important, but you know, some audiences are so quiet, and you get to the end of the gig and you find you have to do three encores 'cause they really liked it, they're only really quiet 'cause they're listening so hard. [MB]

The comments above further emphasize the interwoven relationship between different behaviour settings, used by these performers to create the performance and to make it meaningful. A further implication is that there is no single formula that determines the extent to which the settings interact; the individual identity of the performer and their own experiences of the performance in that particular moment is also critical – perhaps the underpinning notion is that of the sense of 'giving over to it' and working with the web of affordances presented by each unique performance situation.

The unique attributes of each performance certainly provide opportunities to explore the musical material and the affordances of the performance space but the audience have a further impact on the limits of that exploration:

> It's ... almost like an adrenaline junkie ... you just want to climb higher and higher and do more and more extreme things, and I'm working now more and more in settings where it's completely improvised, feeling that, you know, going on stage and just completely working on the parameters you have in this room, with this audience, on this stage etc., and just focusing on that. But the challenge is, obviously, not being self-indulgent and not just ... playing for yourself because ... that's the big ... pitfall of improvised music, where you end up, you know, it's interesting and it's fun, what you're doing, but it doesn't mean anything and it's not relevant. (PFF)

Being mindful of the audience, therefore, has a dual purpose, particularly in this context: the audience can act as part of a behaviour setting in its own right, with audience reactions and energy impacting on the performance choices of the musicians, but it can also play the role of moderator – the musicians are aware of the audience's experience of the performance and are concerned that it remains meaningful and entertaining. Hence, the audience both acts as a source of information for the performers, but also vice versa: the performers act upon the audience; two perception-action cycles interlock (as described in Windsor, 2011, in relation to visual information).

The audience is therefore an integral part of live performance, particularly within a free improvised setting. It is one component of an intricate web of behaviour settings that combine to create a performance – neatly summarized by one of the players as follows:

> I think the audience and the room, and the temperature, your own psychology, you know, they're massive factors, you know, especially when you're improvising, and equally as a duo, I think there's so much scope to feed off that, or the potential for that. [MB]

**Discussion and Conclusion**

This chapter has considered how the contexts of musical improvisation impact on live performances – from the perspective of the performer and the audience. Responding to the affordances of a behaviour setting can create a meaningful performance which is entirely dependent upon a unique combination of the different aspects of venue and people (performers and audience members) present in that moment. Although we have discussed these aspects in specific relation to improvised music, it is likely that behaviour settings impact on all musical performances, regardless of musical genre and that by 'giving over to' the physical and social aspects of particular performance contexts, performers can create meaningful performances for audiences (cf. Gabrielsson, 2010).

This chapter offers a complementary perspective to those offered elsewhere in this volume – demonstrating that just as the layout of particular venues or the atmosphere among the audience impact upon the audience's experience of a live performance, such aspects are significant for performers too. Therefore, considering live performances from an ecological perspective suggests that all aspects of performance contexts are important for *everyone* sharing the experience, and that to consider different behaviour settings in isolation may present an incomplete picture of what makes live performances meaningful.

Improvised music is a useful example for highlighting the impact of the interaction between different behaviour settings because the absence of a full score allows for more opportunity to respond directly to the specifics of any performance context. However, the research demonstrates that an approach to performance which accounts for the experiences of the musicians and the audience simultaneously is critical to the success of a performance (cf. Radbourne et al., 2009). Therefore, an ecological approach offers an opportunity to suggest that the most successful and meaningful live performances depend upon a web of interactions between four features of the performance environment, as shown in figure 9.2

Each aspect of the performance environment affords opportunities for performers who aim to create meaningful performances for the audience (and themselves). Such performance factors can present challenges (such as difficult acoustics or climatological features), but may also enhance a 'planned' performance. By working with the affordances of each of the four elements, performers can create unique and special performances that work for audiences because they are directly relevant and responsive to that moment and place in time; the audience's experience becomes meaningful because they are part of, and witness to, the music's creation. This research furthers our understanding of what makes live music special and considers how performances are shaped by the performance context, just as the audience's experience is enhanced by a similar set of behaviour settings. Less certain, however, is the extent to which our participants are 'typical' as some were particularly self-reflective about the nature of their practice, partly due to having completed PhDs with similar concerns. Similarly, there are still questions about how we can meaningfully 'measure' the impact of the environment on performance, particularly with improvised music. The approach we have taken here, however, provides an informed and considered performer insight into the impact of performance contexts on the creation of a musical performance, highlighting that 'giving over to' all aspects of a performance context (whether physical or social) can create meaningful experiences for everyone that could only be encountered by being there at that moment. Creative music-making transforms spaces for an audience: but the audience itself is part of the space to be transformed, a source of affordance and constraint, a target for

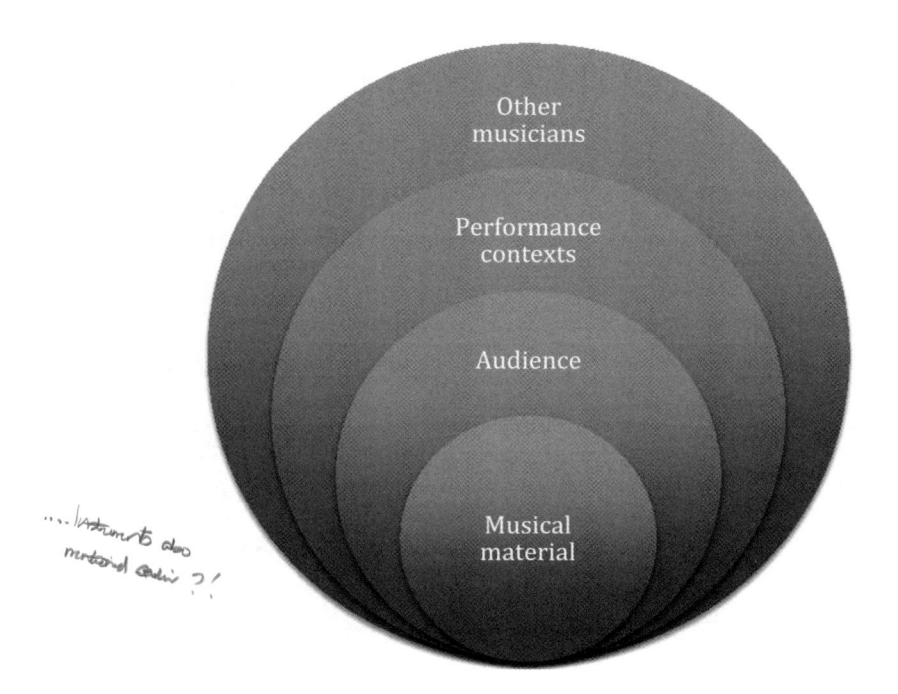

Figure 9.2    Factors influencing live performance/improvisation in context

transformation. As Reed (1996, p. 160) argues (in discussion of William Morris and Pablo Picasso): '(A)rt is a necessary way of enriching everyday experience. Both loved to transform their living places, to design rugs and chairs, plates and wall decorations that expressed how they wished to live'.

It is an error to portray creative music-making as the one-way transmission of information to an audience. It is a piece of work upon a space, which responds to that space and the audience within it as well as transforming it into a less unfamiliar, more challenging setting in which we audience and performers have to learn in real time.

Chapter 10
# Context, Cohesion and Community: Characteristics of Festival Audience Members' Strong Experiences with Music

Sidsel Karlsen

**Introduction**

A widely held belief among theorists and philosophers who have written on, and tried to explain, the phenomenon of festivals is that such events provide frames for their participants' feelings of an extraordinary existence or, in other words, modes of being that cannot usually be accessed in everyday life. For example, the German philosopher Gadamer (1986) describes festivals as events that raise the attendees out of their ordinary existence and into 'a transformed state of being' (p. 59). Likewise, the Russian scholar Bakhtin (1986) writes about festivals as liminal occurrences that produce exceptional frames of time and space – what the Italian theorist Falassi (1987) denotes 'time out of time' (p. 7). Furthermore, Falassi emphasizes reversal, abstinence, intensification and trespassing as the four cardinal points of festival behaviour (p. 3). In other words, festivals offer a self-contained experience that takes participants out of their daily lives and into unusual and out-of-the-ordinary behavioural and existential landscapes.

The exceptional experiences that festivals are thought to provide are also linked to the formation of community in the sense that the events' social function and symbolic meaning is seen to be closely connected to the ideology and worldview of specific communities, to '[their] social identity, [their] historical continuity and [even] to [their] physical survival' (p. 2). Hence, the festival audience members' experiences *during the event* are perceived to have profound meanings and as such to exceed the sphere of the individual and contribute to creating cohesion on the supra-individual level. In addition, should the event happen to be a *music festival*, it also carries potential for providing its attendees with so-called strong experiences with music (SEM; see Gabrielsson, 2010), that is, with intense and sometimes overwhelming emotional reactions to its programmed musical contents.

In this chapter, I will use data and findings from a study of a music festival situated in northern Sweden as a point of departure for investigating the connections between audience members' reported SEM and the festival as a lived community. While the research was originally undertaken in order to explore the particular festival as a source of informal learning (Karlsen, 2007b, 2009; Karlsen and Brändström, 2008), the research sub-questions investigated topics such as how the festival contributed to the construction of its attendees' musical self-narratives as well as to the development of local identity in the municipalities in which it was arranged. Consequently, the extensive data collection included, among other things, audience members' self-reports on festival-related SEM because such experiences were believed to play a potentially significant part in the construction of musical self-narratives. The empirical material also contained a considerable amount of survey, observation and interview-based information (see Karlsen, 2007b, for details about the data collection) on the festival's function in relation to outward branding of and inward reinforcement of cohesion in the affected four municipalities, which bordered on each other: Piteå, Älvsbyn, Arvidsjaur and Arjeplog. These dimensions were seen as important when it came to the event's impact on the development of local identity (see De Bres and Davis, 2001; Delamere, 2001; Gursoy, Kim and Uysal, 2004). In the following, I will first give an account of the findings from the analysis of the festival attendees' SEM self-reports before I move on to describe some of the communal aspects of the festival in question. Thereafter, as stated above, the connections between these two areas of findings will be explored.

**Strong Experiences with Music during Festival Performances**

The festival attendees' self-reports of SEM were collected through the survey among the audience (see Karlsen, 2007b). As part of the questionnaire, the survey participants were presented with the following question and request: 'Music may, on certain occasions open up strong emotional experiences. Have you ever had such experiences during concerts given by *Festspel i Pite Älvdal*? If yes, I would like you to tell me more about it'. Of the 158 participants who answered this question positively, 131 chose to express their experiences through short statements of between one and approximately 50 words. Since the participants were not limited to reporting their experiences during the year of the actual data collection (which was 2005), their statements potentially covered a period of 25 years, this being the lifespan of the festival they attended. As Zentner and Eerola (2010) emphasize, there are numerous methodological challenges connected to self-reports of SEM, and in particular to reports of the retrospective kind as were utilized in this connection. However, sometimes such accounts simply represent 'the most important kind of evidence of emotions' (Sloboda and Juslin, 2010, p. 75) which cannot be accessed in any other way.

The survey participants' statements sometimes took the form of descriptions of their state of mind during the experiences asked about, while 113 of the participants chose not to describe their emotions directly, but rather what caused them. These latter 113 descriptions were taken as a point of departure when analysing the material and identifying 34 factors that impacted on the occurrences of SEM by using the principles of qualitative content analysis (see Kvale and Brinkmann, 2009). Two main categories were constructed – 'contextual factors' and 'intrapersonal factors' – which, when combined, covered 11 subcategories divided into two different levels (see Table 1 below). This inductive coding was followed by a more deductively oriented process (see Karlsen, 2007a), comparing the findings from the festival attendees' self-reports with previous research on SEM (Gabrielsson, 2001; Scherer and Zentner, 2001).

According to Gabrielsson (2001), personal, situational and musical factors may all influence the occurrence of SEM. While *personal factors* include, for example, the listeners' physical or emotional state, cognitive factors and personality-related variables 'such as temperament, maturity, and dispositions' (p. 445), *situational factors* are about physical and social features of the listening situation or venue, special occasions or circumstances, for example being abroad or in an unusual environment when listening, and performance conditions, such as 'music well rehearsed or unrehearsed' (p. 445). Furthermore, *musical factors* may include the perceived quality of the performance and 'the skill, concentration, and involvement' (p. 443) displayed by the musicians, but also structural features of the music itself, such as unexpected chord shifts, timbre, loudness, dynamics, tempo, mode, rhythm, 'beautiful melodies and harmonies, thick texture, increasing tension followed by relaxation' (p. 443) and so on. Scherer and Zentner (2001) make a similar division when they draw up the 'production rules' (p. 365) of experienced emotion when listening to music. In their opinion, such emotions are 'determined by a multiplicative function consisting of several factors: Experienced emotion = Structural features × Performance features × Listener features × Contextual features' (p. 365). Again, structural features refer to attributes of the music itself, in other words 'the building blocks of musical structure' (p. 362) and the 'systematic, configurational changes in sound sequences over time' (p. 364).

Comparing, at first sight, the SEM-inducing factors reported by the festival attendees (Table 10.1) to the findings and models of Gabrielsson (2001) and Scherer and Zentner (2001), it becomes evident that personal and situational factors, or performance, listener and contextual features, are abundantly present in the festival-related material. However, references to musical factors evoking SEM are few, and in those cases when such factors are mentioned, they are mainly connected to the experienced quality of the performance or the skills of the musicians, more than to structural features of the music itself. In fact, only one respondent reported such features being, at least partly, the reasons for the occurrence of SEM: 'Occasionally I am filled with happiness by *understanding* parts of, or whole musical sequences when I have *forgotten* everything around me'. In this quotation, the combination of the cognitive process of understanding and the experience of the suprasegmental feature of 'musical structure and form' (Scherer and Zentner, 2001, p. 364) seems to have been the triggering element. However, unlike in Gabrielsson's (2001) body of data, where descriptions of musical-structural features triggering SEM were quite common and related to 'many different genres' (p. 442), this is the only such example from the festival-related empirical material. What could be the possible explanations of this divergence?

Table 10.1. Factors reported to have impacted on occurrences of festival attendees' SEM

| Main categories | Sub-categories, level 1 | Sub-categories, level 2 | Factors/codes |
|---|---|---|---|
| **Contextual factors** | Frame factors | Event-related frame factors | Time of day (night concerts) |
| | | | Space (church, nature) |
| | | | Size of audience and event |
| | | | Target group adjusted events (children) |
| | | Music-related frame factors | A cappella song |
| | | | Live music |
| | | Audience-related frame factors | Fellow audience members dancing and singing |
| | | Musician-related frame factors | Age of artists (youth) |
| | | | Artistic innocence |
| | Mediative factors | Mediation characteristics | The kind of artists performing |
| | | | Quality |
| | | | Humour |
| | | | The kind of instrument played |
| | | | Soloists |
| | | | Style played |
| | | | Particular piece of music |
| | | | Well-known music (in general) |
| | | | Atmosphere |
| | | | Artists' contact with audience |
| | | | Musicians' enjoyment of playing together |
| | | Results of mediation | Feeling of togetherness |
| | | | To feel involved with the music |

| Main categories | Sub-categories, level 1 | Sub-categories, level 2 | Factors/codes |
|---|---|---|---|
| **Intrapersonal factors** | Cognitive/emotional processes | Emotional work | |
| | | Memory work | |
| | | Associations | |
| | | Cognitive understanding | |
| | Results of cognitive/emotional processes | Insight | |
| | | Bereavement | |
| | | Experienced contrast to own world of work | |
| | | Synesthesia | |
| | Factors based on personal preconditions | Being acquainted with performer | |
| | | Own musicianship | |
| | | Being exposed to something different | |
| | | A surprising experience | |

Firstly, there is a distinct possibility that differences in the sampling of the participants of Gabrielsson's study and mine may have been a contributing factor to the difference in findings. While in Gabrielsson's research one-third of the participants were educated as professional musicians (2001, p. 434) and hence trained to perceive, remember and verbally express the structural features of music, only five (3.8%) of the 131 survey participants who chose to write about their SEM as part of the festival study had a similar background (Karlsen, 2007a, p. 165). One may therefore hypothesize that for amateur musicians and non-musicians, unlike for professional musicians, contextual, listener and performance features may be dominant, or at least play a more significant part with regard to the 'production' (Scherer and Zentner, 2001) of SEM.

Secondly, among the 113 participants who chose to describe what caused their festival-related SEM, the vast majority – 92 respondents – mentioned contextual factors (or, in Scherer and Zentner's words: 'contextual features' and 'performance features') while only 21 mentioned intrapersonal factors (or 'listener features'). This may point towards contextual factors being of special significance for evoking SEM in a festival situation, perhaps connected to the exceptional experiential frames that festivals are thought to produce (Bakhtin, 1986), or simply connected to festival organizers putting a lot of effort into providing contextual richness and diversity for their audience, both with respect to frame factors and mediative factors (see Table 10.1).

Among the contextual factors that seemed to be especially important to the festival attendees' experiences were nature, time of day and venue, often in combination with specific artists. For example, during the festival of 2005, when the fieldwork was undertaken, several concerts were located in a spectacular outdoor venue close to a big waterfall, and this place was mentioned time and again in the SEM statements:

> Storforsen [the name of the waterfall], [name of artists playing], sun, warmth, magic, magnificent. The nature contributed a lot to this amazing music night. I cannot forget this concert with [the musicians'] professional performance.

> [Name of singer] by Storforsen. It fitted so well with the nature.

Others mentioned the church as a venue that for them facilitated a particular experience, sometimes strengthened by concerts being scheduled late at night:

> Among other things resting the soul in the room of the church while surrounded by good music is an experience in itself.

> Especially night concerts in churches – [they] provide an atmosphere that leave traces. I have had different strong musical experiences – the room of the church provides some – the musicians change, yes even the audience [changes].

Moreover, particular artists could be a source of SEM, international as well as local. Here is an example involving a local band that had a big reunion concert during the festival of 2005:

[The members of a local band] have been my idols since I was six years old, when they played in my home village – I know all their songs and have waited for their reunion and concert for over ten years!

Other factors in the contextual category that seemed to be of great importance for evoking SEM concerned different levels of experienced cohesion, either among the musicians themselves or between performers and their audience. Sometimes the size of the audience and the choice of repertoire also played a contributing role:

Last summer at [name of place]. That was cool. The musicians enjoyed playing together to such an extent and I saw that they were impressed by each other.

Concerts with a large audience and well-known music, where musicians and audience together create an atmosphere so that you get goose bumps and teary eyes.

At times, the feeling of togetherness in the festival situation would go beyond the temporarily created festival community as such and extend to a broader experience of belonging to larger groups in society. This lived communality would be described as an SEM-inducing feature in itself, reflected in the situating of the festival in North Bothnia, an area located on the periphery if viewed from the Swedish capital, but with an explicit and distinct regional identity:

To see a band that I never thought I would experience. The feeling of cohesion among people belonging to different age groups and [among] North Bothnians.

It is also evident from Table 10.1 that the festival attendees described a wide range of intrapersonal factors that impacted on their SEM; for example, many performed emotional and memory work (DeNora, 2000) alongside the music presented in concerts, like this person: 'I processed a deep sorrow in my life this summer, among other things through music'.

Others had their experiences boosted through connections to their own professional or amateur musicianship:

Since I previously, as an amateur [musician], have dedicated myself to active engagement with chamber music [in general] and with chamber orchestras in particular, concerts with a good chamber orchestra such as [name of a particular orchestra] mean a lot to me.

However, despite these accounts, the main focus of the SEM statements was, as mentioned above, on contextual factors. Among these were also factors that were strongly connected to audience members' experiences of cohesion and of belonging to a community. As such, festival-related communal dimensions were clearly manifested in the SEM data and played an important role in many of the participants' strong experiences with music. Furthermore, these dimensions could also be detected in other parts of the empirical material, and in the following I will pursue this line of enquiry and describe all the aspects of community found within the festival context.

**The Communal Aspects of Music Festivals**

Through my analysis I came to see the festival as encompassing, co-creating and sustaining three different but interrelated forms of community. First, it functioned as a learning community, or, rather, allowed several learning communities to emerge and function within its frames. Second, as noted above, to some degree it became a vehicle for the outward manifestation of community identity, and thereby a possible tool for the branding of its host municipalities in the larger surrounding society. Third, by drawing on and creating an arena for shared stories and cultural practices and ideals (Ekman, 1999), it also became an occasion for the inward reinforcement of social and cultural community identity, or for the 'deepening, retelling and prolonging [of] already existing community narratives' (Karlsen, 2011, p. 189).

In exploring the festival as a source of informal learning, Lave and Wenger's (1991, see also Wenger, 1998) theory of *situated learning* within *communities of practice* was employed as the epistemological framework of the research. Central features of this theory are that learning happens through 'legitimate peripheral participation', in other words through individuals being 'located in the social world' (Lave and Wenger, 1991, p. 36) of the community in question and interacting with its participants and the activities, identities and artefacts found within its frames. The key to such participation for newcomers is to gain access to the community 'and all that memberships entails' (p. 100), and often what is needed in order to 'become a legitimate participant' (p. 105) is learned through spending time with and observing the community's old-timers or, using the framework's own terminology, the 'full participants' (p. 105) of the community. Furthermore, each community of practice is said to carry the kind of knowledge that provides 'the interpretive support necessary for making sense of its heritage' (p. 98) and thereby also for producing its own future. The historical trace of 'artefacts – physical, linguistic, and symbolic – and of social structures' (p. 58) enables this constitution and reconstitution of the practice over time. Analysing the chosen music festival as a potential community of practice provided insight on the rich learning outcomes and numerous ways of learning among its attendees (see Karlsen, 2007b, 2009). It also enabled a discussion of the festival community's function in relation to society at large by illuminating the questions of who is learning what, from whom and for what purpose.

In addition to understanding the entirety of the festival as a community of practice as such, two sub-communities were identified, both with learning outcomes that, at least to some degree, seemed to have connections to the attendees' SEM. First, the festival encompassed a strong classical music community with members who were very active and who attended a lot of concerts, mainly classical music-related productions but also concerts exhibiting other styles and genres. Hence, the members of this particular sub-community were often full participants (Lave and Wenger, 1991) of the wider festival community in the sense that they had access to large parts of what the total community encompassed. Furthermore, they predominantly belonged to the middle class of their municipalities. A second sub-community emerged around a local band's reunion concert referred to in two of the survey participant SEM-quotations above, about the reunion concert and the experienced cohesion among North Bothnians. In both sub-communities some of the learning outcome on the individual level was connected to audience members learning about themselves – '*who they [were]*' (Karlsen, 2007b, p. 206) – through the emotional, memory and identity work described as the triggers of the SEM categorized under intrapersonal factors (see Table 1).

Another feature that both sub-communities had in common was that a large part of the learning outcome of their participants was connected to 'what it meant to be a person within [a particular] social group' (p. 204) – either the 'group or social class of people who listen to classical music' or 'the group of North Bothnians' – and they also developed knowledge about how to prolong the group's existence, in other words about how to produce its future and reconstitute the community over time (Lave and Wenger, 1991). Drawing on Green's (2010) ideas about the social organization of musical practice, I have argued elsewhere (see Karlsen, 2010) that, based on these and related findings, it is possible to see a music festival as a practice or means by which different groups in society, whether they are social classes or affinity groups, educate their own members. For some members, this group-based education, or perhaps enculturation, included peak experiences when the feelings of togetherness and cohesion, together with the music, co-produced SEM as is evidenced in the quotations above.

The second communal dimension manifested through the festival was that of branding and presenting its host municipalities with respect to the outside world. However, while the festival research literature discusses this dimension quite widely (see Delamere, 2001; Gursoy, Kim and Uysal, 2004; Quinn, 2005; Aronsen, 2006), only two of the host municipalities in this festival seemed to be affected by this dimension at all, and in very different ways. For the small rural municipality of Älvsbyn, one of the concerts by the spectacular Storforsen waterfall (see the quotations above) was an annual happening that the official representatives used very consciously in their marketing of the place, to the extent that many inhabitants thought of it as an independent event and not as part of the bigger festival. For the larger and more urban municipality of Piteå, the music festival constituted one part of building an image of being a 'music town' (see Karlsen, 2007b, p. 150) and of being recognized as such, at least on the national level. Connections between this outward community dimension and audience members' statements about their SEM are few and, if any, they are to be found in the areas of contextual factors and the kind of artists performing. Part of the branding happened through internationally acknowledged musicians being invited to perform at the festival, and references to those musicians' appearance and artistic skilfulness as being the triggering element of SEM appeared in the data. However, this represents only weak evidence of a kind of 'second degree' connection between the outward communal dimension of the festival and the production of SEM, and should not be overemphasized.

The third dimension of community discovered and explored in the festival data was that of inward reinforcement, or of '[t]elling, retelling and celebrating "who we are"' (Karlsen, 2007b, p. 199) among the festival community members, through interactions between the audience, the artists and the festival's programmed content. As with the dimension above, this aspect is also widely covered in the festival research literature (see Frisby and Getz, 1989; Ekman, 1999; De Bres and Davis, 2001; Delamere, 2001; Derrett, 2003; Gursoy, Kim and Uysal, 2004), and in the context of this particular festival this third dimension also had some overlap with the learning community described above. During the festival, through a variety of events, stories about 'us' – especially about the 'us' that covered North Bothnians in general or the inhabitants of the four different host municipalities in particular – were mediated through talks delivered in between the music or directly through the music itself because they were embedded as part of the lyrics. The local band reunion concert mentioned above was one such occasion, and, while I have elaborated on this concert and its significance elsewhere (see Karlsen, 2011), I return to it here in order to provide the reader with an impression of the strong feelings of cohesion and togetherness created in this particular situation. As can be seen from the quotations above, the band – a folk rock group – had been inactive for quite a long time, and this was their first large outdoor concert in over ten years. They shared the stage with a Spain-based band playing mainly Latino-inspired music, and this band was supposed to warm up the audience and get them into the right mood. However, during the first hour of swinging rumba, samba and even reggae, the audience barely moved, but continued to chat, sit on the lawn and eat food from their picnic baskets. Only when the local band came on stage (and continued to play for three hours), did the audience get on their feet, cheered wildly, and then, for the rest of the concert, danced and sang along. The festival attendees knew the lyrics of all the songs, which reflected the spirit of the region: the independence and strength needed for survival in an Arctic context, the resistance against anything that was being imposed from the southern capital area, and the strong, joint agency among the inhabitants of the nearby municipalities.

Although technically an outsider, being Norwegian by birth and moving to Northern Sweden to pursue my doctoral studies, I was drawn into this maelstrom of cohesion and celebration as an observing researcher, and wrote:

> This is about ... what it means to be an inhabitant of the Lapland regions – this is about *who we are*, we, the strange fellows who choose to live our lives close to the Arctic Circle. And for the first time since I moved to this area a year and a half ago, I feel ready and willing to take on the identity of [someone living in this municipality] ... and learn, deeply, what it means to be one. (Karlsen, 2011, pp. 184–5)

My account reveals and reflects my own SEM during this particular event, certainly triggered by the strong feeling of togetherness that arose among all the participants of this outdoor concert. However, I was not the only person there having such experiences. This particular concert was directly referred to in at least seven of the statements describing the factors impacting on the survey participants' SEM. In hindsight, I believe that this occasion – a couple of days later described by a local journalist as having a 'revivalist meeting atmosphere' (Pettersson, 2005) – represents an example of what Frith (1996) describes as groups getting 'to know themselves *as groups* (as a particular organization of individual and social interests, of sameness and difference) *through* cultural activity' (p. 111). As with every successful revival meeting, this intense celebration of 'who we were' also produced peak experiences, or SEM, among some of the participants.

**Music Festivals, Community and SEM: What is at Stake?**

Writing on music and emotion from an anthropological perspective, Becker (2001) proposes ideas that can give insights into the connections between music festivals, the creation of community and SEM, and where the situated and situational dimensions of learning are also included. She suggests that the scripts of music and emotion, including those of SEM, can be understood as supra-individual processes, 'in which the relationship between music and emotion needs to be understood as extending beyond the minds and bodies of single musicians and listeners, that is as a contextually situated social practice' (p. 151). Consequently, in her view, emotions relating to music 'can be usefully viewed as being about an individual within a community, rather than being exclusively about internal states' (p. 151). Developing the idea of the supra-individual further, Becker claims that the music and emotion scripts allow for biological processes to take place, in other words processes which unfold according to their own laws and structures, and which hence have an 'autopoietic organization' (p. 152). This again enables groups of people 'who are focused on a common event and who share a common history of that event [to] act, react, and to some extent think in concert without sacrificing their bounded personal identities' (p. 152). Engaging in such interactions, an individual's being and ontology will be changed, and this change manifests itself as experiences of learning:

> [N]ew domains of knowledge, knowledge gained through interactive behaviours, through doing. Music listeners as well as musicians undergo a learning process in which they imitate physical and mental gestures that ultimately transform both their inner structures as well as their relations to everything beyond the boundaries of their skins. (Becker, 2001, p. 152)

Following Becker's (2001) ideas and viewing those through the framework of socio-cultural learning theory as presented above (Lave and Wenger, 1991; Wenger, 1998), it is evident that when music is brought into the midst of the scene of a community of practice or is what such a community is said to be ultimately about – as it most often is in the situation of a music festival – it has the potential to enhance and intensify some of its communal features. To this script belong also SEM, and whether they are triggered by contextual or intrapersonal factors, they are experienced, as Becker (2001) notes, by individuals within a community, and they have a strong potential to transform. To refer once again to my own personal experiences: the revival meeting band reunion concert did in fact have a long-standing impact on my feelings of belonging towards Piteå and North Bothnia, it *did* transform my inner structures in the sense that a strong emotional bond to the area, its people and their joint spirit was created, a bond which had not been there previously. Even now – at the time of writing it is more than four years since I moved south (and cried my heart out when I left) – I can feel the longing of belonging as I write, read what I write and remember what I lived. Although my experiences were personal, they were also lived and thought 'in concert' (p. 152), and the knowledge gained through them was certainly achieved through 'interactive behaviours' (p. 152). This was also the case for the survey participants whose SEM were triggered by other contextual features, such as nature or being inside a church, and it is likely that similar bonds were created between them and the localities and surroundings in which the SEM occurred.

So, if music plays such an indelible part in creating community, why is it that its structural features are not present in the festival attendees' accounts of their SEM, why is it not *remembered*? And, if a community of practice seemingly *is* about the music – as with a music festival – but music only constitutes a small part of what is remembered and learned when being situated within it, what is then learned apart from that and what does that tell us about the community? Giving a tentative answer to the first question, it may be the case that in the festival situation, which, according to Falassi (1987) is permeated with numerous rites, the ritualistic features of the event foreground the *functions* of music (Merriam, 1964) – perhaps especially those of 'emotional expression' (p. 222), of 'contribution to the continuity and stability of culture' (p. 225) and of 'contribution to the integration of society' (p. 226) – more so than the music itself in terms of its structural features. Hence, the latter are simply not recalled. Furthermore, while the festival study participants also reported learning music (see Karlsen, 2007b, 2009), it was evident through the theoretical framing of the findings that much of what was learned was connected to participation in and sustaining future production of communities of practice. However, much of this learning outcome went beyond the festival community as such, and was connected to the social groups or larger communities that stood behind the festival and made it happen. Hence, to reiterate a point made above, the festival became a means by which different groups in society educated their own members.

Thus, we are back where we started, with a festival being about a community's ideology, worldview and 'physical survival' (Falassi, 1987, p. 2), and with SEM contributing to a music festival's transformative powers (Gadamer, 1986) by enabling its attendees to participate on a supra-individual level and experience the festival – its context and modes of cohesion – as a lived community. This combination of intellectual, musical and emotional experience makes the music festival a very powerful ritual.

# Chapter 11
# Interlude – Lasting Memories of Ephemeral Events

Karen Burland and Stephanie Pitts

As we have seen in the previous section, attending live performances can be a special experience. Live events can be totally immersive, have emotional significance and offer a sense of belonging, identity and community. It might be assumed that live events can create strong and lasting memories to be revisited long into the future, and that the music itself is a large component of the memory. Comparable research investigating emotional responses to private music listening (alone, or at home, for example) suggests that memories and associations of music with particular moments in time, or people, can hold lasting significance (Gabrielsson, 2010), even when other memory functions are in decline (cf. work on Alzheimer's by Cuddy and Duffin, 2005). However, we know from the preceding chapters that live performance is perceived quite differently from private music listening because it is a multi-dimensional experience; the venue, the environmental conditions, other audience members and the musicians all impact on the audience's enjoyment of, and immersion in, the performance. Therefore the extra dimensions associated with a live performance must also form an important part of the individual's impression of the event, and might arguably contribute to richer, more meaningful, memories.

Listeners have been shown to identify with particular genres of music or performers and to use their musical preferences as a 'badge of identity' (Tarrant, North and Hargreaves, 2000). Being an audience member at a live performance can help to enrich and affirm this musical identity, through connections with other audience members, both present and 'virtual'. We have seen in the previous sections that audiences are so much more than the passive onlookers described by Christopher Small (1987; 1998); they are an active part of any performance through their immediate and post-event feedback to the performers, with their contribution to the overall atmosphere of the event having the potential to directly affect the players' confidence and commitment to the performance. Like-minded individuals in an audience have shared interests (particularly in terms of musical taste) and therefore form a kind of community. The community may be temporary and short-lived (although Lucy Bennett's chapter suggests that such communities exist beyond the concert/gig in the virtual world of fan sites), but it offers a sense of belonging which adds a complementary social dimension to what might otherwise be a personal experience. This, in turn, enhances the individual's experience and memory of the event.

A live music performance is, by its very nature, of the moment and transitory; while its multi-dimensional features collide to create a special experience, it is one which is often transient and ephemeral. Given the significance of live music for individuals, it is not surprising that many listeners try to find ways to capture the event physically, in solid form, in order to freeze it in time. The next section considers the ways in which this is done, and so presents another perspective of audiences – as active reviewers and researchers, aiming to capture past events in order to extend and portray their meaning and significance. The purpose of this is threefold: to provide a record of the experience, which may be shared with others; to encapsulate personal responses to the performance which may be compared with others' views; and to capture the meaning of the experience for the individual, perhaps in connection with aspects of personal identity at that moment in time.

Capturing an ephemeral experience in physical form allows memories to be shared, discussed and reviewed with others who share similar memories, values, or identities – thus the community of the music audience, and the musical experience itself, continue to have meaning beyond the performance venue. Indeed, it is precisely the social interactions that individuals have about their musical experiences that can shape our memories of them (van Dijck, 2006). But a physical record also provides a stimulus for remembering a particular performance from the past. A flyer advertising a gig, a ticket stub, a souvenir brochure – all provide a trigger for recalling a particular performance. The links between the physical artefact and memory are the considerations of Sara Cohen's chapter, which begins the next section of the book. Using the maps of musical memories created by her respondents, she has been able to gather information about the ways in which individuals perceive their personal music histories. This is a relatively rare method of data collection in the study of audiences, and offers rich insights into individuals' musical journeys – where they begin and travel – and the ways in which these are intertwined with personal autobiographies.

While Cohen's focus is on personal journeys and memories, considered retrospectively and in relation to specific artefacts and venues, Paul Long's chapter examines two types of 'recording practice'. The first refers to recording a personal account of a performance, reviewing the performance and considering its emotional impact; the second refers to the process of mechanically capturing the sound and visuals of a performance. Long considers the function of these two types of record in the sharing of musical experiences in online communities, exploring the impact of online social interaction on forming and sustaining memories relating to musical performances.

The final chapter of the book offers an insight into what happens when the performers actively seek dialogue and feedback with their audience immediately after a performance. While we can assume that performers are aware of the online activity surrounding their gigs/concerts, it is difficult to ascertain the extent to which they take on board the kinds of feedback offered there, especially since it is often directed at other audience members, rather than the performer him/herself. Melissa Dobson and John Sloboda's research offers fresh insight on the impact of involving the audience directly (and indirectly) in the development of two new works. This is perhaps the logical direction in which audience research is travelling: seeking to ascertain how audiences engage with performances and therefore understand how to enhance the quality of their experience. Arguably this kind of interaction between performer and audience is long overdue, particularly in musics where the two very rarely interact. The 'evaluative triangle' – artist-audience-researcher – is a useful model which has the potential to offer rich insights into audience–performer experiences during live performances.

Chapter 12
# 'The Gigs I've Gone To': Mapping Memories and Places of Live Music

Sara Cohen[1]

## Introduction

This chapter explores the significance of live music by considering how it is remembered and how memories of live music are related to place. Both live music and memory are discussed as social practices and processes and the chapter describes some of the diverse ways in which people actively remember live music events, how these memories are shared and circulated and the social contexts influencing that process. It considers in particular the ways in which live music is remembered in relation to place, whether built music performance venues or geographical places that differ in scale, from the local to the regional and national. More specifically, the chapter explores the relationship between live music, memory and place by focusing on maps featuring places related to England's popular music past, including places of live rock performance. The term 'rock' is used loosely to cover a broad and diverse range of music styles while the notion of a 'map' is also broadly defined in order to compare different forms and practices of maps and mapping. The emphasis is less on what maps represent and more on what they do, who produces them and why. The aim is to consider what this reveals about how live music is remembered and how memories of live music are related to place and, ultimately, about how and why live music matters.

The first of the chapter's three sections focuses on audience members and how they present and map their autobiographical memories of live music, highlighting narratives of remembering music and place that have been conventional to rock

---

[1] The research this chapter is based on was supported as part of the *Popular Music Heritage, Cultural Memory and Cultural Identity (POPID)* project by the HERA Joint Research Programme (www.heranet.info), which is co-funded by AHRC, AKA, DASTI, ETF, FNR, FWF, HAZU, IRCHSS, MHEST, NWO, RANNIS, RCN, VR and The European Community FP7 2007-2013, under the Socio-economic Sciences and Humanities programme. I would like to thank all the research participants who gave us permission to use their interview material and memory maps and also my co-researchers on the POPID team. I am particularly grateful to Les Roberts who worked with me on the England case study and co-authored the publication that provided a starting point for this chapter (Cohen & Roberts, 2013).

culture. The second section considers how such memories are mapped and mobilized across different social and institutional contexts and the different interests this serves, whether it involves the use of rock music and the musical past for the purposes of tourism, heritage and place-marketing or the construction of local communities, 'scenes' and identities. The third and final section draws together the threads of the discussion in order to reflect on the relationship between live music, memory and place, and what the focus on place and social memory has suggested about the specificity of live rock music and its social, cultural and symbolic significance.

**Audience Memories of Live Music and Place**

Between 2010 and 2013 I participated in a project entitled 'popular music heritage, cultural memory, and cultural identity', which was based on collaboration between researchers in England, the Netherlands, Austria and Slovenia, and on comparative research conducted in each of these four countries. The research team in England consisted of me, Les Roberts, a post-doctoral researcher, and Gurdeep Khabra, a doctoral student focusing on English South Asian popular music. The first phase of our research involved interviewing representatives from the music and media industries and tourism and heritage sector, and examining their role in the construction of dominant histories and heritages of English popular music through films, books, exhibitions and so on. The second phase involved research on audiences and *their* music memories and histories, research that provides a basis for the chapter as a whole and a focus for the first section of it. The section begins with an explanation of how the audience research was conducted and the use of map-making as a methodological tool. It then describes how one particular individual mapped their autobiographical memories of live rock music and the places involved, before broadening out to highlight narratives of remembering that were shared by audiences and thus relatively common and conventional.

*Mapping Autobiographical Memories of the Popular Music Past*

As part of our research, audiences were invited to complete a central questionnaire hosted on the main project website in Rotterdam and made available in the language of each of the four countries involved. Through this they answered questions about their background and earliest and most notable musical memories, about places and genres connected to their music memories, and so on. Audiences were also asked to indicate their willingness to be interviewed, which enabled us to follow up on some of the questionnaire responses and explore them in more detail and depth through face-to-face interviews. By May 2013 we had received over six hundred responses from England and explored thirty of them through interviews with the individuals concerned. There were roughly equal numbers of male and female respondents aged between twenty and seventy years of age. Most were white and relatively well educated but they nevertheless varied considerably in terms of their music practices and the extent of their involvement with music, and were from diverse occupational backgrounds. The interviews were conducted across various parts of the country and in locations chosen by the interviewees themselves.

During our early conversations about ways of publicizing and promoting the questionnaire I suggested that we invite audiences to draw us a map of their musical memories. As part of a previous research project on music and urban landscape I had made use of this kind of conceptual, cognitive mapping as a tool for prompting musicians' memories and stories about music (Cohen, 2012a, 2012b). Such hand-drawn maps (also commonly referred to as 'sketch maps' or 'memory maps') have long been used by human geographers, social anthropologists and others to study how people describe places and remember what is where, their subjective sense of space and place, and differences between people in terms of their spatial knowledge and understanding (see Lynch, 1960; Tuan, 1975; Ben-Ze'ev, 2012). While some of the maps drawn by the musicians were rather like conventional cartographic maps, others looked more like pictures, diagrams or flow charts. Some were maps of music and place at particular points in time, but others were more temporal, charting the journeys of individuals and groups through time as well across urban space (how and where the musicians had started out, where they had been and ended up, and so on). These maps were not objective representations of reality but revealed something about the practices and perspectives of those who created them. Most importantly, the act of mapping prompted memories and stories about music, so I wondered if we could apply this approach to our research on audiences, inviting people to map their musical past, and using these maps to explore ways of conceptualising autobiographical memories of and engagements with music.

Les suggested that we test the potential of this approach by producing our own memory maps, and I agreed to give it a go, a decision I immediately regretted when I saw the maps that Les and Gurdeep had produced. My approach had been to limit myself to ten minutes and cover a sheet of notepaper with lines and doodles scribbled in blue biro. Gurdeep, however, had created a fancy, zoomable map using PREZI computer software, while Les produced a large, intricate, multicoloured map drawn by hand on A3 paper, scanned, and edited using Photoshop (see Figure 12.1).

Les told us that although it had taken him longer than he had bargained for, he found the mapping process to be a useful and thought-provoking exercise. He was particularly struck by the fact that he ended up mapping memories of live music, explaining that 'This wasn't especially planned, but records or CDs, other than the act of buying them ... did not really present themselves to me as memory'. Eventually, a project website was produced to inform people about the research, link them to the questionnaire and invite them to draw maps, and Les arranged for our maps to be uploaded onto that site as examples along with a short written statement. As part of his statement Les explained:

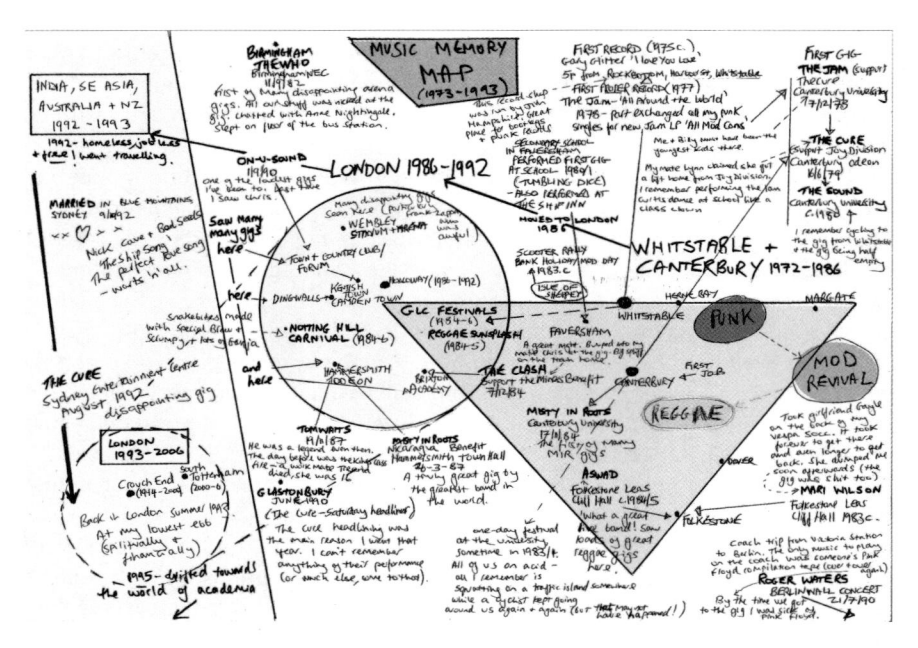

134   COUGHING & CLAPPING: INVESTIGATING AUDIENCE EXPERIENCE

Figure 12.1   Les's memory map

I found it quite difficult at first to determine exactly how to approach the task of mapping my early music memories. In retrospect it now seems obvious, but it only started to work when I learnt to be guided just by what more immediately presented itself as a memory. This was overwhelmingly focused around live music performances; in particular those that involved significant or memorable journeys. In most cases what I found to be memorable were little snippets of details related to specific gigs, but not necessarily the performance or performer. In some cases the gigs remembered weren't even ones I particularly enjoyed.

Figure 12.2, for example, is a close up of a small area on the bottom right-hand corner of the map and a reference to a coach trip from London's Victoria station to Berlin to see Pink Floyd: 'the only music to play on the coach was someone's Pink Floyd tape (over and over again). By the time we got to Berlin I was sick of Pink Floyd'.

Featured elsewhere on the map are references to memories of other events, places and journeys, including travelling to a gig on a Vespa motorbike with his girlfriend seated on the back ('she dumped me soon afterwards and the gig was shit too'); but also to absences from memory, such as the Cure's headlining performance at the 1990 Glastonbury festival, which had been his main reason for going but he found that he now couldn't seem to remember anything about it.

'THE GIGS I'VE GONE TO' 135

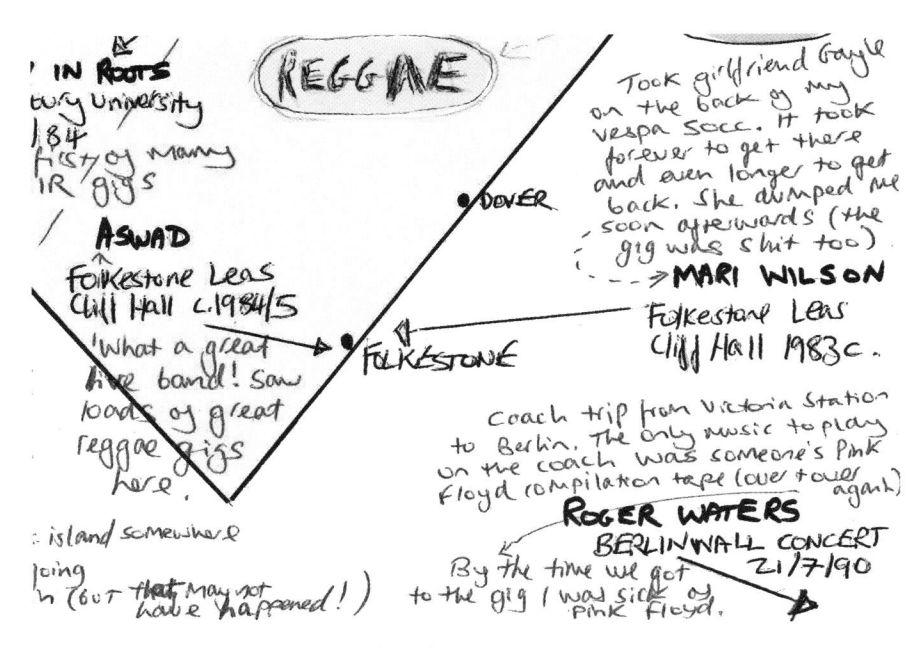

*Figure 12.2 Close-up image of Les's memory map*

*'Going to a Gig': Memories and Journeys of Live Music*

Much like Les's map, the maps and memories of some of our respondents also focused on live music. This map [Figure 12.3] for example, was produced by Ian, a London-based business manager in his late fifties. It is really a collage of ticket stubs from gigs he had attended. He explained that the idea of creating a map had prompted him: 'to see what ticket stubs I had lying around the house and what gigs I had been to and still had the tickets for, and that was a real journey for me. I'd never done that before'.

It had taken Ian a while to gather these tickets together, some of them going back thirty years or more and discovered at the back of drawers, among various piles of paper or stuffed in boxes in his garage, and he talked us through the mapping process:

> [T]icket stubs represent a great (and no doubt lazy) way for me to recall my musical journey. More often than not the tickets have the time, the date, the place and the principal reason of what I'm trying to remember all there right in front of me and therefore the hard work of recollection is all pretty much done. And yet, I find that once I start to put these random components together to form a memory map, the names and dates on the actual tickets themselves stay still, and what is laying seemingly dormant beneath the surface starts to come to life. The different shapes, sizes and colours, the logos, the fonts, the quality of the paper

136   COUGHING & CLAPPING: INVESTIGATING AUDIENCE EXPERIENCE

Figure 12.3   Ian's memory map

all start to trigger more thoughts. The escalating price of tickets over the years. The venues: the dives that remained and the palaces that were closed ... A few of the gigs I have tickets for I can't even remember, a lot of the gigs I have tickets for I will never ever forget.

Organizing these tickets, Ian was struck for the first time by the musical influences he had inherited from his parents and how they had shaped his early memories of growing up in a northern English town. It made him reflect on the influences he might pass on to his own children and that they might carry on with them. As he talked us through his map he related the tickets not only to people but also to performance events and places – from boring folk festivals he used to go to with his parents to dangerous and exciting rock gigs in London during the 1980s – remembered in relation to particular incidents: the time someone got knifed during a performance by the punk band Redskins, and the moment a coin was thrown at the lead singer of The Smiths and he walked off stage after only one song. Particularly vivid were his memories of the car journeys to see bands in places where, as he put it, 'there was always the chance that something special might happen'. He described listening to music as he travelled along and how on one freezing cold January night he even had to sleep in his car. Best of all was a performance by the band Portishead at the Glastonbury festival. The journey there took hours and they then had to wait ages for the band to appear. They were cold and hungry and the rain was heavy but when the band came on the sound was loud, the visuals were fantastic and the performance 'utterly transcended the environment'. But it was the social interaction of live music that appealed to him the most: 'Sometimes I can't even remember the band playing: it's the whole social context around music that is significant for me'.

For Ian, therefore, the process of map-making produced autobiographical memories of encounters with live music that were unique to him, but mediated through stories involving conventional narratives that emerged across our interviews. Like Ian, many respondents described their music influences as 'eclectic', listened to a broad range of music genres and styles, and kept tickets as well as other items of memorabilia from live music events. As Simon Frith (2012) points out, the value of such tickets was determined by how those events had been experienced, and several of our interviewees questioned why anyone would collect music memorabilia that didn't have that personal connection but were instead attached to 'someone else's memory', someone else's experience. These tickets were commonly attached to memories of particular performance venues through narratives of remembering similar to those discussed by Kenny Forbes (2014) who has researched audience memories of the Apollo theatre in Glasgow. Respondents referred to the layout or size of venues, or proximity to the stage and performers, as contributing to the atmosphere of particular events and making them more memorable.

Like Ian, several interviewees expressed surprise that they could recall so little about the musical aspects of such events, which is something that also struck John Street during his research on audience memories of Woodstock festival (2004, p. 31), and Sheryl Garratt who reflects on her memories of being a Bay City Rollers fan in the mid 1970s (1990, p. 402). Occasionally they offered memories of particular moments from the on-stage performance but the musical aspects of the performance tended to be described in rather general terms ('professional and polished' or 'uplifting and powerful'). More importantly, live music events tended to be remembered as a unique social, collective and participatory experience: being part of a crowd and out with friends, participating in the interaction between audience and performers, sharing music and emotion with others in the same place at the same time. They were also commonly remembered in relation to physical, sensual experiences involving cigarette smoke, sticky carpets, sloppy plastic beer cups or the sheer loudness of the music that sometimes meant not being able to hear properly for days afterwards.

In fact remembering live music often involved tales of pleasure and pain, survival and transcendence. Some respondents mentioned returning home from gigs covered in black and blue bruises having been beaten on the legs by security guards (see also Forbes, 2014), but seemingly imprinted on the memory of Ian and other interviewees were the embodied journeys to and from performances, the experience of going along, and people, places and events encountered along the way. There were tales of a hideous train trip to Wembley Stadium; an eight mile walk home after dancing the night away to punk music; the rush to catch the last train home; and travelling to gigs in the back of a butcher's van breathing in the 'smell of blood and perfume'. There were memories of extraordinary journeys connected to a sense of excitement, anticipation and occasion, such as a performance someone had waited years or 'the best part of a lifetime' to see, and the thrill of travelling into a city to go for the first time to a gig or club. Yet there were also memories of regular weekly journeys to the same venue; journeys embedded in patterns of repetition and familiarity that shape music cultures or scenes. For the individuals we interviewed the experience of going to a gig was thus remembered in relation to lived, everyday places and the rituals, routines and journeys involved, as well as places that emerged as somehow special and symbolic, whether the night-time city or particular performance venues.

**Mobilising Memories of Live Music across Social and Institutional Contexts**

Focusing on audiences and their autobiographical maps and memories of live rock music, I have so far highlighted conventional narratives of remembering and some of the common ways in which memories of live music were attached to place. This second section of the chapter considers how such memories are mapped across different social and institutional contexts and the various interests this serves. As Adam Behr (2013) points out, maps have been increasingly integrated into everyday media consumption and there has been a growth in the mapping of music activity, whether by academics, communities and businesses. Les Roberts and I have explored this trend elsewhere (Cohen and Roberts, 2013; Roberts, 2012; Cohen 2012b) and the discussion builds on this work in order to situate the autobiographical maps and memories within a broader, comparative perspective, highlight the dynamics and mobility of music memory, and deepen understanding of the relationship between live music, memory and place. It begins with the use of rock music and the musical past in the marketing of place and then moves on to discuss live music in relation to the construction of local communities and identities.

*Place-branding and Maps of National Popular Music Heritage*

Only some of those who participated in our audience research related music to local or national identity, and few found the term 'heritage' relevant for popular music or their own personal musical past. Like Ian, most referred instead to notions of music 'inheritance' or to 'influences' they could trace back and forth, whether through record collections or YouTube. Over the past few decades, however, official and commercial interests in popular music heritage and tourism have grown in England and beyond, hence a proliferation of books and films about the popular music past, as well as music monuments and plaque schemes, tours and trails, exhibitions and also cartographic maps, some of which Les Roberts and I have discussed in detail (Cohen and Roberts, 2013).

England Rocks! provides one example, an interactive, web-based map produced in 2007 as a tourist marketing tool by the government-funded national tourism agency Visit Britain in collaboration with the British music company EMI. Users were invited to explore birthplaces of gigs and festivals, places referenced in or inspired by song lyrics, and album sleeve locations, so although the map was not focused solely on live music, places of live music heritage were nevertheless prominent. These places were marked on the map with coloured dots but it was not possible to zoom in and explore them in any detail. Instead users could click on fly posters arranged around the maps and on what was designed to look like an urban brick wall, posters that were devised to provide a brief list of relevant facts and information. When we spoke to the Marketing Director of Visit Britain he explained that the map was intended to be broad in coverage, re-branding Britain as an exciting country with a rich and diverse music heritage 'from heavy metal to pop'. But the map focused on existing visitor attractions and constructed a narrow and selective history that was based largely on white, male rock music and, from what we could tell from the notes and designs that were passed on to us, on the personal music tastes and autobiographical memories of the marketing staff involved. It was also based on a small selection of cities and regions, with Liverpool the only city connected to its own page. Various performance venues and festivals, such as Liverpool's Cavern Club and Creamfields festival, were listed on the left-hand side of that page but the accompanying map offered little detail on their precise location.

We came across other maps of English or British popular music heritage that were likewise produced through collaboration between the music and media industries and tourism and heritage sector. They included the 'Where it's At' interactive floor map launched in 2009 as a central exhibit within the British music experience exhibition at London's O2 arena. The map's content had been sourced from a book by the music journalist and rock genealogist Pete Frame entitled *Rockin' around Britain: Rock and Roll Landmarks of the UK and Ireland* (1999). Like the England Rocks! map it featured places of live rock performance and involved a similarly cursory, almost arbitrary engagement with local music geographies, little cartographic detail, and the same selective focus on the popular music past. The main function of these maps seemed to be to symbolize the nation and capitalize on a shared sense of a musical past but only insofar as it resonated with a brand profile of the nation that was likely to have widespread and international appeal in terms of potential tourist consumption (Cohen and Roberts, 2013). In this sense the maps were in many respects similar to maps of music heritage used to market particular English cities, such as the map entitled 'Sound City: a guide to Liverpool's music heritage', which was used to promote Liverpool as European Capital of Culture 2008 (Cohen, 2012c). The maps thus constructed a heritage that seems far removed from the more localized memories, journeys and experiences of our respondents and the diversity of their musical tastes and influences.

## Local Musicscapes and Vernacular Memory

In England these kinds of 'official' maps of popular music heritage have been accompanied by a countervailing trend towards maps aimed at more localised exploration of place and the musical past. Some of the latter are produced in collaboration with official, 'top-down' initiatives but others are produced independently of these initiatives, sometimes in response or resistance to the dominant discourses they represent. We encountered many such maps during our research although they took different forms. They included, for example, smartphone map-based apps, such as 'Soundtrack to London', an app developed through a partnership between the Museum of London and Nokia and launched in 2011. The app provides users with a map of London that enables them to zoom into particular sites and search for music landmarks, including performance venues. These smartphone maps do not necessarily represent a better or more 'authentic' engagement with local music geographies than the England Rocks! map, and some are likewise used to encourage consumers to visit tourist destinations or purchase music downloads. They nevertheless differ from the England Rocks! map in terms of scale and cartographic precision, enabling users to zoom in and explore places and sites in more detail, and to do so while on the move and in situ, rather than sitting in front of a computer or standing around a museum exhibit. They therefore allow for an embodied and embedded engagement with music practices and journeys, shifting the focus away from more abstract cartographic representations of the nation (Cohen and Roberts, 2013).

As part of our research we also encountered many non-professional websites and online resources devoted to English popular music histories and heritages, some of which reflect the growth of interest in community or vernacular mapping (Clifford and King, 1996; Harzinski, 2010; Leslie, 2006; Roberts, 2012; Wood, 2010). We interviewed a number of individuals who were exploring the use of this kind of mapping to actively engage local communities in a collective production of music heritage, including the curators of civic museums and digital archivists concerned to celebrate, preserve and share the popular music heritage of particular English cities. There are several digital archives dedicated to the musical past of Birmingham, for example, as well as numerous websites, blogs, Facebook pages, Twitter feeds, and so on, devoted to specific Birmingham venues; and websites about Birmingham more generally that are not primarily about music but have elicited a wealth of contributions on the subject (e.g. 'Birmingham Music Heritage 1965–1985', 'Home of Metal' and 'Soho Road: to the Punjab'). Featured on the website 'Birmingham: it's not shit' was one virtual musical map of the city that was created using Google Maps. It was populated by the site's users who had been invited to upload their memories of the local music past and attach them to particular places on the map. Like the smartphone map apps the map enabled a detailed focus on local music histories and geographies, but unlike the apps the emphasis here was on audience perspectives and involving users in the mapping process.

This resonates with our own use of maps as part of our audience research, and also with the work of Jez Collins, who established the digital Birmingham Music Archive in an effort to address what he saw as the neglect of Birmingham and its music heritage in dominant and official histories of English popular music, such as that constructed by the England Rocks! map. He and his colleague Paul Long (Long and Collins, 2012) argue that these kinds of community-based archives are motivated by the failure of mainstream heritage narratives and collections to reflect and actively represent community histories, stories and knowledge. In establishing his own archive his aim was to put Birmingham 'on the map' (ibid.) in a metaphorical sense, and he described himself as a 'DIY heritage activist'. Visitors to his site are invited to help to build a repository of information and material related to the city, creating a body of local knowledge that he and Long describe as 'a layering and detailed texturing of activity in the city and the places in which music was sought out and experienced' (ibid., p. 152). Through individual and collective memory, Collins (2013b) suggests, users map out places and spaces, often no longer in existence, 'with a fondness which invokes civic pride' (p. 148).

Performance venues, as Collins (2013a) points out, are a particularly rich focus for conversational threads on his website, which unfold as individuals upload and exchange stories of live music and the local musical past. Here, for example, are a couple of comments about one Birmingham club called 'Mothers' uploaded by two individuals who frequented it during the 1980s. Their comments illustrate, once again, autobiographical memories of live music and the places involved:

> Venues like this will never be seen again, the bands and acts today demand large auditoriums with thousands in the crowd. We used to queue up down the alley at the side of the club for maybe 10 minutes to get in. Fantastic memories.

> I was only 14 years old at the time but managed to get in, and remember my shoes sticking to the carpet ... got absolutely smashed on 2 halves of their cider and haven't been able to touch the stuff from that day to this.

## Memory, Place and the Significance and Specificity of Live Rock Music

Throughout this chapter I have discussed different kinds of maps featuring places of live rock performance in England. The focus has been on memory and the popular music past, beginning with maps based on the autobiographical memories of particular individuals before moving on to maps of the nation, and then returning back down again via more localized maps to the individual and autobiographical. The chapter has explored these various maps in order to consider not only how live music is remembered by audiences but also how such memories are mapped and mobilized across various social and institutional contexts. This has enabled four general and concluding points about the significance and specificity of live music and the relationship between live music, memory and place. The first point concerns the social and symbolic significance of live music events, and the places to which they are related.

The individuals who participated in our research presented memories of encounters with music that were complex, diverse, and unique to each person. A few of them explained that music had not played a significant role in their life and was not particularly important to them, while others described music as their life and explained how it had defined the kind of person they were and their sense of self. The vast majority of responses fell in between these two extremes and while their involvement with live music varied quite considerably, all of our respondents presented memories of listening to recorded music. As with memories of live music they remembered listening to recorded music in particular spaces and places and related these memories to specific social events, people and relationships. There were also common references to journeys. The individuals we interviewed, for example, remembered listening to music through Walkmans or iPods during regular journeys by foot, bus or train, and almost all of them responded to questions about their 'earliest memories' by describing songs or albums they remembered listening to in the family car. Unlike the process of remembering live music, therefore, there was an emphasis on private spaces and on the rituals and routines of domestic and family life, with memories of listening to music recordings not only in the car but in the bedroom, family kitchen and garden shed, and so on. There was also more emphasis on particular lyrics, musical sounds and songs that had a personal and often emotional resonance, and that acted as a memory prompt. This was particularly apparent in the ways in which some respondents talked about their personal collections of music recordings and related memorabilia, such as posters, and when they spoke of remembering friends or relatives who had died or their past experiences of personal illness and depression.

Live music events tended to be remembered rather differently, even though they were remembered in many diverse ways and not always as a positive experience or in relation to a sense of nostalgia. There were nevertheless conventional narratives of remembering and for many people, as illustrated by the responses of Ian and other interviewees, live music was clearly remembered as a unique collective and participatory experience. For some, live music symbolized key moments or periods in their lives, whether their first ever night-time venture into the city with a group of friends or a time when they were free from the responsibilities of parenthood and able to go out and socialize with others on a regular basis. Memories of live music were thus related to social, emotional and sensual experiences as well as the embodied experience of going along to gigs or festivals. They illustrate, as Ruth Finnegan (1989) points out, how music can be regarded as something special while also embedded in the rituals and routines of everyday life, including the regular routes or 'pathways' people take across space and through life. Memories of live music thus invoked a dynamic, fluid sense of place and were at the same time related to places that symbolized the experiences involved. As Frith (2012) so aptly states:

What people recall about gigs is getting there and spilling out into the streets, the shape of the space, the distance or closeness of the band. Live music memory like live music itself has to happen in a particular place, and in memory the place shape[s] the music just as at the event itself the music shapes the place. And in memory too there are always other people involved – friends, lovers, a kind of network of changing relationships which become imbricated in the way a gig lives on.

Van Dijck (2006, p. 369) points out that autobiographical memories of music are shaped through social interaction and commonly shared with others, and as part of our research we explored some of the many ways in which memories of music were shared among audiences. This can involve the repetition and circulation of stories, anecdotes and myths about live music performance and the musical past not only through word-of-mouth and face-to-face interaction but also through fanzines, radio and film documentary, lyrics and visual images, online interaction and social media networks, as illustrated by the numerous sites devoted to memories and histories of music in Birmingham. Research conducted for an earlier project on music and landscape in Liverpool benefited considerably from the wealth of information on live music and the local music past provided through such sites (Cohen, 2012b). Frith (2012) thus refers to:

> the remarkable blossoming of local music archive material on the web ... Every British city, town and region, it seems, has people putting together exhaustive historical accounts of their local venues, bands and gig (most sites illustrated liberally with concert posters and ticket stubs). Such sites are a treasure trove of oral history; they provide not just factual information – who played where and when – but emotional insights too.

Collins (2013a), who established the Birmingham Music Archive, describes the kind of memory work motivated by such sites, and how they attract ever increasing amounts of uploaded historical materials, including links to official band sites and other tribute pages; embedded video from YouTube and occasional streams of music; and digitized photographs, ticket stubs, posters and other ephemera from personal collections. They also motivate a kind of online communication described by Collins as 'often scrappy in nature', involving comments made with little care or attention to language or even detail. 'Names, sounds, scenes and places are cited and users call on others to add detail for their own sometimes vaguely recalled fragments of experience'. This kind of prompting, he argues, produces conversational exchanges between individuals and within groups that give rise to 'multiple perspectives on the past' as well as the creation of community. When researching live music and landscape in Liverpool I was particularly struck by the ways in which such memories and conversational exchanges accumulated around particular music venues, and how venues often provided 'a physical idiom for defining a particular social group and the relationships involved, and for expressing feelings of belonging or not belonging to that group and a wider community or music 'scene' (Cohen, 2012a, p. 595).

This attachment of music memory to place, whether to music venues, cities or local communities and 'scenes', occurred across various music genres but was particularly prevalent within rock culture. The second point, therefore, is that the ways in which live music is remembered, as well as the value of these memories and how they are related to place, is shaped by specific social and cultural contexts, including genre-based cultures and the social and ideological conventions involved. Stories of live music and of 'going to a gig' (or on tour) have certainly played a central part in the discourses and mythologies of rock culture, and within rock culture live music has been closely associated with the concept of authenticity. Frith (2007, p. 8) thus argues that live music 'remains vital for almost all music genres', while for those involved with rock, jazz, and folk performance it is regarded as 'the truest form of musical expression'. He attributes this to the fact that 'A live concert is not simply a transitory experience but symbolizes what it means to be a music fan' and can also represent a community (ibid., pp. 5–7).

For Phillip Auslander (1999, p. 160), the authenticity of live rock performance is connected to the rock ideology of the 1960s and 1970s, the shifting interplay between recordings and live performances, and the way that live performance came to authenticate the sound on the recording. Auslander argues that within a mediatized culture and wider cultural economy, live events can thus have cultural value and to have experienced those events can give cultural prestige (ibid., p. 37): 'being able to say that you were physically present at a particular event constitutes valuable symbolic capital – certainly, it is possible to dine out on the cachet of having been at Woodstock, for example'. Yet while Auslander argues that this symbolic value of live events 'is completely independent of the experiential quality of the event itself' (ibid. p. 57), the ways in which such events are remembered and represented suggests otherwise. Audiences who visited Liverpool's legendary Cavern Club during the early 1960s, for example, may have gained a sense of prestige simply by being there but have also remembered experiences of discomfort (such as the dampness and the smell of the toilets) that have contributed to the mythology and authenticity of that club, much like collective memories of other legendary rock clubs of the 1960s, 70s and 80s (Cohen, 2011; Forbes, 2014).

These autobiographical and collective memories have fed into published histories of rock music in which live music performance venues are commonly used to represent key places and moments in rock's chronological development (Cohen, 2011). Dominant histories of Liverpool popular music promoted through books and films, for example, have tended to focus on three totemic clubs: the Cavern, a club made famous by the Beatles who performed there on a regular basis during the early 1960s; Eric's, a club associated with the post-punk scene of the late 1970s and early 1980s and with bands such as Echo and the Bunnymen; and Cream, a club that played a significant role in the international development of electronic dance music during the late 1980s and early 1990s, helping to pioneer a new kind of global dance corporation. This illustrates the focus on rock and on particular 'revolutionary' moments in conventional popular music histories (Negus, 1996, p. 140), and galleries dedicated to each of these three clubs formed the core of a major exhibition on the history of Liverpool popular music launched in 2008 (Cohen, 2012c).

Such histories have fed into constructions of rock as local and national heritage, such as the England Rocks! Map, and this illustrates the third point, which is that memories of live music are circulated and mapped across various social and institutional contexts, and that this can change the ways in which they are presented, valued and attached to place. Through the England Rocks! map memory was absorbed into heritage, and popular music heritage was 'officially' and instrumentally used to market and brand the nation as a whole in order to boost niche forms of cultural tourism and promote the work and profile of the music industries. These maps did not allow for detailed exploration of local music geographies but used them to serve an ideology of nationhood that primarily celebrated white, English, male rock. The smartphone map apps and community-based maps, on the other hand, attended (although in different ways) to music and memory as a more localized experience. They may reinforce 'official' accounts of popular music history or provide counter mappings, but they represent a more material and site-specific engagement with local music geographies. The community-based maps engaged users in the mapping process and in a collective production of vernacular memories of music and place. Similarly, for Ian and other individuals who participated in our project, the process of map-making produced autobiographical, vernacular memories of music that were conflated with experience, including the lived and embodied experience of going along to gigs and places encountered along the way.

The fourth and final point, therefore, is that maps and map-making can provide a useful tool for research on the relationship between live music, memory and place. As part of our own research we have made use of maps and map-making as a methodological tool for prompting audience memories of music and place; in fact the anthropologist Marc Augé (2002) describes maps as a 'memory machine'. By analysing different forms and practices of mapping the musical past (whether online maps, map apps or maps created on paper by hand) this chapter has considered how memories of live music are presented, mobilized and circulated. This has revealed some of the different ways in which live music is remembered, valued and attached to place, as well as the individuals, groups and institutions involved in this process and the various interests it serves.

# Chapter 13
# Warts and All: Recording the Live Music Experience[1]

Paul Long

**Introduction**

Once the last notes have been sounded and the house lights have been raised, what meanings do the audience take away with them from the concert? In what ways is the performance, its context and experience, remembered by attendees? What meanings do live music events have for other music lovers who were *not* present at specific concerts and yet are able to hear them through various media or hear *about* them from those who *were* in attendance?

This chapter explores the aftermath of the concert and offers some answers to these questions by suggesting how the concert can be understood in terms of recording practices. Here, recording practices can be defined in two intimately related ways. On one hand, recording refers to the impressions, emotions, accounts, assessments and variety of other practices in which the experience of the concert is mapped and memorialized by attendees. On the other hand, a process of recording is manifest in the mechanical capturing of the sound and image of musical events. The resulting variety of artefactual forms includes film, TV and radio programmes as well as those things habitually referred to as the Record: vinyl, tape, CD and digital compression files such as the MP3. In addition, there are artefacts such as photographs, concert programmes, posters and even T-shirts displaying the dates of festivals, tours and so on, which register the occasion of the event and, for many, become integral to its commemoration and perhaps its mythologization. The relationship of these recording practices is most immediately evident in the nature of live texting and tweeting among fans (see Lucy Bennett's chapter in this volume) that suggests that a record of memorialization and its circulation begins *during* the concert itself, thanks to modern mobile devices.

These modes of recording may entail individualized responses for making sense of live music performances and are explored here for the ways in which they are used to facilitate sharing and interaction between music consumers. The label of consumer serves to signal that the interactions with live music discussed here

---

[1] Thanks are due to Lisa Wiedemann, HafenCity Universität Hamburg for help with the development of this chapter. Thanks also to DJs Michael Boland and James Allsworth for insights into live recordings of club nights.

take place in the context of an industrial structure of production and promotion in which economic transactions impact on the nature of meaning and exchange between audience members.

Research for this chapter draws upon the online practices of music consumers, exploring their identification with concerts and constructions of performance. Central to this discussion are ideas of witness, authority and authenticity evidenced in individual accounts and collective recollections of performances, their meaning, qualities and legacy. Online sites such as *All About Jazz*, *Talk Classical*, and a myriad of social media forums devoted to specific venues and the performances of popular music artists past and present, attest to a prodigious range of reflective activity, underlining the continued importance of live music in the digital age. It would be premature to suggest that this activity indicates an explosion of interest in music per se and the live event in particular, yet it does make visible a considerable variety of statements to other consumers and of course to the researcher. The detailed dedication to an array of genres and live events by consumers online extends beyond the familiar focus of cultural studies on popular culture by incorporating accounts from audiences for classical music and jazz as well. Likewise, this study extends beyond the allied focus of cultural studies on spectacular groups of fans and subcultures associated with specialized aspects of music, as evidenced in work by Paul Hodkinson (2002) on goth, or Natalie Purcell (2003) on death metal fans. As Antoine Hennion cautions, 'Love, passion, taste, practices, habits, mania' indicate the lexicon of those who might not fit the image of the 'connoisseur' and whose attachments 'are no weaker or less indispensable or vital for those who value them, and warrant as much attention' (2001, p. 2).

**Remembering the Concert**

This section explores how testimonies and memory practices frame the legacy and understanding of what live music events mean for individuals, reconvening as well as extending audiences after the event in online communities of interest. A starting point is to understand the ephemerality of the concert, performance, show or 'gig'. Paul Grainge suggests that, as a concept, the ephemeral connotes 'the evanescent, transient and brief; in definitional terms, it describes anything short-lived' (2011, p. 2). As the online concert streaming site *World Concert Hall* persistently reminds subscribers through its promotional notices on Twitter: '*Right now*, an all #Reich concert with himself and a world premiere from #London [ ... ] *Right now*, von Eckardstein plays #Mendelssohn [ ... ] *Right now*, #Bach's Cantatas and #Schelle from #Bruges' (my emphasis). To receive and read such notices alongside those from attendees present within concert halls in London or Bruges, or from those listening at a physical remove from the venue as performances are streamed to them online (or, as Bennett details in her chapter, simply hearing *about* the concert), is to register that the 'right now' is already history, a moment passed never to be regained.

The live concert then is a specific temporal and spatial event in which, as Philip Auslander notes, the music produced is an intangible cultural expression (2008, p. 148). Nonetheless, and as comments on social media sites and in forums dedicated to music alone attest, once the experience of performance is over, a great deal of attention is afforded to recalling it, exploring and evaluating the nature of that experience. In fact, the process is habitual enough to have generated a market in scrapbooks dedicated to it – 'Just the Ticket ... ticket stub organizer' – and even smartphone applications like StagePage for just this purpose. The StagePage 'app' promises to 'Keep live music alive'. It allows users to upload mementos and pictures that can be shared by email or social media sites, prompting 'a trip down your live music memory lane' ('Alexcel', *evolver.fm*, 2013).

The ephemeral nature of the live event inflects its meaning in the memories of concert-goers. 'Mark' at the *Good Music Guide Classical Music Forum*, writes at a moment in which he is 'buzzing as I usually am right after a concert', describing his view of 'music's creation as a kind of act of magic'. In the same thread, 'Novi' reflects on the immediacy of responses by musicians to a venue's environment, of the intimacy of performance, 'I feel there's something almost personal in this relationship between player and audience that is also quite spontaneous'. For 'Bass Clef', a recent concert is recalled as a transcendent experience, in which 'I just sat transfixed in awe – everyone around me melted away so I became unaware of them, it was just me and the performers and the music' (*Good Music Guide Classical Music Forum,* 2013).

Such singular moments are often defined against the fixity and perceived limits of the mechanical recording. As 'Andante' at *Talk Classical* suggests: 'there is a magic in a live performance (warts and all) that you will never get in a recording, even a recording of a live performance. The atmosphere cannot be recorded, even the cough from four rows back, adds to the ambience, a recording is always a compromise' (*Talk Classical,* 2013). That the live performance offers unfiltered access to the essence of music is an idea endlessly repeated in its recollection, as individuals describe experiences of ephemeral events never to be repeated. 'Mimi Michel' of Queens, New York, writes of the pleasure of attending a performance of a Beethoven Piano Concerto. This account notes that while the performers struck a number of wrong notes, such instances add drama and particularity to events:

> This is what live performance shows us: The most important goal is not absolute perfection, but a performance memorable for extraordinary depth and beauty, sustained throughout, no matter the bumps along the way. If anything, those very human bumps make a performance more interesting and vibrant, not less (posted at Angel, *WZQR*, 2013).

In a discussion of the ephemerality of visual media, Amelie Hastie suggests that attention to its attendant detritus might 'maintain or restore a sense of materiality in relation to it' (2007, p. 172). For her, such 'detritus' takes on textual and sensorial form, inclusive of memories of places and the impressions we have of them as well as the kinds of souvenirs one has of ephemeral moments such as ticket stubs or promotional items. A sense of materiality is useful here for comprehending the accretion of concert memories and perspectives posted online as well as for the part that materials generated by and around the concert play in the process of recollection. 'Solitary Wanderer' at *Good Music Guide*, for instance, writes of a collection of old concert programmes, 'When I looked through them recently I enjoyed reliving some of the fine performances I've experienced over the past few years'. 'Brewski' adds: 'I still have programs from things like Herbert von Karajan's concerts at Carnegie Hall back in the 1980s, and some particularly memorable Met performances ... they're great memory triggers'. 'Seargeant Rock' underlines the indispensable yet ephemeral nature of such material, lamenting the fact that 'Unfortunately nearly every program I had before I joined the army at age 20 has been lost. Mom threw them away when I was overseas, thinking they were useless clutter and worthless'.

Beyond the citing of such detritus, a feature of social media sites is the facility for uploading and sharing such materials, demonstrating that to their owners, these are valued personal memorabilia. Triggers and anchors for collective memory focused on the concert include audio-visual recordings of concerts, posters, ticket stubs, photographs but also code for the embedding into web pages of video and music files cross-referenced from a prodigious array of other online locations. Consider, for instance, Facebook groups like the *Birmingham Odeon Memorial*, a site dedicated to a cinema-cum-concert venue in Birmingham, UK. To scroll down this typical site is to encounter an endless series of scans of tickets, posters and personal photographs of performances. There are recollections of events, and questions and clarifications about setlists at particular concerts, all generated by the community that has been gathered in this site. While some posts generate lengthy discussion of the original performance, often the image of artefacts serves as a totem for approval and recognition for the poster and event among the community. This recognition is registered in user 'Likes' for a post or remarks such as this comment on images of a Judas Priest gig of 1981: 'I was in the balcony for the gig with my mom & dad ... in my defence i was 12' (Birmingham Odeon Memorial, Facebook, 2012). Uploading such material announces the individual's authority and witness to performances, while recognition and acknowledgement from others who shared the experience confirms it.

Such Facebook groups are indicative of how collective memory of concerts is serviced by, and services, many more than those who were ever part of the original audience for the event. As a result, memory work becomes a potential site of struggle for credentials and authority in which claims to witness support one's status as a music aficionado. An example from the founding moment of British punk rock illustrates this point. When the Sex Pistols reformed in 1996 Charles Shaar Murray noted in his review for *Mojo* magazine that the band played before a crowd of 30,000, a figure greater than the total of their original UK concert audiences. As an aside he adds 'though if you assembled everybody who'd claimed to have seen 'em at the Screen On The Green in '76 you'd-a needed Wembley

Stadium to fit 'em all in' (Shaar Murray, 1996). A similar perspective is captured in the title of David Nolan's book about the Sex Pistols' gig at Manchester's Lesser Free Trade Hall in June 1976, *I Swear I Was There*. In one interview the author comments on the fact that in spite of the tiny audience, many more have since claimed to have been present that night. Pondering the reasons for such claims, his answer endorses the hyperbole of the book's subtitle, *The Gig That Changed The World*:

> Perhaps because people desperately want to be part of something which is so clearly and so obviously identified as a point of change. It's so easy to identify, June 4th 1976, that's the point where [music] took a left hand turn. That's why I suppose it becomes quite enticing to want to have been there (Quoted by Singleton, 2006).

Whether musical cultures are changed in such instances is a moot point, but as Tim Wall has argued, such ideas service themes of disruption and fracture in the ways in which histories of pop are constructed (Wall, 2013, pp. 3–22). To pinpoint a moment in such a manner and to which so few were privy, to claim that '*I* was there!' functions as a means of distinction (Bourdieu, 1984). The authenticity of the concert experience – as detailed in this volume by Jennifer Radbourne, Katya Johanson and Hilary Glow – is a quality that is in turn afforded those who shared in that experience. Online, anyone is able to report on any event and in each case, varying degrees of cultural capital are both deployed and accrued that echo the offline conversations music consumers have among themselves. For instance, the *Smuggled Sounds* blogspot reproduces an account from 'Beverley' of her 'precious memories' of attending a performance by George Michael recorded for MTV's *Unplugged* programme. This witness is one who 'would like to share some recollections of a most special and magical occasion'. She recalls the tight security, and the instructions to the audience about their choice of clothing and expected behaviour. The exclusivity and relative intimacy of the concert underwrites the privilege of witnessing the moment that marked Michael's return to performance after a hiatus:

> Looking around the other people present, it was obvious that there was a great mix of fans and people from all aspects of the music industry, including some of the DJs from London's Capital Radio. We were led to our seats around 7.45pm. The atmosphere was really electric, people were just so excited at the prospect of George singing live again! My husband and I were seated about halfway back in the studio, right in the centre of our row, and about four seats away from the VIP area, where we saw George's parents and other family members (Beverley at *Smuggled Sounds*, 2013).

Whether attendees numbered 4, 40, or 400, as at this event, does not detract from the finite audience able to recall any one concert, the nature of the experience they shared and the authority afforded by having been present. Indeed, this is illustrated by a current project to memorialize the Woodstock Festival of 1969. The festival is described as 'a symbol of an entire generation', although as an ongoing attempt to register the names and memories of the original audience in an 'Official Woodstock Registry' records, around 400,000 attended. Even among this number, and as the Bethel Woods site notes, a dedicated 35,000 were all that remained to see Jimi Hendrix's performance, elevated from among so many celebrated sets amid 'three days of legendary performances, unimaginable mud, and unforgettable experiences' (Woodstock Festival History at *Bethel Woods Center for the Arts*, 2013).

The nature of the Woodstock history accords with the kind of heritage projects detailed by Sara Cohen (in this volume) in which particular places and spaces are the focus for memory practices. Likewise, the scope of this activity highlights how the ambition of such projects is enabled in part by digital technologies and by online cultures of 'crowd sourcing'. As I have suggested elsewhere (Collins and Long, 2014), the practices of such online communities and the digital architecture that supports them can be thought of in terms of the ideas of José van Dijck as 'cultural frames for recollection' that 'do not simply invoke but actually help construct collective memory' (2006, p. 358). Beyond the DIY use of Facebook for groups dedicated to memorializing venues or particular concerts or the variety of music forums across the internet, this structuring is emulated in the applications mentioned already as well as enterprises such as *Songkick*. Ostensibly a retail point for concert tickets, *Songkick* aims also to represent 'the life-changing experience of seeing your favorite bands live'. It offers a managed site for the recording of memories, involving the sharing of materials and facilities for engagement with 'others who were there'. Here, the epistemological ambition is considerable, aiming to 'put every single concert or festival that's ever happened online'. At the time of writing, *Songkick* claims to have spent a year accumulating information on over one million concerts from the last 50 years and is 'well on our way to becoming the definitive live music resource online' (*Songkick*, 2013). The overall effect of such activity is not only to identify individual moments of musical history as significant for individuals and the collective, but serves also to underline the value of the live event.

**The Concert Recording**

In the ecology of music culture then, the intangible nature of live performance, its experience and understanding, can be understood in terms of a dynamic relationship between scarcity and plenty. The scarcity of the event is a product of its ephemerality, a condition that affords authority and authenticity to those who have experienced and witnessed it. Counterpoising this scarcity is the fixity and potential plenty of the mechanical recording of the performance and its circulation. This section explores the status that *this* kind of recording of live music events has for thinking about the aftermath of the concert. Whether officially sanctioned by artists and music companies, or – as 'bootleg' – unofficial in nature, how do these kinds of records make meaning? How do they inflect the relationship between consumers and the memorialization and mythologization of the live performance? How are live recordings understood in relation to ideas of the audience, of witness, authority and the evaluation of music?

Considering the specificity of the musical recording, Stephen Cottrell describes a potential subfield of scholarship in the form of 'phonomusicology', simply 'the study of recorded music, including its contexts of production and patterns of consumption' (Cottrell, 2010, pp. 16–17). Such an approach allows for an analysis of some of the confusions over the relationship between event and record. As Hennion observes of the concert: when compared with the musical recording, it 'has a more pronounced social status, varying depending on the genre, but represents a definite focus, a benchmark, whether it is a rock or a classical concert' (Hennion, 2001, p. 13). As we have seen in the previous section, this privileging has the effect of locating the live performance as a site of authenticity and integrity. As discussed by Jeremy Wallach (2003, p. 47), the live performance is an experience to be romanticized as if removed from the mechanics of the music industry, a process that fixes and dilutes performance in the form of a secondary 'Recording'.

Some of the issues resulting from this relationship are illustrated with reference to the fact that the history of music production has, for the most part, involved the capturing of artists performing in the studio much as they would do in a concert hall. Such comparisons are contentious, however: the critic Evan Eisenberg has insisted that it is only live recordings that capture events; 'studio recordings, which are the great majority, record nothing' (cited in Elsdon, 2010, p. 147). Of course, as Michael Chanan has described (1995, pp. 137–155), so much music is originated by the technology of the studio, and presents what is in effect a simulacrum of performance: as Baudrillard would have it, a copy with no original (Baudrillard, 1994/2003, p. 5). Nonetheless, the mechanical recording process has inflected the status and understanding of performance – in the concert hall or studio. 'Waldvogel' of the *Talk Classical* forum registers this idea in a discussion of the technological limitations of historical recordings, relating one historical illustration in which:

> Louis Armstrong recorded West End Blues with his Hot Five in 1928. The performance has no bass instruments at all – the piano has to provide the rhythm. The drums are restricted to what sounds like drumsticks being tapped together. This occurred because recording techniques of the time would be overwhelmed by any loud sounds in the bass range.

Such circumstances have political resonance for the production, consumption and study of music, in making sense of the genre of jazz in this instance, by exploring ideas of its essence and history. As argued by Jed Rasula (1995) for instance, issues here concern the fidelity of such mechanical recordings – studio or 'live' – to 'authentic' notions of jazz, which is understood to be a music created anew in each and every live performance. The fixity of the recording threatens this quality as well as the way in which the history of jazz performance is written.

A rejoinder to this kind of argument comes from Simon Frith (2007) who has pointed out that it is misleading to consider music to be an object appropriated by a mode of industrialization – of which the recording is the acme. It is in fact its *result*. Frith suggests that 'Twentieth-century popular music means the twentieth-century popular record; not the record of something (a song? a singer? a performance?) which exists independently of the music industry, but a form of communication which determines what songs, singers, and performances are and can be' (Frith, 2007, p. 94). This attention to the popular can be extended to a wider music culture as a means of understanding the relation of music recordings with live events, resonating with Hennion's description of 'discomorphosis'. Hennion suggests that concert-going is no longer a dominant mode of encountering music: 'people listen now through the many other versions in their head; they have come to hear a particular performer whom they have heard on disc, playing a "repertoire" which has increasingly come to resemble a record company's "catalogue"' (Hennion, 2001, p. 16). The concert is a point of comparison and assessment in a continuum with recordings with which we are already familiar or indeed, may turn to for comparison after the fact of the concert.

'Solitary Wanderer' of the *Good Music Guide* forum illustrates this discomorphosis in reflecting on the value of the record in an assessment of one concert: 'I must say that the live experience was better. But it was essential to have learned them first to appreciate them properly'. In the same thread, 'Soundproof' writes that while 'There's an immediacy to the live performance that I prefer ... I need to go to live concerts in order to recognize when I'm hearing an approximation when listening at home'. Similarly, contributors to a forum dedicated to Van Morrison tell of how they discovered this artist on record and how this led them to his live shows. 'Ed, Washington' writes:

> In recent years, I have had the privilege to finally attend his shows. And I am thankful that when I finally did, I was up on just about his entire catalogue and thoroughly enjoyed whatever he chose to play. Atlantic City 2005, Virginia 2006 and DC 2009 are nights I will not soon forget.

'John F' tells of how he became hooked on Morrison's recordings before finally attending a concert, and a very significant one too:

> By the time Van appeared at the Troubador in L.A. in 1973, I had everything I could get my hands on from Them-time on. My girlfriend Laura Greenwood and I attended two of the Troubador shows, parts of which went into the "Too Late to Stop Now LP". [ ... ] In fact, the second, slightly higher-pitched female scream that slips in there just after Van finishes "Domino" is Laura.

Supplementing his audible presence and witness of the Van Morrison concerts captured on that record, John F also uploads several images of Morrison in concert from the 1970s taken by his now deceased partner.

While we should acknowledge the ontological, aesthetic and political issues presented by the idea of a 'live' recording – as outlined by Peter Johnson (2010, pp. 37–51) for instance – it is useful to treat such artefacts and their variety as presenting ideas about what constitutes music performance. Such ideas are important to listeners and the understanding of performance whether they have ever attended a concert or not. The individual 'live' recording captures not only aspects of any event but contributes also to a generic category of the representation of performance and a wider culture of consumption and interpretation in which such recordings are received and understood. This idea is evidenced in a discussion of the favourite live albums of community members at *All About Jazz*. As 'Guy' notes 'It's interesting that what we consider to be a "classic live album" was often just a night at the gig (and sometimes not even a great one!)'.

The live recording perforce fixes and memorializes, reinforcing a sense of its ephemerality by the process of preservation and selection from out of any other possible instances of an artist's performance. In turn, the live recording potentially assembles and addresses an audience, the majority of whom (if any) have no original reference point for the event captured. This does not prevent them from evaluating the recording in terms of its authentic qualities of performance, or for the ways in which it evokes a feeling of participation and communion with an event and indeed for the ways in which responses to it can be recorded and shared in turn. For instance, 'Jazzterday', writing about Dave Brubeck and Gerry Mulligan's *Live At The Berlin Philharmonie* enthuses that 'The sheer excitement of this classic performance (both on the artists' and the audience's side) is brought forward in a way that makes you feel like you were in the concert yourself'. At *Good Music Guide*, 'Sid James' writes of the great jazz performances of the past captured on record, that 'listening to the recording you can kind of picture the event while you are listening. Especially when the audience are clapping along to him singing a tune. It kind of crystallizes a moment in history'.

Based on such observations, we can think of the sound of the audience, band announcements and interactions, extended (or shortened) versions of familiar songs and other ambient noises as generic features of the live recording and which give it meaning. For instance, 'Ladyrebeca' writes at *Good Music Guide* of having a preference for jazz music:

> 'so I appreciate the moment-in-time live recording. I think a live audience spawns creativity that may otherwise manifest itself in a less interesting form (in, say, a studio) … On the Miles Davis Complete Plugged Nickel recordings, I *love* hearing the old cash register chiming in the background. It's also become an additional instrument. And there's this one guy who yells out, "Yeeeeaaaahh Miiiiles" during the clapping. Always makes me smile'.

The Davis recording referred to here signals how particular sites have become associated with live recordings and in turn afford authenticity. In jazz culture and alongside Chicago's Plugged Nickel, are venues such as Birdland, Newport and Greenwich Village's the Village Vanguard, 'the seat of live jazz since the 1940s', where 'Ninety-one live recordings have been made between 1957 and 2001, chronicling the whole of the history of jazz' (Bailey, 2005). Rock and soul music have their iconic venues such as the Fillmore, Marquee or the Apollo, which are sites associated with a long list of recordings, official or otherwise. In turn, these recordings have been earmarked and canonized as examples of significant moments in popular music, capturing and fixing ideas of performance.

Live recordings are regularly consecrated in the oeuvre and history of individual artists as well as in a wider music culture. Such recordings stand as monuments to moments in time that have served to fix an idea of the concert and in turn become 'ideal'. They contribute to a collective memory of what constitutes a live performance, even though for the majority for whom such material has meaning, it is the recording that is the point of reference for any recollection. C. Michael Bailey gives a sense of the time capsule quality of the live recording for rock music in an assessment of his 'top ten' performances. Writing of Joe Cocker's *Mad Dogs and Englishmen* he suggests that it is fortunate that this band did not survive to make further recordings or to tour: 'their music would have become old. This way, one may listen to this music 30 years later and still hear it fresh as if it had just been extracted from the LP shrink-wrap' (Bailey, 2004).

At this point we can consider further the live recording as a product of the music industry, re-framing it like the event it depicts in terms of scarcity. Of course, any one recording is endlessly reproducible, potentially accessible to an infinite number of listeners but will always present the *same* recording. Historically, music companies have managed the flow of product to the market and have been unwilling to provide further material that might dilute the exploitable value of the core commodity. While officially sanctioned live recordings may be scarce therefore, audience demand for the experience they offer is not necessarily assuaged by such releases or attendance at live performances by the artists captured, a situation which may help explain the value of the bootleg and allied practices for the memory of the concert for consumers.

Clinton Heylin's history of the bootleg indicates how illicit production and circulation is important mainly to specialized collectors in providing copies of studio productions such as unreleased songs and alternative takes of familiar material. The major market in the field of jazz and rock, however, is for recordings of live performances: 'These are generally complete live performances, bum notes and all – something legitimate record companies have often baulked at releasing – captured crudely from the audience or perhaps from an unmixed "board" tape' (Heylin, 1996, p. 9). Heylin's history and the contemporary demand for recordings of the scarce concerts of pianist Grigory Sokolov signals that classical performance is subject to the same pressures as popular forms (as reported by Rhodes, 2011). While Heylin is concerned with a micro-economy of bootlegging, an organized network of alternative production and values when compared to the legitimate music industries, here we can attend to the importance of individual practices of recording the experience of the concert. Across various online sites there are prodigious examples of the results of attempts by concert-goers to capture events on film and audio. Like the Twitter feeds documented by Bennett elsewhere in this volume, such material stands as a mode of witness – that the recorder was present and here is the evidence. Sharing recordings online, sometimes uploaded during the concert itself, invites others to participate in the evaluation of a performance whether they were in attendance or not. Some of this material is but a few seconds long, some presented in documentary style, including sequences leading up to the concert, the event itself, as well as its aftermath, including comment and critique. While clips sometimes go 'viral', viewing figures recorded on Vimeo or YouTube are often miniscule, yet online sharing facilities and proximity means that audience members – and those who were not in attendance at events – are able to access and collate footage of the same moments. The emulation of the process informs the officially produced film of the Beastie Boys in concert *Awesome; I Fuckin' Shot That!* (Dir. A. Yauch, 2006). In this instance, 50 audience members were given video cameras to shoot a gig from their perspective and from which the film was assembled.

While digital capture by smart phones offers often very good image and sound quality, results are rarely presented in imitation of professional recordings or as a fair copy of any event. That such recordings compare poorly with professionally produced recordings is in part due to the prohibitions in venues on such activity. For instance, the covert nature of most personal recording leads to amateurish qualities in framing, of a lack of perspective, unbalanced sound quality and so on. Nonetheless, such material is an important touchstone for memories of concerts and their mythologization and, as a result, quality of recording is sometimes relegated to a secondary consideration. One might argue that the negligible quality of such recordings is itself an aesthetic benchmark of authenticity, at once testament to the moment it captures but removed absolutely from any sense that it is an analogue conveying the experience; nonetheless, a desirable object for those seeking communion with the event.

Heylin suggests that to collectors, bootlegs are often valued for their 'authentic take' when compared to official releases with a 'retinue of post-production credits' (Heylin, 1996, p. 9). His celebration of bootlegging as a form of rebellion is at one with Neumann and Simpson's (1997) description of the same practice in terms of deviance and critique of the restrictive nature of the cultural industries. In this analysis, bootleggers themselves describe their practices 'in terms of an elusive notion of getting closer to the "authentic", the "real", and overcoming the distances set by the commercial recording industry'. While I would argue that there are distinctions to be made between the kind of bootlegging described by Heylin, Neumann and Simpson and some of the work encountered online in the course of this research, the process of capture and preservation is usefully described as a search for the lost 'aura' of the ephemeral event in which 'Bootleg recordings seem to provide a marker for a meaningful experience that would otherwise be lost' (1997, p. 338).

**Conclusions**

This chapter attests to some of the ways in which the concert experience – encountered in person or at a remove – is recorded and memorialized across a range of online activity. Given the fleeting nature of the live music event, one might argue that its meaning is only ever conveyed and understood as a result of the materiality of its recording and interactions between attendees and others eager to hear about it after the fact. That this activity is so prodigious suggests that this account is but a starting point for further research about the aftermath of the concert.

Further work might attend to the nuanced distinctions between musical genres and their consumption, particularly between classical and pop forms. The status of the live recording in classical music for instance is complicated by what Johnson (2010) describes as the naturalistic approach to its capture in which the presence of technology is elided. At another end of the music spectrum, the performances of DJs, mixologists, turntablists and so on, present interesting challenges to the notion of the concert. 'Live' tapes produced by such artists are generally taken from the sound desk and avoid ambient sounds of crowd and venue.

Having been present at live performances matters a great deal to consumers and operates in terms of a personal and communal attachment to artists, musical repertoires, communities and particular events. This presence has value in the dynamics of individual and wider taste cultures and the formation of audience identity and collective memory. To paraphrase, the accrued impression is of a statement of 'I was there ...', which is coupled with the implicit 'you *should* have been there' or 'you *had* to be there', in any statement or exchange about live performances. The desire for the live recording, officially sanctioned or otherwise, testifies to a response to the last two statements and a yearning to retrieve and explore this shared experience.

# Chapter 14
# Staying Behind: Explorations in Post-performance Musician–Audience Dialogue

Melissa C. Dobson and John Sloboda

This chapter reports on a pilot research and development project designed to explore the potential of post-performance dialogues between musicians and audiences at live events. The defining characteristic of the events studied is that audience feedback is given in response to questions formulated by the musicians involved, designed to provide information of genuine artistic interest and relevance to those concerned. Audience members are, thereby, drawn into a relationship which has elements of a focus group, or consultancy, rather than the more common 'ask the performer' model of post-performance events, which maintains the more traditional boundaries in which the performers give and the audience gratefully receives. In the kind of event being reported here the tables are turned: it is the audience who gives and the musicians who receive, thus offering the opportunity of a more explicitly collaborative two-way relationship between artist and audience.

Classical musicians generally have rather limited means of obtaining direct and detailed feedback from their live audiences. This is often restricted to applause at the end of the piece and the somewhat intangible 'feel of the room'. This is in contrast to some other genres of music, where through movement, clapping, or vocalizing, performance conventions allow audience members to respond in real time to the music-making unfolding on stage (Small, 1998). For example, audience members in jazz performance can be seen as active participants, with their responses to a musician's (often improvised) performance forming a 'communication loop' between performers and listeners (Berliner, 1994, p. 459), while studies of 'pub rock' (Bennett, 1997; Björnberg and Stockfelt, 1996) stress the rapport built between performers and audiences as a defining feature of performances in this context, especially when performers encourage audience participation in the form of 'singing along' to songs which have gradually assumed a local significance (Bennett, 1997). In contrast, it is common for classical performances to take place in which the performers do not address the audience verbally for the full extent of their time spent on stage (for further discussion on the effects of musicians talking to their audiences during a concert, see e.g. Kolb, 2001; Pitts, 2005b; Tomes, 2004).

We are living in a time when Western audiences for live classical music are steadily declining (National Endowment of the Arts, 2008). At such a time, a deeper understanding of audience reactions is not only of intrinsic intellectual interest, but is hopefully of direct practical use to musicians seeking to engage audiences and enhance the quality of their experience. Arts marketing research, for example, has highlighted the importance of the social dimension to concert-goers, and has suggested that discussions and forums which allow audience members to extend the concert experience in a social capacity elevate their experience in the concert hall. Gainer (1995) conducted in-depth interviews with ten regular attenders of the live performing arts to gain further insight into the role of 'ritual' in consumer behaviour. She found that sharing social experiences, including using arts events to 'build bridges' with distant acquaintances, or even just being able to talk about experiences of attendance with others who attend similar events, were key motivations for attending arts performances. Gainer concludes that in some cases, 'the market for the live performing arts appears to be a market in the venue for social interaction, and not always a market in the performance on the stage' (p. 258), with individuals motivated to subscribe to concerts with another person or in groups in order to provide a regular forum for social interaction (p. 256). In work aiming to find better parameters with which to define the quality of a performance from the audience's perspective, Radbourne, Glow, Johanson and White (2009) identified four key factors which held the potential to enhance or detract from the audience experience at classical concerts and theatre productions, one of which was 'collective engagement', noting the benefits of performers acknowledging the audience's presence, of a sense of shared response between audience members, and of the ability to articulate that response through talking to others present (see their chapter elsewhere in this volume).

In theatre, a common feature of performances is the post-performance discussion, in which members of the cast and creative team answer questions from the audience: a format which allows audience members to share their responses to the production they have just witnessed (Heim, 2012). At the time of writing, this practice is not yet common in classical music performances in the UK. More widely, although anecdotal evidence suggests that post-concert discussions may be more prevalent in other countries – for instance Germany – these events have not yet been properly documented or researched. Audience members at most classical concerts may therefore attend a pre-concert talk (sometimes, but not always, given by the performers) and/or may informally discuss their responses after the performance, perhaps particularly in concert series where subscribers inhabit the same seats in the auditorium both within and across seasons, providing a vehicle through which informal discussion with one's neighbours may flourish (O'Sullivan, 2009). However, providing a more organized forum after concerts where responses to the music and performance can informally be discussed would situate the concert as a more social experience for those to whom being able to share their responses with others is important (Radbourne, Johanson and Glow, 2010). For new audience members in particular, being able to talk informally with other attenders and the performers themselves might provide one channel through which the knowledge and skills relating to classical music listening in the concert hall can be informally learnt, as has been demonstrated in the relatively analogous field of theatre reception research by Scollen (2008).

There are important ways in which greater interaction between musicians and audiences may be of benefit to performers, too, and it is this slant which forms our primary focus in this chapter. There is a tendency in the field of music psychology to collect detailed evaluative responses from music listeners without reference to the specific concerns or interests of the musicians involved, even when the event is a live performance. Moreover, research interrogating the concept of performance quality has traditionally sought the perspectives of those whose role it is to formally evaluate a performance (e.g. competition adjudicators or examiners for graded practical music examinations), placing emphasis on technical facility, accuracy and interpretation (see Thompson and Williamon, 2003) rather than also considering the potentially broader conceptualization of performance quality that audience members may bring to a performance (Dobson, 2010).

One notable exception to these trends is the set of papers published in a special issue of *Music Perception* in 2004, exploring dimensions of audience response to live performances of a new work, *Angel of Death*, by the composer Roger Reynolds, who collaborated with a team of psychologists and musicologists to investigate whether 'listeners actually hear what the composer intended for them to hear (and what the musicologists thought they would hear)' (Levitin and Cuddy, 2004, p. 167). The process of the work's genesis was truly collaborative: experimental studies were used to investigate aspects including listeners' perceptions of thematic structure and the effects of instrumentation change on memorization of the musical materials, the results of which were provided to the composer to use in producing the final version of the work (ibid., p. 168). Audience appraisals of the work were then collected at two premiere performances, using hand-held devices through which audience members could provide continuous responses (see McAdams et al., 2004). In his reflection on the process overall, Reynolds (2004) notes the reassurance of discovering that listeners perceived the formal structure in his piece as he had hoped, before setting out the following paradox:

> The historical-social fact is that we live in a time in which the composer's premises, the issues that engage him or her, differ markedly from the experience and capacities of the majority of serious music-listeners. This is even true if one limits the audience to those with wide experience in contemporary music. [...] At the same time, the materials, strategies, and, therefore, prospects open to composers are of unprecedented richness. The essential ethic of the creative process will not allow one to act in violation of one's own aesthetic sensibility. (Reynolds, 2004, pp. 354–5)

Reynolds concludes that processes such as the one explored in the *Angel of Death* project hold the potential to provide a useful source of perspective for composers when grappling with this dilemma, and recommends that this approach be taken by a range of living composers, with the potential for 'a sufficient weight of evidence [to] be accumulated so that some influence on the course of musical practice and thought might be exerted' (ibid., p. 355).

Our approach seeks to build on this work (a) by looking at a range of works across a range of events rather than just one work; (b) by including performers as well as composers in the research process; and (c) by focusing on the direct flow of verbal information and views between musicians and audience in the immediate post-performance period, thereby providing the musicians with direct feedback from audience members, and with the opportunity to follow up on their responses and ask further questions of the audience there and then. The pilot work reported in this chapter looks at the potentials that can be realized when musicians themselves take a lead in the formulation of the research questions that are posed to the audience, and are centrally involved in the review of the data so obtained. We seek to explore the benefits and challenges for musicians involved in (a) playing a role in this type of research process, and (b) the act of engaging in a public post-concert dialogue with one's audience – the effects of 'talking' on stage. Documenting musicians' experiences with – and responses to – this unfamiliar process, our stance was deliberately explorative, gathering initial findings which can be used to inform further hypothesis-driven research in the future. Our approach can be summarized in terms of its positioning on four key research dimensions, which are contrasted to what we have called the dominant model, which is the one more commonly found in psychological studies of responses to music (see Table 14.1).

Table 14.1   The positioning of the present research and the 'dominant' model on four key research dimensions

|  | **Dominant model** | **This research** |
| --- | --- | --- |
| **Object of study** | Performers or listeners separately | Performers and listeners in interaction |
| **Focus of study** | Individuals and their internal processes | Group processes, involving artists, audience and researchers |
| **Data gathering context** | Controlled/closed (e.g. pre-recorded music in lab, experiments, questionnaires, structured interviews) | Open (live music performance events, semi-structured group discourse) |
| **Primary agenda** | Researcher-led | Artist–researcher collaboration |

**Method**

We have now worked across five different artistic projects in a process which involves (a) discovering artistically relevant questions which can be validly posed to audience members, (b) collaboratively devising appropriate means of collecting this data (always a post-performance discussion, augmented in two cases by a questionnaire), (c) jointly reviewing the outcomes of the event, and the audience data, and (d) obtaining reflective feedback from those involved regarding the value of being involved in the exercise. A summary of the five projects is shown in Table 14.2 below.

Table 14.2    Details of the five pilot research events

| Date/location | Event | Artistic collaborator / Data collected |
|---|---|---|
| **July 2011**<br>**Guildhall School** | (A) 'For Summer is a come O and Winter is a gone O' Premiere of new composition, performed by chamber ensemble, conducted by student composer. | Composer /<br>Audience questionnaire, Post-concert discussion, Debrief interview with composer |
| **November 2011**<br>**Guildhall School** | (B) 'Movers and Shakers' Workshop to explore potentials of music-related movement for audience members during a Bach solo violin suite performance. | Directors, performer /<br>Audience questionnaire, Post-concert discussion |
| **February 2012**<br>**Guildhall School** | (C) 'The Seven Deadly Sins' New student production of Kurt Weill's ballet chanté, with orchestra and singer/actors. | Directors, performers /<br>Post-concert discussion, Group debrief interview with singer/actors and performer-researcher liaison |
| **May 2012**<br>**Wallace Collection (of period swords)** | (D) 'Combattimento' A site-specific staging of Monteverdi's one-act opera with student orchestra and singer/actors. | Directors, performers /<br>Post-concert discussion, Group debrief interview with director and some performers |
| **June 2012**<br>**Queen Elizabeth Hall** | (E) 'Debut Sounds' A London Philharmonic Orchestra concert of new works by young composers. | Composers /<br>Post-concert discussion, Debrief interview with the composers' mentor |

Specific events researched with this model include premieres of new compositions, innovative staging of opera and music theatre, and an event where audience members were invited to move during the performance (through both structured movement coaching and opportunities for free movement), rather than stay seated. A range of research methods was deployed, as appropriate to each event.

In the space available here we employ a case study approach to illustrate what this process has yielded in two of these events: Event A was the world premiere of a composition for small instrumental ensemble. Our collaborator was the composer himself, who also conducted the performance. Event C was a new staging of Kurt Weill's ballet chanté, *The Seven Deadly Sins*. Our collaborators were the directors, the actor/singers, and the conductor of the orchestra.

**Case Studies**

*Event A – For Summer is a Come O and Winter is a Gone O*

***Method***
Our primary collaborator, a student composer at the Guildhall School of Music & Drama, wrote a single-movement piece for a four-instrument ensemble (oboe, viola, percussion, piano) whose inspiration was a traditional day of celebration in the composer's home town, characterized by distinctive rituals involving folk music and dance. The town is Helston in Cornwall and the day is known as 'Flora Day' held on 8 May every year. The style of the composition was of mainstream acoustic 'new music' within the classical tradition. In the programme note available to the audience, the composer wrote: 'The day sees the local people dance a processional dance around the town led by a brass band at set times throughout the day. [...] For this piece I have decided to derive all of the material from the tune called the Flora Dance and I have played with the different levels at which the tune is heard within the music'. He then went on to briefly characterize some of the elements of the day that specifically informed the composition. The primary question of interest to the composer was whether audience members' knowledge of the programmatic background to the composition was a significant factor in their appreciation of the work.

Beginning about two months ahead of the premiere, and in consultation with the researchers and his composition tutor, the composer devised four simple questions which were posed to the audience in a questionnaire which was handed out just before the piece was performed. Audience members were encouraged to look at these questions but not to actually write anything until the performance was over. They were also invited to come to a different room immediately after the end of the concert to 'meet the composer' and discuss their responses in more detail.

There were 27 people in the audience. Fifteen audience members completed the questionnaire, and nine of these attended the post-concert discussion which lasted around 40 minutes. The discussion was recorded. Twenty-four hours after the discussion, the composer was interviewed about his experiences of this process, and this interview was also recorded as part of the research process. Thematic analysis of the questionnaire data and transcripts was undertaken.

***Findings***
In response to the main question posed by the composer ('Was the programme note which described the event which inspired this piece helpful to you in appreciating

or enjoying this piece?') the 13 of the 15 respondents answered that the programme note was 'somewhat useful but not essential' in appreciating or enjoying the piece.

Elaborative discussions around this theme in the post-performance event confirmed that the piece 'stood by itself' as an aesthetic entity, and that the programmatic scaffolding assumed a subsidiary role in the appreciation of the piece. There were also mixed responses relating to whether the folk tune could be identified in the piece, with the majority of questionnaire respondents answering that they were 'not sure' that they were able to identify the tune. The post-performance discussion facilitated more detailed comments on this topic, with audience members saying that while they mostly could not identify the folk tune, they appreciated knowing about and recognizing the various events of the Flora Day, as these provided a clear structure and sense of progression through the piece.

This was useful feedback for the composer, who felt that this experience of learning about what his audience could and could not discern in the work would change his future compositional practice: 'when I'm writing a bar which I think, "oh, that's clever", then I'll think, actually that's not really going to come across. So, I think in the practice of my composition, that's when I'll really learn most about what I've learnt from this'. He also valued the fact that the feedback he received was an immediate response, unfettered by consequent rumination on the part of the audience member:

> I think that's what's exciting for me in a way about getting feedback straight after the piece, it's not thought out – you haven't got to wait three days' time and go 'yes, this bit worked, because of this' – it's very raw, I think that's the bit that really excites me.

Although the research process did elicit immediate responses from the audience, a number of audience participants in the post-performance discussion reflected on how the process of reading the programme note and seeing the questionnaire in advance had changed the way they listened to the performance, either by listening out for certain features …

> I found that [the programmatic structure of the piece] a lot clearer than the tune, which I found – I was listening really hard because I had read the questionnaire, but I couldn't hear it.

… or by listening in a more analytical mode than usual:

> I was very aware afterwards, saying oh, right, I've got to do a questionnaire […] so perhaps it would have been nice to be given the questionnaire as you walked out, maybe, so that you didn't know what questions, you just had a heightened awareness, because otherwise it was just like, having to say oh, this is directly relevant to the programme or not, which is a shame in a way, because it meant you couldn't sit back and enjoy the piece.

Interestingly, however, in his debrief interview the composer described how setting the audience a specific evaluative task in advance of the performance was an unexpected benefit for him, by enhancing his experience of the quality of their attention to the piece: 'I liked the idea that people were really listening to the piece in a very detailed way [...] It might be a selfish composer speaking, but I liked the idea that people were really trying to understand it and trying to have something constructive to say about what they found'. Here, the fact that the research process in itself changed the way in which participants engaged with the stimulus – in research terms, a feature which is negative yet unavoidable – was in artistic terms of significant benefit to the composer.

*Event C – The Seven Deadly Sins*

**Method**

Kurt Weill's *The Seven Deadly Sins* is a satirical sung ballet, composed to words by Bertolt Brecht, and first performed in 1933. The plot depicts the fortunes of two American sisters in the Great Depression who set out from their family in Louisiana to earn enough money to send home to allow the family to build a little house on the Mississippi. The work is primarily a critical commentary on the way in which capitalism dehumanizes people and commodifies personal relationships.

The creative team consisted of a student artistic director, a student musical director/conductor, and two staff members acting as project advisors. A member of the research team (JS) met with the creative team six months ahead to discuss the collaboration. Thereafter one of the staff members in the team (an experienced social-science researcher) acted as performer–researcher liaison, and took primary responsibility for generating and passing on a set of agreed questions for the post-performance discussion from the creative team:

- What do you think the message of the work that you have just seen is? Is the message still relevant today?
- Does Weill's music contribute to this message?
- What were some of the effects of this work and how we staged it on you the audience?
- How did you experience these? (For instance, did it bring the message out, or did it alienate/patronize you?)
- Do we still believe that theatre has the capacity to provoke political change amongst its audiences – or is it just another cultural commodity?

The creative team decided to invite a well-known classical performer/teacher to chair a post-performance discussion as the means of obtaining audience feedback. A member of the research team (JS) held two pre-event briefing meetings with the chair.

The post-performance discussion took place in the performance space immediately after the performance, and involved, in addition to the chair, three members of the creative team, and two of the singer/actors. The discussion lasted about 30 minutes. Over half the audience remained for the discussion, which was pre-announced at the start of the performance; a good range of the audience contributed to the discussion, and no one individual was perceived to dominate. A few weeks afterwards, post-event feedback was elicited from the artist participants in the discussion, four of whom attended a one-hour recorded meeting with the researchers, while one sent written comments by email. Thematic analysis of this feedback was undertaken.

### *Findings*
Just as the student composer in Event A had found that the research process itself had exerted an unexpected positive effect, the participants in *Seven Deadly Sins* found that the very process of formulating questions for the post-performance discussion (or for some members of the cast, just knowing that they had been formulated by others in the creative team) shaped the way they approached the rehearsal process:

> Conductor: But it was good though [...] because once we had those questions, it enabled us to shape the performance as well. So it gave us a direction for this [post-performance discussion] and a direction for the performance.

> Singer/Actor: It enabled us to make much clearer choices in the setting and things like that, yeah, certainly.

The cast members felt that having a set of questions in itself played an important role during the rehearsal process, regardless of whether the post-performance discussion had actually taken place:

> Singer/Actor: I think, whenever you're staging a performance and you're working with direction and things like that, you're always trying to give something to the audience. But having these questions, whether or not they were for a post-performance talk, without taking away from them in any shape or form, I think, you know, having to think about how we were staging things was really a good opportunity for us to think about what we were doing. However, I would be very interested to see, if we didn't necessarily have a post-performance discussion, if we would be able to do the same kind of thing with a set of questions, and not have feedback from them.

Unsurprisingly, the student director of the production was more focused on the tangible benefit of receiving audience feedback in the discussion, believing that post-performance events could have value in the development of new productions, especially if they were to take place in a workshop style during the rehearsal process – then allowing time for suggestions and feedback from the workshop discussion to be incorporated into the final production:

> Director: It was a real eye-opener into what worked and what wasn't so clear. [It] would be great for a new production in the late stages of rehearsals to have one of these types of event to further enhance their communication with the audience [...] I definitely think that there is a future for this type of dialogue between an audience and production prior to the performances going to the public. [It] provides so much insight into what exactly works from an audience's point of view. When you are the performer/director you get so involved in the performance yourself that you almost can no longer see it with a blank slate.

From a directorial point of view, then, the research process was predominantly positive, providing valuable feedback that held the potential to enhance future performances.

For other performers, participating in the post-performance discussion presented some challenges, relating to either the pace and/or nature of a change in their roles. The conductor of the performance described being more nervous about participating in the discussion than he was about the actual performance, and would have preferred more time to adjust between the end of the performance and the beginning of the discussion: 'it's a strange headspace to be in, suddenly conducting, and [then] turn around and open your mouth'.

For one student singer in particular, taking part in the post-performance discussion created an unexpected change of his own perceived status in relation to the audience:

> Singer/Actor: It was just odd. I had never experienced it before. It was almost as if instead of walking through the stage door after the performance, you walked through the audience door.

However, he recognized that his willingness to take part in a post-performance discussion of this nature would vary depending on a number of factors, including whether or not he felt the performance had gone well. Interestingly, a post-performance discussion following a performance that had not gone well could be seen as even more valuable, presenting an opportunity 'to redeem yourself':

> Singer/Actor: It's almost like, when you start the performance, the audience have high status and the performer has low. And that status is then substantiated throughout the performance and it grows, and then the audience has a lower status. When you leave the auditorium, you then come out and you feel as if you have quite high status over and above an audience. To have this [post-performance discussion], balanced it out, I felt, and we were then back on the same [...] and I think in a purely selfish, diva way, I wasn't too chuffed about it. [laughter] But then, I think if it had gone terribly, I think I would have been overly chuffed to sit down and talk to every member of the audience, and say, "I wouldn't have done that in rehearsal".

Overall, this participant felt ambivalent about the post-performance talk, indicating that he would be willing to do it again, but this was strongly dependent on performance context: he would not be willing to repeat the process at a performance that was seen as 'high-profile' or large-scale, but would happily take part in a context that, like this student production, was perceived to be relaxed and 'low-key'. The key message from this participant was that taking part in the post-performance discussion changed the nature of his experience of the performance as a whole, describing how it 'detracted from the post-performance high [...] To be completely honest it took away from my ego'.

There were also issues of social hierarchies and status in how the post-performance discussion itself was run. In the case of this project, placing the creative artist at the centre of the research involved having to bend our ideal research process to work with the reality of the context in which the performance was taking place. Our other pilot post-performance events have been chaired by one of the research team, meaning that, as much as possible within a fairly open discussion, we have retained control of the questions that have been asked of the audience.

In this project the creative team arranged for a well-known classical performer – who was an outsider to this research process – to chair the discussion, as his presence and name (as a 'classical music celebrity') was seen as an important publicity tool in enticing audience members to attend. However, for us, this situation meant that we had decreased control over the questions asked in the discussion, and over the ways the questions were framed – with the chair asking questions of both the panel and the audience, with less being asked of the audience than we had initially intended when devising the research.

From the performers' perspective, none of them had taken part in a discussion of this kind before, and they appreciated being guided in the discussion by the chair. In retrospect, they felt that they would have valued greater opportunities to ask their own questions of the audience about specific aspects of the production; one raised an interesting point about where authority lay in the discussion, noting that continuing to ask her own questions of the audience would have constituted encroaching on the chair's territory:

> Staff Project Advisor: I did ask a question of the audience. I think I wouldn't have been comfortable to keep on coming up with more audience questions. Because then the question is, am I trying to take over [the chair's] job. [*pause*] I suppose, [he] was chairing it, but he wasn't actually, he hadn't really been involved in the work.

Finally, the participants considered the audience's place in the perceived hierarchy created by the performance and the post-performance event. Some of the performers reported that they felt that audience members were unclear about the purpose of the post-performance discussion, raising the question of whether the audience should have been alerted in advance to expect questions to be asked *of them*. Another reported that the inclusion of a post-performance event changed audience members' expectations and aims of the evening, moving the event from 'pure entertainment' to a potential learning experience:

> Singer/Actor: I think, from my experience with my friends that came along, it changed the way that they approached the piece. They didn't go out to be entertained. They went out to have some input. And it wasn't in a negative way. They were ready for a post-performance [event], but it wasn't like they were getting dressed up to go to the West End. It was that they were getting dressed up to go to a School and have an after-show production talk, which changed the way they approached it.

This idea of going out to 'have some input' is interesting, given that it pertains to the usual mode in classical music performances (and post-performance events) whereby the performers 'give' and the audience 'receives', even when the medium of this reception in a post-performance discussion is more actively directed by questions from the audience. How might altering this dynamic – to an emphasis on artists directing questions to their audiences – change the balance of power between performers and audiences? How might audience expectations of, and approaches to, classical music performance change?

One possible factor is a facilitation, created by being asked questions themselves, of increased audience–audience interaction and peer learning:

> Singer/Actor: What I was told was [the audience] enjoyed [...] their own ideas came more into fruition through matching, you know, similar ideas of listening to other [people] speak and going, 'oh yes, that's right, that's what I was trying to, you know, that's how I was trying to string it together' and, you know, perhaps it gave them clearer ideas and it helped them to understand the piece, through other people's understanding, which then again, you know, in turn helped us.

There is therefore scope in this exploration of post-performance events to create a model whereby the process of performers posing questions to audiences (rather than vice versa) still generates a sense of input, dialogue and learning between audience members – so creating a feedback cycle that is valuable to musicians and audience members alike.

**Concluding Discussion**

From the two short case studies presented here, we have mapped some of the benefits and challenges experienced by musicians participating in this process of research, including: the potentially positive impact of the research activity on the creative process; both positive and negative aspects of receiving verbal feedback directly after a performance, including the necessary expansion of the musician's performance persona from 'one who plays' to 'one who talks'; and issues of social hierarchies, authority and power (for performers, in curation, in audience expectations).

All of the five studies, of which we have described two in more detail, involved students and/or staff at a higher education institution for the advanced training of professional musicians and actors. This allows our research, in addition to attempting to meet normal academic goals, to take full advantage of a conservatoire's unique position as a meeting place between researchers, professional musicians and other creative professionals, advanced teachers, and the students they teach. This position allows us to observe professional performance and the development of emerging professionals. But more than this, it also enables us to help shape innovative practice. The practice we can influence most directly is that occurring within the conservatoire, both its teaching and learning practice, but also the considerable amount of artistic practice that emanates from the staff and students.

We see research as an integral part of an ongoing process whereby new means of relating to audiences are being devised, trialled, and embedded in the culture. We believe that a progressive conservatoire can be a crucible for pushing professional boundaries as well as evolving educational practices, and allowing experimentation in a context that is somewhat protected from the harsh winds of commercial imperative. As modern audiences increasingly seek active and engaged roles, the successful musician of the twenty-first century will arguably be the one who welcomes and encourages a closer and more personal engagement with the people they are performing to. As conservatoire training adapts to reflect this change – recognizing the importance of musicians' behaviour during these liminal stages of the performance event – so musicians at the start of their careers will be better equipped with skills and experience that allow them to engage positively and constructively with their audiences. One of our aims is to help encourage an environment in which musicians are much more likely to engage directly with their audiences to obtain tailored and valued feedback. We would like to see a situation where it is normal for the kinds of process we have researched to happen in public concert halls. Such work would require fewer divisions between research and curation – and greater collaboration between arts organizations and research institutions – than is currently the norm. We hope this chapter has indicated how this could reap considerable benefits for all parties involved.

We accept that these preliminary findings cannot necessarily be generalized, especially as we have predominantly worked in this pilot research programme with students – who are orientated towards receiving feedback – rather than professional musicians. However, this was a pilot research study documenting for the first time, as far as we are aware, some of the reported benefits and problems of post-performance events for the creative artists involved in classical music performances. Findings from these student projects may be used to encourage professional musicians to take part in future research on this topic. Of course, applied or action research of this kind must still be subjected to the critical scrutiny of peers in relation to its research rigour. However, there is also a different tightrope we must walk. On the one hand, an important constraint on such research is the need to respect the artistic process and not import research processes that come to dominate or distort the artistic outcomes. On the other hand, the very introduction of this interactive research process does have the capacity to alter the artistic process itself, as the data showed. Our priority is to produce research which is rigorous but, importantly, directly useful to the musicians involved. We hope that future research could be used to develop a system of performance evaluation for use in the training of musicians in which aspects of performances which have been shown to be of value to audiences themselves (rather than to examiners or adjudicators) are taken into account.

It is also important to recognize that the inclusion of a post-performance event in which verbal feedback is sought may change the experience of the concert for audience members, too. As Edward Said (2008, p. 307) has suggested, in comparison to other art forms music is both 'the most directly affecting and expressive as well as the most esoteric and difficult to discuss' (cf. Adorno, 1976, p. 4; Mitchell and MacDonald, 2009). This prevailing notion that music's ineffability makes it difficult to express one's responses to it (see Hewett, 2003) suggests that asking individuals to discuss their listening experiences in a group environment may mean they take some time to become confident in doing so, and therefore that the type of feedback that artists receive may be self-selecting, with only seasoned concert-goers – familiar with musical terminology and willing to voice their assessments of the performance in public – contributing. There is, therefore, an agenda of audience development which also needs to be explored. Can we provide experiences and support which empower audience members to be more active, confident and effective in providing feedback? Heim (2012) describes a process of priming and encouraging post-show theatre audiences to participate as 'critics', engendered through deliberately breaking out of the 'question and answer' model of discussion to create meaningful dialogue between audience members themselves. However, a key principle in this approach was that none of the cast or creative team were present at the discussions, which were moderated by a neutral facilitator – therefore, the artists were unable to respond directly to any feedback volunteered, and a dialogue between artists and audience members was not established.

One practice that musicians could profitably learn from is the 'Critical Response Process' introduced primarily in the context of dance by Lerman and Borstel (2003). In this process, audience members receive explicit training and induction into their role as constructive critics, and are invited by a facilitator to comment behind closed doors on work in progress, prior to its final shaping and public release. The process follows four key steps, starting with invitations for audience members to articulate statements of meaning about the work they have just experienced. Artists are then able to ask questions of their audience, with help from the facilitator in forming these questions as required; in the third step the tables are turned and the audience is invited to ask neutral questions of the artists. Finally, the process concludes with 'permissioned opinions', in which audience members must first declare which aspect of the work their opinion relates to (e.g. musical form, instrumentation or dynamic range), giving the artist the opportunity to then say whether or not they wish to hear the opinion.

Another potential approach is to 'reduce the threat' to individual audience members and artists by, for instance, having artists move between smaller groups of audience members for conversation and feedback, essentially asking audience members to engage as collaborators rather than 'subjects' by eliciting each other's responses and experiences in a collective dialogue which includes the artist. The use of informal small-group or one-on-one discussions, rather than large-group situations which may be inhibiting to many audience members, may be enabling for all concerned, and may be one means of tapping into the kinds of spontaneous responses between audience members which can often be heard in foyer spaces immediately after a performance (cf. Heim, 2012; Radbourne, Johanson and Glow, 2010). This approach could be combined with the collection of quantitative or qualitative data from audience members privately during the performance, possibly using continuous response methods.

We are yet quite far away from a culture in which audience members themselves are enabled to become co-participants in the design of feedback procedures. Yet the full and active engagement of all three corners of the evaluative triangle – artist–audience–researcher – does not seem an unrealistic dream. We hope that this research project is one small step in the direction of achieving that.

# Chapter 15
# Postlude

Karen Burland and Stephanie Pitts

The chapters in this book draw together, for the first time, complementary perspectives on what it means to be an audience member. Regardless of musical genre, or performance context (music festival, concert hall or converted/adapted spaces), the authors have demonstrated the varied ways in which audiences contribute to live performances. The research portrays a picture of audiences as actively seeking meaningful musical experiences which they try to preserve and share with others. There are a number of factors that determine the extent to which they find such special moments during live performances, and, as we discuss below, it may be these aspects that audiences seek to re-experience at future events – thus we may think of audience behaviour as a cyclical process of experiencing-preserving-revisiting – and this cycle offers an insight into what it means to be an audience member and why this might matter.

For some audience members, the experience of live music is entirely dependent upon 'being there' – for them there is something special about the feel of venue, the atmosphere of the event, the proximity to performers or other audience members that enables immersion in the music and in some cases leads to 'flow' experiences. For such individuals, these are experiences which cannot be expressed using words – the 'feel' of the occasion is significant and meaningful. However, one suggestion emerging from this book is that the experience of live performance is not simply, and only, dependent upon an individual actually 'being there'; audiences can engage with live performances, in real time, but remotely, relying on others to share their experiences online (e.g. by texting or tweeting), thereby extending the audience 'community' in ways previously unimaginable (even as recently as the 1990s). This suggests that being part of a community of like-minded others is an important aspect of being an audience member; communities offer a sense of belonging but also contribute to personal identities as they offer opportunities for identification with different groups of individuals – whether those groups relate to musical preferences (Long), national identity (Karlsen), or cultural values (Pitts). For some, the importance of communities may only be relevant during the performance itself, but others like to extend the experience by joining online fansites or forums dedicated to exchanging and sharing responses to gigs and concerts. This kind of activity emphasizes the social nature of audience experience, and indicates that, for many, discussions and debates (and disagreements!) with others can enhance and solidify our responses to live performances (Dobson and Sloboda; Burland and Windsor).

It can therefore be argued that live performance is meaningful whether individuals engage in person or remotely, but that the types of experience may be different, even if they are complementary. For example, we have seen that situational factors (that is, the venue, the environmental conditions, the interactions with other audience members/performers) offer unique and special experiences to audience members and these aspects are entirely dependent upon 'being there' in the moment. However, aspects of community, belonging and identity also emerge from live performance contexts, but these may be experienced remotely (via online activity) as well as by being at the event itself. There is little research which compares the nature of musical responses to performances experienced live or remotely but it would be logical to assume that 'being there' leads to more meaningful memories than remote engagement. Indeed, there is some evidence for this in Lucy Bennett's chapter which deals most specifically with online activity during performances: she suggests that in many instances the responsibility to record performances and pay attention to a mobile phone detracted from total immersion in the experience, even though those doing the recording were aware of the service they were offering other fans. Therefore, we suggest that the most meaningful experiences for audience members relate to a combination of social, personal and situational factors, but that the latter have a more powerful impact on an individual's engagement and response during a performance.

As suggested above, and throughout the book, responses to performances last longer than the event itself and the ways in which audience members try to preserve their memories may be personal (through scrapbooking, mapping, or storing ticket stubs in a box), social (through sharing video/audio recordings, discussing and reviewing the concert with others), face-to-face, or remote (via contributions to fansites and forums). Such activities shape our memories of performances (van Dijck, 2006) and inevitably become entwined with our biographies: as Sara Cohen discussed in her chapter, looking back at ticket stubs collected over the years brings back memories relating not only to particular gigs (including very specific aspects relating to buildings and a sense of place) but to aspects of personal identity and history too. Preserving the memories of gigs online also contributes to an individual's sense of identity as it offers a sense of authority and status for having been there to witness a particular event taking place. Once again, the experience of 'being there' is perceived to be a privilege which sets apart those who were there and those who were not; the act of preserving an event emphasizes its significance for the individual and, when the memories are shared, highlights that others have missed out on a special experience.

When live performances are perceived as special and meaningful, the act of preserving them in some form allows for individuals to revisit the experience in the immediate or distant future. However, if the situational factors are as significant to the experience as we suggest above, then it is perhaps unlikely that any kind of record will truly preserve the memory. Therefore, individuals may choose to re-experience live performance in order to enhance and supplement memories of past events and to create new ones.

**Personal & social experiences of live performance**
- Community/connecting with others
- Identity
- Belonging

**Live performance: being there**
- Participation/agency
- Importance of venue and atmosphere
- Experiencing "Flow" or emotional responses

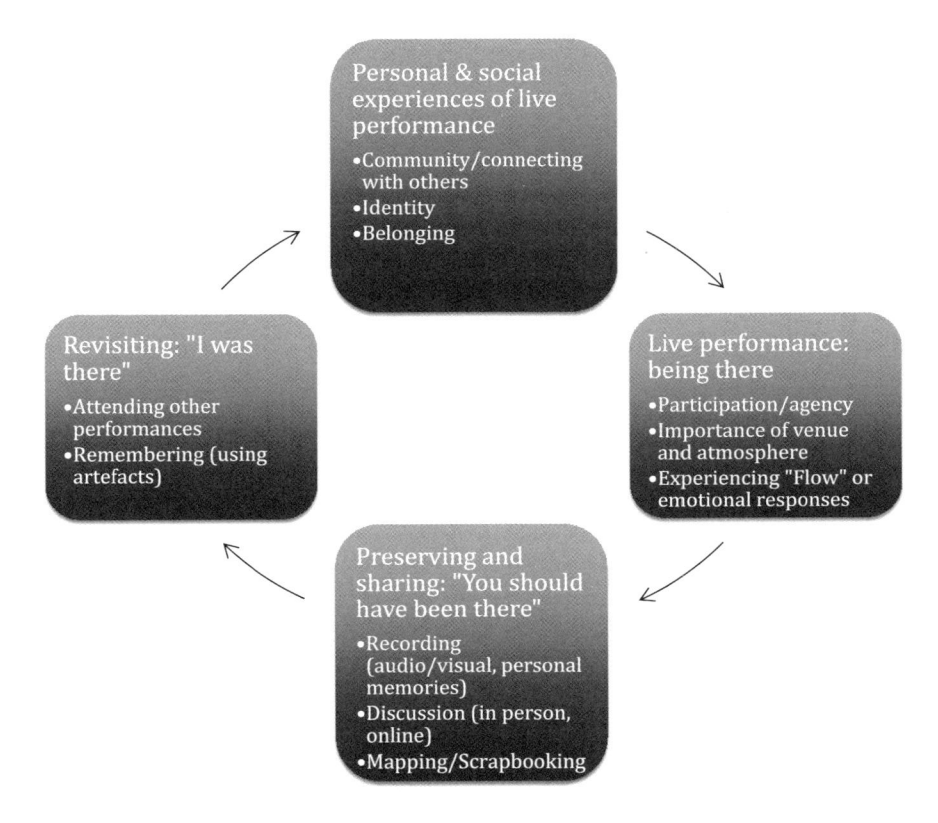

**Preserving and sharing: "You should have been there"**
- Recording (audio/visual, personal memories)
- Discussion (in person, online)
- Mapping/Scrapbooking

**Revisiting: "I was there"**
- Attending other performances
- Remembering (using artefacts)

Figure 15.1　The cyclical process of being an audience member

Attendance at live performances offers audience members access to a potentially rich and fulfilling experience in which they have a sense of agency and can have an impact on the experiences of the performers and other audience members. Audiences are therefore active participants in live performances and their engagement during and after events is significant when reflecting on what it means to be an audience member. One way in which we might depict the cyclical process of being an audience member is shown in Figure 15.1.

This process models the preceding discussion, highlighting the difference between social and personal experiences during live performances (whether in the venue or experienced remotely) and the more situational factors experienced directly as a result of 'being there'. We view each of the segments as an extension of the live performance while acknowledging that not all audience members will be dedicated to preserving and sharing memories of particular events as extensively as others.

One of the questions we have kept in mind throughout the creation of this book is 'What does it mean to be an audience member and why does it matter?', and it is the second half of this question that is due some additional consideration now. In a society where there is concern about dwindling audiences for arts events and a climate of ever-decreasing funding for the arts, it is important to research and understand the value of live music for individuals and society. While there is an element of understanding how to encourage more people to attend concerts and gigs and therefore how to increase profit, we consider this research to be about much more than that. This book demonstrates that audiences are active in the ways in which they engage with live music and this sense of agency is an important aspect of their experience. It also demonstrates that people will become repeat attenders if they have a meaningful or enjoyable experience, exemplified by the commitment some show to preserving and sharing their memories. Organizations and musicians alike can learn about what audiences value in their experiences of live music and therefore how they may enhance or repeat such aspects in future events, thus ensuring that future audience members also have meaningful and enjoyable experiences. Finally, and perhaps most importantly, live music is meaningful for individuals on a personal level, as it provides a sense of community, belonging and identity and thus has the potential to contribute to aspects of well-being.

Understanding the importance of 'being there' may also offer additional understanding of our emotional responses to music. Alf Gabrielsson has already gone some way in addressing this in relation to his work on strong experiences with music (SEM; 2010), but it is possible that empirical investigations of music and emotion may benefit from considering the impact of contextual and situational factors on our experiences of attending live music performances, as responses may be quite different to those experienced while listening at home, for example. While this book has not focused on measures of emotional responses during live performance explicitly as a way to understand what it means to be an audience member, there is evidence from Kate Stevens and her colleagues that responses to live performances are enhanced by visual components, particularly in relation to movement. Their work also highlights that technology is advancing such that measuring audience responses in real time is possible and now relatively unobtrusive.

The methodological approaches utilized within the book are varied and many authors have offered innovative techniques for capturing the ways in which audiences are active participants in live music events. There is a clear move towards understanding the meaning of live events for audience members on a personal level, moving far beyond simply profiling the demographics of audiences at different types of event. This book contains methods that gather retrospective responses to events using interviews, questionnaires, and mapping; real-time measurements of emotional responses; information gathered by examining online forums and fansites; and discussions between performers and audience immediately (or shortly) after an event has taken place. It is our hope that research in this area continues to use and develop innovative methods for understanding what it means to be an audience member in the 21st century, pursuing the idea of individuals as active participants in the creation of live music events. Considering such questions from the perspective of the performer will inevitably offer additional useful insights into the impact of audiences on live performances, as demonstrated in the chapters by Melissa Dobson and John Sloboda, and Karen Burland and Luke Windsor.

We have tried to offer insights into the entire cycle of the live music experience – from designing venues, to marketing events, through the actual experience of the event to its eventual evaluation – highlighting the complex array of factors that influence the process and experience of organizing music events and being an audience member. Adopting a holistic approach to audience research which considers these elements as intertwined is one of the challenges of future research in this area, but one which should lead to a deeper and more meaningful insight into the value and power of live music.

# References

Adorno, T.W. (1976). *Introduction to the sociology of music*. Translated by E.B. Ashton. New York: The Seabury Press.

Alexcel (n.d.). *StagePage*. Retrieved 1 February 2013 from evolver.fm/appdb/app/stagepage.

*All About Jazz* (1 June 2007). *What's your favourite live album*? [Forum message] Retrieved 2 February 2013 from http://forums.allaboutjazz.com/showthread.php?p=305455.

American Marketing Association (2007). *Definition of marketing*. Retrieved 2 September 2013 from http://www.marketingpower.com/AboutAMA/Pages/DefinitionofMarketing.aspx

Amos, T. and Powers, A. (2005). *Piece by piece: A portrait of the artist*. London: Plexus.

Andersson, A. and Andersson, D. (2006). *The economics of experiences, the arts and entertainment*. Cheltenham: Edward Elgar.

Angel, A. (31 May 2012). *Top five faked classical performances*. Retrieved 1 February 2013 from http://www.wqxr.org/#!/articles/top-5105/2012/may/31/top-five-faked-classical-performances/.

Antonietti, A., Cocomazzi, D. and Iannello, P. (2009). Looking at the audience improves music appreciation. *Journal of Nonverbal Behaviour*, 33(2), 89–106.

Aronsen, M. (2006). *Quart 06 – mer enn musikk. Verdiskapning og ringvirkninger* [*Quart 06 – more than music. Appreciation and cumulative effects*]. Kristiansand: Agder Research.

Attali, J. (1985). *Noise: The political economy of music*. Minneapolis: University of Minnesota Press.

Augé, M. (2002). *In the metro*. Minneapolis: University of Minnesota Press.

Auslander, P. (2008). *Liveness: performance in a mediatized culture*. London: Routledge.

Auslander, P. (2002). Live from cyberspace: Or, I was sitting at my computer, this guy appeared he thought I was a bot. *PAJ: A Journal of Performance and Art*, 24(1), 16–21.

Australia Council for the Arts (2010). *More than bums on seats: Australian participation in the arts*. Retrieved 9 January 2013 from www.australiacouncil.gov.au

Bachorik, J.P., Bangert, M., Loui, P., Larke, K., Berger, J., Rowe, R. and Schlaug, G. (2009). Emotion in motion: Investigating the time-course of emotional judgments of musical stimuli. *Music Perception*, 26(4), 355–364.

Bagozzi, R. (1975). Marketing as exchange. *Journal of Marketing*, 39(4), 32–39.

Bailes, F. and Dean, R.T (2012). Comparative time series analysis of perceptual responses to electroacoustic music. *Music Perception*, *29*, 359–75.

Bailey, C.M. (2004). *Joe Cocker: Mad dogs and Englishmen*. Retrieved 2 February 2013 from http://www.allaboutjazz.com/php/article.php?id=14764#. UTmUmaX9Ka40.

Bailey, C.M. (2005). *Sonny Rollins: A night at the Village Vanguard*. Retrieved 2 February 2013 from http://www.allaboutjazz.com/php/article.php?id=18623#. USygqKX9JE8.

Bailey, D. (1992). *Improvisation, its nature and practice in music*. First published 1980. British Library.

Bakhtin, M. (1986). *Rabelais och skrattets historia* [*Rabelais and the history of laughter*]. Uddevalla: Anthropos.

Barker, M. (2013). 'Live at a cinema near you': how audiences respond to digital streaming of the arts. In J. Radbourne, H. Glow and K. Johanson (Eds) *The audience experience: A critical analysis of audiences in the performing arts* (pp. 17–34). Bristol: Intellect.

Barker, R.G. (1968). *Ecological psychology: Concepts and methods for studying the environment of human behavior*. Stanford: Stanford University Press.

Barker, R.G. and Schoggen, P. (1973). *Qualities of community life*. San Francisco: Jossey-Bass.

Barrett, E. and Bolt, B. (Eds) (2007). *Practice as research: Approaches to creative arts enquiry*. London: I.B. Tauris.

Barsade, S.G. (2002). The ripple effect: Emotional contagion and its influence on group behavior. *Administrative Science Quarterly*, *47*, 644–675.

Barsalou, L.W. (2008). Grounded cognition. *Annual Review of Psychology*, *59*, 617- 645.

Bartenieff, I. and Lewis, D. (1980). *Body movement: Coping with the environment*. New York: Gordon & Breach Science Publishers.

Baudrillard, J. (1994/2003). *Simulacra and simulation*. Translated from French by Sheila Faria Glaser. Ann Arbor, University of Michigan Press.

Baym, N. (2011). *Nancy Baym: An interview with Richie Hawtin: Building global community*. Retrieved 5 April 2013 from http://blog.midem.com/2011/02/nancy-baym-an-interview-with-richie-hawtin-building-global-community/.

Baym. N. (2012). Fans or friends? Seeing social media as musicians do. *Participations*, *9*(2). Retrieved 18 June 2013 from http://www.participations.org/Volume%209/Issue%202/17%20Baym.pdf.

Becker, J. (2001). Anthropological perspectives on music and emotion. In: P.N. Juslin and J.A. Sloboda (Eds), *Handbook of music and emotion: Theory, research, applications* (pp. 135–60). New York: Oxford University Press.

Behnke, R.R., Sawyer, C.R. and King, P. E. (1994). Contagion theory and the communication of public speaking state anxiety. *Communication Education*, *43*(3), 246–251.

Behr, A. (2013). *Mapping the maps*. Retrieved July 2013 from http://livemusicexchange.org/blog/mapping-the-maps-adam-behr/.

Ben-Ze'ev, E. (2012). Mental maps and spatial perceptions: The fragmentation of Israel-Palestine. In L. Roberts (Ed.), *Mapping cultures: Place, practice, performance* (pp. 237–59). Basingstoke: Palgrave Macmillan.

Bennett, A. (1997). 'Going down the pub!': The pub rock scene as a resource for the consumption of popular music. *Popular Music*, 16(1), 97–108.

Bennett, A. and Peterson, R.A. (Eds) (2004). *Music scenes: Local, translocal, and virtual*. Nashville: Vanderbilt University Press.

Bennett, L. (2012). Patterns of listening through social media: Online fan engagement with the live music experience. *Social Semiotics*, 22(5), 545–557.

Berliner, P.F. (1994). *Thinking in jazz: The infinite art of improvisation*. Chicago and London: The University of Chicago Press.

Beverley. (25 August 2009). *George Michael – Unplugged*. [Web log post]. Retrieved 1 February 2013 from http://live-bootleg.blogspot.co.uk.

*Birmingham Odeon Memorial*. Retrieved 3 December 2013 from http://www.facebook.com/groups/65349726819

Björnberg, A. and Stockfelt, O. (1996). Kristen Klatvask Fra Vejle: Danish pub music, mythscapes and 'local camp'. *Popular Music*, 15(2), 131–147.

Blake, M. (2007). *Pigs Might Fly: The inside story of Pink Floyd*. London: Aurum.

Boone, R. and Cunningham, J.G. (1998). Children's decoding of emotion in expressive body movement: The development of cue attunement. *Developmental Psychology*, 34(5), 1007–1016.

Botti, S. (2000). What role for marketing in the arts? An analysis of arts consumption and artistic value. *International Journal of Arts Management*, 2(3), 16–27.

Bourdieu, P. (1979/1984). *Distinction*. Translated from French by Richard Nice. Cambridge, MA: Harvard University Press.

Brand, G., Sloboda, J., Saul, B. and Hathaway, M. (2012). The reciprocal relationship between jazz musicians and audiences in live performances: A pilot qualitative study. *Psychology of Music*, 40, 634–651.

Braun, V. and Clarke, V. (2006). Using thematic analysis in psychology. *Qualitative Research in Psychology*, 3, 77–101.

Brooks, P. (2008). Remediation of moving bodies: Aesthetic perceptions of a live, digitised and animated dance performance. *Culture, Language and Representation*, 6, 85–99.

Brown, A. and Novak, J. (2007). *Assessing the intrinsic impacts of a live performance*. Cambridge, MA: WolfBrown.

Bruno, A. (2011). *Superglued Sneak Peek: App, Unveiling At SXSW, Finds Gigs Based On Location, Friends, Preferences*. Retrieved 5 April 2013 from http://www.billboard.biz/bbbiz/industry/digital-and-mobile/superglued-sneak-peek-app-unveiling-at-sxsw-1005073062.story.

Bull, M. (2000). *Sounding out the city: Personal stereos and the management of everyday life*. Oxford: Berg.

Bull, M. (2005). No dead air! The iPod and the culture of mobile listening. *Leisure Studies*, 24(4), 343–355.

Burland, K. and Pitts, S.E. (2010). Understanding jazz audiences: listening and learning at the Edinburgh Jazz and Blues Festival. *Journal of New Music Research*, *39*(2), 125–134.

Burland, K. and Pitts, S.E. (2012). Rules and expectations of jazz gigs. *Social Semiotics*, *22*(5), 523–43.

Byrne, C., MacDonald, R.A.R. and Carlton, L. (2003). Assessing creativity in musical compositions: Flow as an assessment tool. *British Journal of Music Education*, *20*(3), 277–290.

Calvo-Merino, B., Jola, C., Glaser, D.E. and Haggard, P. (2008). Towards a sensorimotor aesthetics of performing art. *Consciousness and Cognition*, *17*, 911–922.

Camurri, A., Lagerlöf, I. and Volpe, G. (2003). Recognizing emotion from dance movement: comparison of spectator recognition and automated techniques. *International Journal of Human-Computer Studies*, *59*(1–2), 213–225.

Carah, N. (2010). *Pop brands: Branding, popular music, and young people*. New York: Peter Lang Publishing.

Castellano, G., Mortillaro, M., Camurri, A., Volpe, G. and Scherer, K. (2008). Automated analysis of body movement in emotionally expressive piano performances. *Music Perception*, *26*(2), 103–119.

Cavicchi, D. (1998). *Tramps like us: Music and meaning among Springsteen fans*. New York: Oxford University Press.

Chan, L.P., Livingstone, S.R. and Russo, F. A. (2013). Facial mimicry in response to song. *Music Perception*, *30*(4), 361–367.

Chanan, M. (1995). *Repeated takes: A short history of recording and its effects on music*. London and New York: Verso.

Chanan, M. (2002). Television's problem with (classical) music. *Popular Music*, *21*(3), 367–374.

Chesher, C. (2007). Becoming the Milky Way: Mobile phones and actor networks at a U2 concert. *Continuum: Journal of Media and Cultural Studies*, *21*(2), 217–25.

Clarke, E. (2005). *Ways of listening: An ecological approach to the perception of musical meaning*. Oxford: Oxford University Press.

Clifford, S. and King, A. (Eds) (1996). *From place to place: Maps and parish maps*. London: Common Ground.

Clopton, S.W., Stoddard, J.E. and Dave, D. (2006). Event preferences among arts patrons: implications for market segmentation and arts management. *International Journal of Arts Management*, *9*(1): 48–59.

Clynes, M. (1989). Methodology in sentographic measurement of motor expression of emotion – two-dimensional freedom of gesture essential. *Perceptual and Motor Skills*, *68*(3), 779–783.

Cohen, S. (2011). Cavern journeys: music, migration and urban space. In J. Toynbee and B. Duek (Eds), *Migrating Music* (pp. 235–250). London: Routledge.

Cohen, S. (2012a). Live music and urban landscape: Mapping the beat in Liverpool. *Social Semiotics*, *22*(5), 587–603.

Cohen, S. (2012b). Urban musicscapes: Mapping music-making in Liverpool. In L. Roberts (Ed.). *Mapping cultures: Place, practice, performance* (pp. 123–143). Basingstoke: Palgrave Macmillan.

Cohen, S. (2012c). Bubbles, tracks, borders and lines: Mapping music and urban landscape. *Journal of the Royal Musical Association*, *137*(1), 135–171.

Cohen, S. and Roberts, L. (2013). Heritage rocks! Mapping spaces of popular music tourism. In S. Krüger and R. Trandafoiu (Eds), *The globalization of musics in transit: Musical migration and tourism* (pp. 35–58). London: Routledge.

Collins, J. (2013a). A pile of my history, found in my parents' attic: Online music memories. Paper presented at *The Cultural Memory of Sound and Space*, University of Turku, Finland.

Collins, J. (2013b). Multiple voices, multiple memories: Public history-making and activist archivism in online popular music archives. Paper presented at *Popular Music Heritage, Cultural Memory & Cultural Identity*, 31 January–1 February 2013, University of Rotterdam, The Netherlands.

Collins, J. and Long, P. (2014). 'Fillin' any blanks I can' Online archival practice and virtual sites of musical memory. In L. Roberts, M. Leonard, S. Cohen and R. Knifton (Eds), *Sites of Popular Music Heritage* (pp. 81–96). London: Routledge.

Connolly, M. and Krueger, A.B. (2006). Rockonomics: the economics of popular music. *The Milken Institute Review*, *9*(3), 50–66.

Corbett, J. (1995). Ephemera underscored: Writing around free improvisation. In K. Gabbard (Ed.), *Jazz among the discourses* (pp. 217–240). Durham, USA: Duke University Press.

Cottrell, S. (2010). The rise and rise of phonomusicology. In A. Bayley (Ed.), *Recorded music: Performance, culture and technology* (pp. 15–36). Cambridge: Cambridge University Press.

Cowan, J. K. (1990). *Dance and the body politic in Northern Greece*. Princeton: Princeton University Press.

Csikszentmihalyi, M. (2008). *Flow: The psychology of optimal experience*. London: HarperCollins.

Cuddy, L.L. and Duffin, J. (2005). Music, memory, and Alzheimer's disease: is music recognition spared in dementia, and how can it be assessed? *Medical Hypotheses*, *64*(2), 229–235.

Davidson, J.W. and Good, J.M.M. (2002). Social and musical coordination between members of a string quartet: An exploratory study. *Psychology of Music*, *30*, 186–201.

Davis, C.J., Bowers, J.S. and Memon, A. (2011). Social influence in televised election debates: A potential distortion of democracy. *PLoS ONE*, *6*(3), e18154.

De Bres, K. and Davis, J. (2001). Celebrating group and place identity: A case study of a new regional festival. *Tourism Geographies*, *3*(3), 326–37.

Dean, R.T. and F. Bailes. (2010). Time series analysis as a method to examine acoustical influences on real-time perception of music. *Empirical Musicology Review*, *5*, 152–75.

Dean, R.T., Bailes, F. and Schubert, E. (2011). Acoustic intensity causes perceived changes in arousal levels in music: An experimental investigation. *PLoS ONE*, *6*, e18591.

Decety, J. and Meyer, M. (2008). From emotion resonance to empathic understanding: A social developmental neuroscience account. *Development and Psychopathology*, *20*(4), 1053–1080.

Delamere, T.A. (2001). Development of a scale to measure resident attitudes toward the social impacts of community festivals, part II: Verification of the scale. *Event Management*, 7, 25–38.

Deller, R. (2011). Twittering on: Audience research and participation using Twitter. *Participations: Journal of Audience and Reception Studies*, *8*, 216–245.

Demeijer, M. (1989). The contribution of general features of body movement to the attribution of emotions. *Journal of Nonverbal Behavior*, *13*(4), 247–268.

DeNora, T. (2000). *Music in everyday life*. Cambridge: Cambridge University Press.

Derrett, R. (2003). Making sense of how festivals demonstrate a community's sense of place. *Event Management*, *8*, 49–58.

Detenber, B. H. and Reeves, B. (1996). A bio-informational theory of emotion: Motion and image size effects on viewers. *Journal of Communication*, *46*(3), 66–84.

Dobson, M. (2010). *Between stalls, stage and score: An investigation of audience experience and enjoyment in classical music performance* (Unpublished PhD thesis). University of Sheffield, UK.

Dobson, M.C. and Pitts, S.E. (2011). Classical cult or learning community? Exploring new audience members' social and musical responses to first-time concert attendance. *Ethnomusicology Forum*, *20*(3): 353–383.

Du Gay, P., Hall, S., Janes, L., Mackay, H. and Negus, K. (1997). *Doing cultural studies: The story of the Sony Walkman*. London, Sage Publications.

Duffett, M. (2003). Imagined memories: webcasting as a 'live' technology and the case of Little Big Gig. *Information, Communication and Society*, *6*(3), 307–25.

Earl, J. (2005). *British theatres and music halls*. Princes Risborough: Shire Publications.

Earl, P.E. (2001). Simon's travel theorem and the demand for live music. *Journal of Economic Psychology*, *22*, 335–358.

Egermann, H., Pearce, M.T., Wiggins, G.A. and McAdams, S. (2013). Probabilistic models of expectation violation predict psychophysiological emotional responses to live concert music. *Cognitive, Affective and Behavioural Neuroscience*, *13*(3), 553–553.

Egermann, H., Sutherland, M. E., Grewe, O., Nagel, F., Kopiez, R. and Altenmüller, E. (2011). Does music listening in a social context alter experience? A physiological and psychological perspective on emotion. *Musicae Scientiae*, *15*(3), 307–323.

Ekman, A.-K. (1999). The revival of cultural celebrations in regional Sweden: Aspects of tradition and transition. *Sociologica Ruralis*, *39*(3), 280–93.

Ekman, P. and Rosenberg, E.L. (Eds) (1997). *What the face reveals: Basic and applied studies of spontaneous expression using the Facial Action Coding System (FACS)*. London: Oxford University Press.

Elliott, R. (1997). Existential consumption and irrational desire. *European Journal of Marketing*, 31(3/4), 285–296.

Elliott, R. and Wattanasuwan, K. (1998). Brands as symbolic resources for the construction of identity. *International Journal of Advertising*, 17(2), 131–144.

Elsdon, P. (2010). Jazz recording and the capturing of performance. In A. Bayley (Ed.), *Recorded music: performance, culture and technology* (pp. 146–164). Cambridge: Cambridge University Press.

Evans, G. (1997). Performance indicators in the arts – state of the arts or art of the state. In Conference Proceedings, *International Association for the Management of Arts and Culture (AIMAC)*. San Francisco: Golden Gate University, 441–51.

Falassi, A. (1987). Festival: Definition and morphology. In A. Falassi (Ed.), *Time out of time. Essays on the festival* (pp. 1–10). Albuquerque: University of New Mexico Press.

Farrugia, R. and Gobatto, N. (2010). Shopping for legs and boots: Tori Amos's original bootlegs, fandom, and subcultural capital. *Popular Music and Society*, 33(3), 357–375.

Fasel, B. and Luettin, J. (2003). Automatic facial expression analysis: a survey. *Pattern Recognition*, 36, 259–275.

Ferguson, S., Schubert, E. and Stevens, C. (2010). Movement in a contemporary dance work and its relation to continuous emotional response. In K. Beilharz, A. Johnston, S. Ferguson and A.Y.-C. Chen (Eds), *Proceedings of the 2010 Conference on New Interfaces for Musical Expression (NIME 2010)*. Broadway, Sydney, Australia.

Finnegan, R. (1989). *The hidden musicians: Music-making in an English town*. Cambridge: Cambridge University Press.

Fodor, J.A. and Pylyshyn, Z.W. (1981). How direct is visual perception? Some reflections on Gibson's 'ecological approach'. *Cognition*, 9, pp. 139–196.

Forbes, K. (2014). 'You had to be there': Memories of the Glasgow Apollo audience. In S. Cohen, M. Leonard, L. Roberts and R. Knifton (Eds), *Sites of popular music heritage* (pp. 143–59). London: Routledge.

Frame, P. (1999). *Rockin' around Britain: Rock and Roll landmarks of the UK and Ireland*. London: Omnibus Press.

Fredrickson, W.E. (2000). Perception of tension in music: Musicians versus nonmusicians. *Journal of Music Therapy*, 37(1), 40–50.

Freedman, J.L. and Perlick, D. (1979). Crowding, contagion, and laughter. *Journal of Experimental Social Psychology*, 15(3), 295–303.

Frisby, W. and Getz, D. (1989). Festival management: A case study perspective. *Journal of Travel Research*, 28, 7–11.

Frith, S. (1988). *Music for pleasure: Essays in the sociology of pop*. Cambridge: Polity Press.

Frith, S. (1996). Music and identity. In S. Hall and P. du Gay (Eds), *Questions of cultural identity* (pp.108–127). London: Sage Publications.
Frith, S. (2007). Live music matters. *Scottish Music Review*, *1*(1), 1–17.
Frith, S. (2007). *Taking popular music seriously: Selected essays.* Aldershot: Ashgate.
Frith, S. (2012). *Live music and memory*. Retrieved July 2012 from http://livemusicexchange.org/blog/live-music-and-memory/.
Fritz, B.S. and Avesec, A. (2007). The experience of flow and subjective well-being of music students. *Horizons of Psychology*, *16*(2), 5–17.
Front of House (2006). *Parnelli Innovator Honoree, father of festival sound.* [online]. Retrieved 20 January 2013 from http://www.fohonline.com/index.php?option=com_contentandtask=viewandid=579andItemid=1
Gabrielsson, A. (2001). Emotions in strong experiences with music. In P.N. Juslin and J.A. Sloboda (Eds), *Music and emotion. Theory and research* (pp. 431–49). New York: Oxford University Press.
Gabrielsson, A. (2010). Strong experiences with music. In P.N. Juslin and J.A. Sloboda (Eds), *Handbook of music and emotion. Theory, research, applications* (pp. 547–74). New York: Oxford University Press.
Gadamer, H.-G. (1986). The festive character of the theatre. In R. Bernasconi (Ed.). *The relevance of the beautiful and other essays* (pp. 57–65). Cambridge: Cambridge University Press.
Gainer, B. (1995). Ritual and relationships: Interpersonal influences on shared consumption. *Journal of Business Research*, *32*, 253–260.
Garratt, S. (1990). Teenage dreams. In S. Frith and A. Goodwin (Eds), *On record: Rock, pop and the written word* (pp. 399 – 409). New York: Pantheon.
Gibson, J.J. (1950). *The perception of the visual world.* Boston, MA: Houghton Mifflin.
Gibson, J.J. (1966). *The senses considered as perceptual systems.* Boston, MA: Houghton Mifflin.
Gibson, J.J. (1977). The theory of affordances. In R. Shaw and J. Bransford (Eds), *Perceiving, acting, and knowing: Toward an ecological psychology* (pp. 67–82). Hillsdale, NJ: Lawrence Erlbaum Associates.
Gibson, J.J. (1979). *The ecological approach to visual perception.* Boston: Houghton Mifflin.
*Good Music Guide Classical Music Forum* [online]. Retrieved 1 January 2013 from http://www.good-music-guide.com.
Grainge, P. (2011). *Ephemeral media: Transitory screen culture from television to YouTube.* London: Palgrave Macmillan.
Granger, C.W. (1969). Investigating causal relations by econometric models and cross-spectral methods. *Econometrica: Journal of the Econometric Society*, *37*(3), 424–438.
Green, L. (2010). Research in the sociology of music education: Some introductory concepts. In R. Wright (Ed.) *Sociology and music education* (pp. 21–34). Farnham: Ashgate.

Gunn, S. (1997). The sublime and the vulgar: the Hallé concerts and the constitution of 'high culture' in Manchester c. 1850–1880. *Journal of Victorian Culture*, *2*(2), 208–228.

Gursoy, D., Kim, K. and Uysal, M. (2004). Perceived impacts of festivals and special events by organizers: an extension and validation. *Tourism Management*, *25*, 171–81.

Hanna, S.P. and Del Casino, V.J. (2003). Introduction: Tourism spaces, mapped representations, and the practices of identity. In S.P. Hanna and V.J. Del Casino (Eds), *Mapping tourism* (pp. ix-xxvii). Minneapolis: University of Minnesota Press.

Harbor, C. (2013). *The birth of the music business: Public commercial concerts in London 1660–1750* (Unpublished PhD thesis). Royal Holloway, University of London, UK.

Harland, J. and Kinder, K. (1999) *Crossing the line: Extending young people's access to cultural venues*. London: Calouste Gulbenkian Foundation.

Harzinski, K. (2010). *From here to there: A curious collection from the Hand Drawn Map Association*. New York: Princeton Architectural Press.

Hastie, A. (2007). Introduction: detritus and the moving image: ephemera, materiality, history. *Journal of Visual Culture*, *6*(2), 171–174.

Heft, H. (2001). *Ecological psychology in context: James Gibson, Roger Barker and the legacy of William James's radical empiricism*. Mahwah, NJ: Lawrence Erlbaum.

Heim, C. (2012). 'Argue with us!': Audience co-creation through post-performance discussions. *New Theatre Quarterly*, *28*(May), 189–197.

Hennion, A. (2001). Music lovers: Taste as performance. *Theory, Culture and Society*, *18*(5), 1–22.

Henry, R. (2000). Dancing into being: the Tjapukai Aboriginal Cultural Park and the Laura Dance Festival. *The Australian Journal of Anthropology*, *11*(2), 322–332.

Hewett, I. (2003). *Music: Healing the rift*. London: Continuum.

Heylin, C. (1996). *Bootleg: the secret history of the other recording industry*. New York: St. Martin's Press.

Hills, M. (2002). *Fan cultures*. London: Routledge.

Hocking, J.E. (1982). Sports and spectators: Intra-audience effects. *Journal of Communication*, *32*(1), 100–108.

Hodgkins, C. (2009). *Problems arising from changing demographics*. Retrieved 10 January 2012 from http://www.jazzservices.org.uk

Holt, F. (2010). The economy of live music in the digital age. *European Journal of Cultural Studies*, *13*(2), 243–261.

Hodkinson, P. (2002). *Goth: identity, style and subculture*. Oxford: Berg.

Holbrook, M.B. and Hirschman, E. (1982). The experiential aspects of consumption: Consumer fantasies, feelings and fun. *Journal of Consumer Research*, *9*, 132–140.

Holden, J. (2004). *Capturing cultural value: How culture has become a tool of government policy.* London: Demos.
Huron, D. (2004). Music-engendered laughter: An analysis of humor devices in PDQ Bach. In *Proceedings of the 8th International Conference on Music Perception and Cognition (*pp. 700–704). Evanton, Illinois.
Hutchins, E. (1995). *Cognition in the wild.* Cambridge, MA: The MIT Press.
Hytönen-Ng, E. (2013). *Experiencing 'flow' in jazz performance.* Aldershot: Ashgate.
Jackson, S.A. (1992) Athletes in flow: A qualitative investigation of flow states in elite figure skaters. *Journal of Applied Sport Psychology* 4(2), 161–80.
Jaffe, J.C. (2010). *The acoustics of performance halls: Spaces for music from Carnegie Hall to the Hollywood Bowl.* New York: W.W. Norton and Company.
Jakobs, E., Manstead, A.S. and Fischer, A.H. (2001). Social context effects on facial activity in a negative emotional setting. *Emotion, 1*(1), 51–69.
James, J. (2000). *Made to move research report.* Judith James Consultancy. Sydney, Australia: Australia Council for the Arts.
Jeckell, B.A. (19 February 2005). Amos Expresses Herself with New Album, Book. Retrieved from http://www.billboard.com/articles/news/64106/amos-expresses-herself-with-new-album-book.
Jenson, J. (1992). Fandom as pathology: The consequences of characterisation. In L.A. Lewis (Ed.), *Adoring audience: Fan culture and popular media* (pp. 9–29). London: Routledge.
Johnson, J. (2002) *Who needs classical music? Cultural choice and musical value.* New York: Oxford University Press.
Johnson, P. (2010). Illusion and aura in the classical audio recording. In A. Bayley (Ed.), *Recorded music: performance, culture and technology* (pp. 37–51). Cambridge: Cambridge University Press.
Jola, C., Pollick, F. E. and Grosbras, M-H. (2011). Arousal decrease in 'Sleeping Beauty': Audiences' neurophysiological correlates to watching a narrative dance performance of 2.5 hrs. *Dance Research, 29,* 378–402.
Jones, B. T. (1995). *Last night on Earth.* USA: Pantheon Books.
Joy, A. and Sherry, J. (2003). Speaking of art as embodied imagination: A multisensory approach to understanding aesthetic experience. *Journal of Consumer Research, 30*(2), 259–282.
Karlsen, S. and Brändström, S. (2008). Exploring the music festival as a music educational project. *International Journal of Music Education, 26(*4), 363–73.
Karlsen, S. (2007a). Festival audience's strong emotional experiences with music. In: F.V. Nielsen, S.G. Nielsen and S.–E. Holgersen (Eds), *Nordic Research in Music Education. Yearbook 9 2007* (pp. 153–67). Oslo: NMH–publikasjoner.
Karlsen, S. (2007b). *The music festival as an arena for learning: Festspel i Pite Älvdal and matters of identity.* Retrieved 29 November 2012 from http://epubl.ltu.se/1402–1544/2007/60/.
Karlsen, S. (2009). Learning through music festivals. *International Journal of Community Music, 2*(2/3), 129–41.

Karlsen, S. (2010). Revealing musical learning in the informal field. In R. Wright (Ed.), *Sociology and music education* (pp. 193–206). Farnham: Ashgate.

Karlsen, S. (2011). Music festivals in the Lapland region: Constructing identities through musical events. In L. Green (Ed.), *Learning, teaching, and musical identity. Voices across cultures* (pp. 184–96). Bloomington, IN: Indiana University Press.

Katsilometes, J. (18 April 2009). The Killers rock is in raucous opening of new Joint at Hard Rock Hotel. *Las Vegas Sun*. Retrieved 15 January 2013 from http://www.lasvegassun.com/blogs/kats-report/2009/apr/18/killers-rock-us-raucous-opening-new-joint/.

Kay, R. H. and LeSage, A. (2009). Examining the benefits and challenges of using audience response systems: A review of the literature. *Computers and Education*, 53, 819–827.

Keegan-Phipps, S. (2009). Folk for art's sake: English folk music in the mainstream milieu. *Radical Musicology*, 4. Retrieved 5 September 2013 from www.radical-musicology.org.uk/2009/Keegan-Phipps.pdf.

Kolb, B. (2001). The effect of generational change on classical music concert attendance and orchestras' responses in the UK and US. *Cultural Trends*, 11(41), 1–35.

Kotler, P, Armstrong, G, Harris, L and Piercy, N (2013) "Principles of Marketing". 6th edition. London: Pearson.

Kotler, P. and Scheff, J. (1997). *Standing room only: Strategies for marketing the performing arts*. Boston, MA: Harvard Business School Press.

Kozinets, R.V. (2002). Can consumers escape the market? Emancipatory illuminations from Burning Man. *Journal of Consumer Research*, 29(1), 20–38.

Kronenburg, R.H. (2010). Live architecture: The design of portable buildings for live music performance. *Architectural Research Quarterly*, 14(4), 304–316.

Kronenburg, R.H. (2012). *Live architecture: venues, stages and arenas for popular music*. Oxford: Routledge.

Krueger, J. (2011). Doing things with music. *Phenomenology and the Cognitive Sciences*, 10, 1–22.

Krumhansl, C.L. (1998). Topic in music: An empirical study of memorability, openness and emotion in Mozart's string quintet in C major and Beethoven's string quartet in A minor. *Music Perception*, 16(1), 119–134.

Kubacki, K. and O´Reilly, D. (2009). Arts marketing. In E. Parsons and P. Maclaran (Eds) *Contemporary Issues in Marketing and Consumer Behaviour* (pp. 55–71). Oxford: Butterworth-Heinemann.

Kubacki, K. and Croft, R. (2005). Paying the piper: a study of musicians and the music business. *International Journal of Nonprofit and Voluntary Sector Marketing*, 10, 225–37.

Kvale, S. and Brinkmann, S. (2009). *InterViews. Learning the craft of qualitative research interviewing*. Thousand Oaks: Sage Publications.

Larry.Cool. (13 July 2010). The Arena put Manchester on top of the world [Article response]. *Manchester Evening News*. Retrieved 19 January 2013 from http://

menmedia.co.uk/manchestereveningnews/life_and_style/s/1301523_the_arena_put_manchester_on_top_of_the_world.
Larsen, G. (2014). Consuming the arts. In D. O'Reilly, R. Rentschler and T. Kirchner (Eds), *The Routledge companion to arts marketing*, (pp. 183–93). London: Routledge.
Larsen, G., Lawson, R. and Todd, G. (2010). The symbolic consumption of music. *Journal of Marketing Management*, 26(7/8), 671–685.
Lave, J. and Wenger, E. (1991). *Situated learning: Legitimate peripheral participation*. Cambridge: Cambridge University Press.
League of American Orchestras (2009). *Audience demographic research review*. Retrieved 9 January 2013 from http://www.americanorchestras.org.
LeBlanc, A., Jin, Y.C., Obert, M. and Siivola, C. (1997). Effect of audience on music performance anxiety. *Journal of Research in Music Education*, 45(3), 480–496.
Lees, N. and Stevens, K. (2002). Recognising emotion in voice and face: Do audio-visual features integrate? *Australian Journal of Psychology*, 54(1), 56.
Lerman, L. and Borstel, J. (2003). *Liz Lerman's Critical Response Process: A method for getting useful feedback on anything you make, from dance to dessert*. Takoma Park: The Dance Exchange.
Leslie, K.C. (2006). *A sense of place: West Sussex parish maps*. Chichester: West Sussex County Council.
Levitin, D.J. and Cuddy, L.L. (2004). Editorial: Introduction to the *Angel of Death* project. *Music Perception*, 22(2), 167–170.
Lingel, J. and Naaman, M. (2012). You should have been there, man: Live music, DIY content and online communities. *New Media and Society*, 14(2), 332–349.
Löbert, A. (2012). Fandom as a religious form: On the reception of pop music by Cliff Richard fans in Liverpool. *Popular Music*, 31(1), 125–141.
Long, P. and Collins. J. (2012). Mapping the soundscapes of popular music heritage. In L. Roberts (Ed.), *Mapping cultures: Place, practice, performance* (pp. 144–159). Basingstoke: Palgrave Macmillan.
Lynch, K. (1960). *The image of the city*. Cambridge. MA: MIT Press.
MacKinnon, N. (1993). *The British folk scene: Musical performance and social identity*. Buckingham: Open University Press.
Madsen, C.K. (1998). Emotion versus tension in Haydn's Symphony no. 104 as measured by the two-dimensional continuous response digital interface. *Journal of Research in Music Education*, 46, 546–554.
Madsen, C.K. and Fredrickson, W.E. (1993). The experience of musical tension: A replication of Nielsen's research using the continuous response digital interface. *Journal of Music Therapy 30*, 46–63.
Marshall, L. (2003). For and against the record industry: An introduction to bootleg collectors and tape traders. *Popular Music*, 22(1), 57–72.
Martin, V., Bunting, C. and Oskala, A. (2010) *Arts engagement in England 2008/09: Findings from the Taking Part survey*. Retrieved 9 January 2013 from http://www.artscouncil.org.uk

McAdams, S., Vines, B.W., Viellard, S., Smith, B.K. and Reynolds, R. (2004). Influences of large-scale form on continuous ratings in response to a contemporary piece in a live concert setting. *Music Perception*, *22*, 297–350.

McCarthy, K., Ondaatje, E., Zakardi, L. and Brooks, A. (2004). *Gifts of the muse*. Boston: Rand Corporation.

McCormick, N. (21 February 2011). Adele soars to top of charts after Brits performance. *The Telegraph*. Retrieved from http://www.telegraph.co.uk/culture/music/music-news/8337781/Adele-soars-to-top-of-charts-after-Brits-performance.html.

Meagher, J. (5 December 2008). The O2: Welcome to the Future. *Irish Independent*. Retrieved from http://www.independent.i.e./entertainment/day-and-night/the-o2-welcome-to-the-future-1564580.html.

Menin, D. and Schiavio, A. (2012). Rethinking musical affordances. *Avant*, *3*, 202–215.

Merchant, A., Ford, J.B. and Sargeant, A. (2010). Charitable organizations' storytelling influence on donors' emotions and intentions. *Journal of Business Research*, *63*(7), 754–762.

Merriam, A.P. (1964). *The anthropology of music*. Evanston, IL: Northwestern University Press.

Millard, W.J. (1992). A history of handsets for direct measurement of audience response. *International Journal of Public Opinion Research*, *4*(1), 1–17.

Minor, M.S., Wagner, T., Brewerton, F.J. and Hausman, A. (2004). Rock on! An elementary model of customer satisfaction with musical performance. *Journal of Services Marketing*, *18*(1), 7–18.

Mitchell, H.F. and MacDonald, R.A.R. (2009). Linguistic limitations of describing sound: Is talking about music like dancing about architecture? In A. Williamon, S. Pretty and R. Buck (Eds), *Proceedings of the International Symposium on Performance Science 2009* (pp. 45–50). Utrecht, The Netherlands: European Association of Conservatoires (AEC).

Morris, B.J. (2001). Anyone can be a lesbian: The women's music audience and lesbian politics. *Journal of Lesbian Studies*, *5*(4), 91–120.

Music Week (4 March 2011). *X Factor shines alone amid disappointing NAA figures*. Retrieved 20 January 2013 from http://www.musicweek.com/news/read/x-factor-shines-alone-amid-disappointing-naa-figures/045140.

Myerscough, J. (1998). *The economic importance of the arts in Britain*. London: Policy Studies Institute.

Nagel, F., Kopiez, R., Grewe, O. and Altenmüller, E. (2007). EMuJoy: Software for continuous measurement of perceived emotions in music. *Behavior Research Methods*, *39*, 283–290.

National Endowment of the Arts (2008). *2008 survey of public participation in the arts*. Retrieved from http://www.arts.gov/research/2008-SPPA.pdf

Negus, K. (1996). *Popular music in theory: An introduction*. Cambridge: Polity Press.

Negus, K. (2002). The work of cultural intermediaries and the enduring distance between production and consumption. *Cultural Studies*, *16*(4), 501–515.

Neumann, M. and Simpson, T.A. (1997). Smuggled sound: Bootleg recording and the pursuit of popular memory. *Symbolic Interaction*, *20*(4), 319–41.

New Musical Express (4 March 2009). *Cardiff venue closed down*. Retrieved 11 June 2013 from http://www.nme.com/news/various-artists/43208.

Nielsen, F.V. (1987). Musical tension and related concepts. In T.A. Sebeok and J. Umiker-Sebeok (Eds), *The semiotic web '86. An international year-book*. Berlin: Mouton de Gruyter.

O'Reilly, D. (2011). Branding the arts and entertainment. In B. Walmsley (Ed.), *Key issues in the arts and entertainment industry* (pp.47–67). Oxford: Goodfellows.

O'Reilly, D. and Kerrigan, F. (2013). A view to a brand: Introducing the film Brandscape. *European Journal of Marketing*, *47*(5/6), 769–89.

O'Reilly, D., Larsen, G. and Kubacki, K. (2013). *Music, markets and consumption*. Oxford: Goodfellows Publishers.

O'Sullivan, T. (2009). All together now: A symphony orchestra audience as a consuming community. *Consumption, Markets and Culture*, *12*(3), 209–223.

Oakes, S. (2003). Demographic and sponsorship considerations for jazz and classical music festivals. *The Services Industries Journal*, *23*(3), 165–178.

Opie, I. (1993). *The people in the playground*. Oxford: Oxford University Press.

Pettersson, B. (2005). Ett fall för filosofiska rummet [A case for the room of philosophy]. *Piteå-Tidningen*, 12 November, editorial.

Pitts, S.E. (2005a). *Valuing musical participation*. Aldershot: Ashgate.

Pitts, S.E. (2005b). What makes an audience? Investigating the roles and experiences of listeners at a chamber music festival. *Music and Letters*, *86*(2), 257–69.

Pitts, S.E. and Burland, K. (2013). Listening to live jazz: An individual or social act? *Arts Marketing*, *3*(1), 7–20.

Pitts, S.E., Dobson, M.C., Gee, K.A. and Spencer, C.P. (2013). Views of an audience: Understanding the orchestral concert experience from player and listener perspectives. *Participations: Journal of Audience and Reception Studies*, *10*(2), 65–95.

Pitts, S.E. and Spencer, C.P. (2008) Loyalty and longevity in audience listening: Investigating experiences of attendance at a chamber music festival. *Music and Letters*, *89*(2), 227–238.

Purcell, N.J. (2003). *Death metal music: The passion and politics of a subculture*. Jefferson, North Carolina: McFarland Publishing.

Quinn, B. (2005). Arts festivals and the city. *Urban Studies*, *42*(5/6), 927–43.

Radbourne, J. (2002). Social intervention or market intervention? A problem for governments in promoting the value of the arts. *International Journal of Arts Management*, *5*(1), 50–61.

Radbourne, J., Glow, H., Johanson, K. and White, T. (2009). The audience experience: measuring quality in the performing arts. *International Journal of Arts Management*, *11*(3), 16–29.

Radbourne, J., Johanson, K. and Glow, H. (2010). Empowering audiences to measure quality. *Participations: Journal of Audience and Reception Studies*, 7(2), 360–379.

Rasula, J. (1995). The media of memory: The seductive menace of records in jazz history. In K.Gabbard (Ed.), *Jazz among the discourses* (pp. 134–64). Durham and London: Duke University Press.

Reason, M. (2004). Theatre audiences and perceptions of 'liveness' in performance *Participations: Journal of Audience and Reception Studies 1*(2). Retrieved from http://www.participations.org/volume%201/issue%202/1_02_reason_article.htm.

Reason, M. (2012). Artistic enquiries: kinesthetic empathy and practice-based research – Introduction. In D. Reynolds and M. Reason (Eds) *Kinesthetic empathy in creative and cultural practices* (pp. 195–197). Bristol: Intellect.

Reason, M. and Reynolds, D. (2010). Kinesthesia, empathy, and related pleasures: An inquiry into audience experiences of watching dance. *Dance Research Journal*, 42(2), 49–75.

Reed, E.S. (1996). *The necessity of experience*. New Haven and London: Yale University Press.

Reybrouck, M. (2005). A biosemiotic and ecological approach to music cognition: Event perception between auditory listening and cognitive economy. *Axiomathes*, 15(2), 229–266.

Reynolds, R. (2004). Epilog: Reflections on psychological testing with The Angel of Death. *Music Perception*, 22(2), 351–356.

Reynolds, D. (2012). Kinesthetic empathy and the dance's body: Fom emotion to affect. In D. Reynolds and M. Reason (Eds) *Kinesthetic empathy in creative and cultural practices* (pp.121–136). Bristol: Intellect.

Rhodes, J. (26 March 2011). The greatest living pianist. *Spectator*. Retrieved 4 November 2012 from http://www.spectator.co.uk/features/6808878/the-greatest-living-pianist/.

Rieser, M. (2011). *The mobile audience: media art and mobile technologies*. Amsterdam: Rodopi.

Roberts, L. (2012). Mapping cultures: A spatial anthropology. In L. Roberts (Ed.), *Mapping cultures: Place, practice, performance* (pp.1–25). Basingstoke: Palgrave Macmillan.

Roscanuck83 (November 2012). Comment. *Nirvana – The Point Theatre, Dublin, Ireland 1992 (FULL)*. Retrieved 10 January 2013 from http://www.youtube.com/watch?v=74bKupYf4N8.

Rose, N. (1954). Some comments on motion picture research. *Journal of the University Film Producers Association*, 6(3), 3–8.

Rose, F. (April 2009). Nine Inch Nails iPhone app extends Reznor's innovative run, *Wired*. Retrieved 5 April 2013 from http://www.wired.com/underwire/2009/04/trent-reznor-wa/

Rossel, J. (2011). Cultural capital and the variety of modes of consumption in the opera audience, *Sociological Quarterly*, 52, 83–103.

Rostron, J. (16 April 2010). Cardiff needs a venue like The Globe. *The Guardian*. Retrieved 19 January 2013 from http://www.guardian.co.uk/cardiff/2010/apr/15/the-globe-cardiff-music-venues-la-roux-jamie-t.

Rothschild, A.R. and Graber, R.E. (1999). *Live at Fillmore East: A photographic memoir*. New York: Thunder's Mouth Press.

Russell, J.A. (1980). A circumplex model of affect. *Journal of Social Psychology*, 39, 1161–1178.

Russell, J.A., Weiss, A. and Mendelsohn, G.A. (1989). Affect Grid: a single-item scale of pleasure and arousal. *Journal of Personality and Social Psychology*, 57, 493–502.

Said, E.W. (2008). *Music at the limits: Three decades of essays and articles on music*. London: Bloomsbury.

Sanders, J.T. (1997). An ontology of affordances. *Ecological Psychology*, 9(1), 97–112.

Scherer, K.R. and Zentner, M. (2001). Emotional effects of music: production rules. In P.N. Juslin and J.A. Sloboda (Eds), *Music and emotion. Theory and research* (pp. 361–92). New York: Oxford University Press.

Schlager, K. (4 June 2005). Cell Phone is Newest Star on Touring Circuit, *Billboard*. Retrieved from http://www.billboard.com/biz/articles/news/1411227/cell-phone-is-newest-star-on-touring-circuit.

Schubert, E. (1999). Measuring emotion continuously: Validity and reliability of the two-dimensional emotion-space. *Australian Journal of Psychology*, 51, 154–165.

Schubert, E. (2004). Modeling perceived emotion with continuous musical features. *Music Perception*, 21, 561–585.

Schubert, E., Vincs, K. and Stevens, C.J. (2013). Identifying regions of good agreement among responders in engagement with a piece of live dance. *Empirical Studies of the Arts*, 31(1), 1–20.

Scollen, R.J. (2008). Regional voices talk theatre: Audience development for the performing arts. *International Journal of Nonprofit and Voluntary Sector Marketing*, 13(1), 45–56.

Sevdalis, V. and Keller, P.E. (2011). Captured by motion: Dance, action understanding, and social cognition. *Brain and Cognition*, 77(2), 231–236.

Sgouros, N.M. (2000). Detection, analysis and rendering of audience reactions in distributed multimedia performance. In *Proceedings of the 8th ACM International Conference on Multimedia* (pp. 195–200). New York: Association for Computing Machinery (ACM).

Sgouros, N.M. (2003). Analysis, management and indexing of distributed multimedia performances based on audience feedback. *Multimedia Systems*, 8(6), 470–481.

Shaar Murray, C. (August 1996). The Sex Pistols and Friends: Finsbury Park, London, *Mojo*. Retrieved 11 March 2013 from http://www.rocksbackpages.com/Library/Article/the-sex-pistols-and-friends-finsbury-park-london.

Shaw, R. and Turvey, M.T. (1981). Coalitions as models for ecosystems: A realist perspective on perceptual organization. In M. Kubovy and J. Pomerantz (Eds), *Perceptual organization* (pp. 343–415). Hillsdale, NJ: Lawrence Erlbaum.

Sheridan, M. and Byrne, C. (2002). Ebb and flow of assessment in music. *British Journal of Music Education*, *19*(2), 135–143.

Singleton, P. (2006). David Nolan discusses the new upgraded version of his book *I Swear I Was There* with Phil Singleton. *God Save the Sex Pistols*. Retrieved 3 November 2012 from http://www.philjens.plus.com/pistols/pistols/pistols_swear.html.

Sloboda, J.A. and Juslin, P.N. (2010). At the interface between the inner and outer world: Psychological perspectives. In P.N. Juslin and J.A. Sloboda (Eds), *Handbook of music and emotion. Theory, research, applications* (pp. 73–97). New York: Oxford University Press.

Small, C. (1987). Performance as ritual: Sketch for an enquiry into the true nature of a symphony concert. In A.L. White (Ed.), *Lost in music: Culture, style and the musical event* (pp. 6–32). London: Routledge and Kegan Paul.

Small, C. (1998) *Musicking: The meanings of performing and Listening*. Hanover, NH: Wesleyan University Press.

Smith, H. and Dean, R.T. (Eds) (2009). *Research-led practice, practice-led research in the creative arts*. Edinburgh: Edinburgh University Press.

Sogon, S. and Izard, C.E. (1987). Sex differences in emotion recognition by observing body movements: A case of American students. *Japanese Psychological Research*, *29*(2), 89–93.

Songkick (n.d.) Retrieved 1 March 2013 from http://www.songkick.com/info/aboutwww.songkick.com.

Stevens, C., Schubert, E., Haszard Morris, R., Frear, M., Chen, J., Healey, S., Schoknecht, C. and Hansen, S. (2009). Cognition and the temporal arts: Investigating audience response to dance using PDAs that record continuous data during live performance. *International Journal of Human-Computer Studies*, *67*(9), 800–813.

Stevens, C., Schubert, E., Wang, S., Kroos, C. and Halovic, S. (2009). Moving with and without music: Scaling and lapsing in time in the performance of contemporary dance. *Music Perception*, *26*(5), 451–464.

Strauss, N. (9 December 1998). A Concert Communion With Cell Phones; Press 1 to Share Song, 2 for Encore, 3 for Diversion, 4 to Schmooze, *The New York Times*. Retrieved 12 December 2011 from http://www.nytimes.com/1998/12/09/arts/concert-communion-with-cell-phones-press-1-share-song-2-for-encore-3-for.html?pagewanted=allandsrc=pm.

Street, J. (2004). This is Your Woodstock: Popular Memories and Political Myths. *Remembering Talk Classical*. Retrieved 5 March 2013 from http://www.talkclassical.com.

Tarrant, M., North, A.C. and Hargreaves, D.J. (2000). English and American adolescents' reasons for listening to music. *Psychology of Music*, *28*, 166–173

Tepper, S.J. and Ivey, B. (2008). *Engaging art: The next great transformation of America's cultural life.* New York: Routledge.

Thompson, S. and Williamon, A. (2003). Evaluating evaluation: Musical performance assessment as a research tool. *Music Perception, 21*(1), 21–41.

Tomes, S. (2012). *To talk or not to talk.* Retrieved 25 March 2013 from http://www.susantomes.com.

Tomes, S. (2004). *Beyond the notes: Journeys with chamber music.* Woodbridge: The Boydell Press.

Tuan, Yi Fu. (1975). Images and mental maps. *Annals of the Association of American Geographers, 65*, 205–13.

Tzokas, N. and Saren, M. (1999). Value transformation in relationship marketing, *Australasian Marketing Journal, 7*(1), 52–62.

Upright, C.B. (2004). Social capital and cultural participation: Sousal influences on attendance at arts events. *Poetics, 32*, 129–143.

van Dijck, J. (2006). Record and hold: Popular music between personal and collective memory. *Critical Studies in Media Communications. 23*(5), 357–374.

Vargo S. and Lusch, R. (2004). Evolving to a new dominant logic for marketing. *Journal of Marketing. 68*(January), 1–17.

Vines, B.W., Krumhansl, C.L., Wanderley, M.M. and Levitin, D.J. (2006) Cross-modal interactions in the perception of musical performance. *Cognition, 101*, 80–113.

Wagener, A. (2012). *Why do people (not) cough in concerts? The economics of concert etiquette.* Association of Cultural Economics International: Working Paper Series. Downloaded 13 November 2013 from www.culturaleconomics.org/awp/AWP-05-2012.pdf

Waksman, S. (2011). Selling the nightingale: P.T. Barnum, Jenny Lind and the management of the American crowd. *Arts Marketing: An International Journal, 1*(2), 108–120.

Walker-Kuhne, D. (2005). *Invitation to the party: Building bridges to the arts, culture and community.* New York: Theatre Communications Group.

Wall, T. (2013). *Studying popular music culture* (2nd edition). London, Thousand Oaks, Delhi and Singapore: Sage.

Wallach, J. (2003). The poetics of electrosonic presence: Recorded music and the materiality of sound. *Journal of Popular Music Studies, 15*(1), 34–64.

Warman, J. (27 August 2010). How music festivals are singing the changes. *The Guardian.* Retrieved 20 January 2013 from http://www.guardian.co.uk/business/2010/aug/27/music-festivals-record-industry

Watkins, E.E. (2007). Instant fame: Message boards, mobile phones, and Clay Aiken. *Association of Internet Researchers Conference 6.0.* Retrieved 18 June 2013 from http://aladinrc.wrlc.org/handle/1961/5241.

Weale, R. (2006). Discovering how accessible electroacoustic music can be: The intention/reception project. *Organised Sound, 11*, 189–200.

Whatley, S. (2012). The poetics of motion capture and visualization techniques: The differences between watching real and virtual dancing bodies. In D. Reynolds and M. Reason (Eds), *Kinesthetic empathy in creative and cultural practices* (pp. 263–279). Bristol: Intellect.

Wenger, E. (1998). *Communities of practice. Learning, meaning, and identity.* Cambridge: Cambridge University Press.

Westwood, M. (28 May 2013). The newly liberated audience. *The Australian.* Retrieved 7 June 2013 from http://www.theaustralian.com.au/arts/the-newly-liberated-audience/story-e6frg8n6-1226651634463.

Windsor, W.L. (2000). Through and around the acousmatic: The interpretation of electroacoustic sounds. In S. Emmerson (Ed.), *Music, electronic media and culture* (pp. 7–33). London: Ashgate.

Windsor, W.L. (2004) An ecological approach to semiotics. *Journal for the Theory of Social Behaviour*, *34*(2), 179–198.

Windsor, W.L. (2011). Gestures in music-making: Action, information and perception. In A. Gritten and E. King (Eds), *New Perspectives on Music and Gesture* (pp. 45–66). Ashgate: Farnham.

Windsor, W.L. and de Bézenac, C. (2012). Music and affordances. *Musicae Scientiae*, *16*, 102–120.

Wood, Denis (2010). *Rethinking the Power of Maps*. New York: The Guilford Press.

Bethel Woods Center for the Arts (n.d.). *Woodstock Festival History: August 15–16–17–18, 1969.* Retrieved 10 March 2013 from http://www.bethelwoodscenter.org/museum/festivalhistory.aspx.

*World Concert Hall.* Retrieved 5 March 2013 from http://www.worldconcerthall.com.

Wundt, W. (1874/1905). *Fundamentals of physiological psychology.* Leipzig: Engelmann.

Yin, R.K. (2003). *Case study research. Design and methods.* Thousand Oaks: Sage Publications.

Zentner, M. and Eerola, T. (2010). Self-report measures and models. In P.N. Juslin and J.A. Sloboda (Eds), *Handbook of music and emotion. Theory, research, applications* (pp. 187–221). New York: Oxford University Press.

Ziegler, C., Bevilacqua, F., Bastien, M., Mirzabekiantz, E., Bermúdez, M. (2007). *Double Skin/Double Mind* DVD-ROM – workshop developed by Emio Greco | PC. Amsterdam, The Netherlands: Emio Greco | PC and AHK.

# Index

acoustics 37, 38, 39, 42, 101, 105–7
affordances 102, 106–14
amateur musician 121
American Marketing Association (AMA) 8–9
arenas 35, 38–9
arousal 74, 77–9
artefacts 128, 135–7, 142, 147, 150, 155
attendance
    barriers 13, 32
    motivations 13, 22, 23, 25, 27, 32, 160, 172
atmosphere 39, 45, 101, 111, 113, 120, 121, 125, 127, 149, 159, 175–6
audience as participants 2, 53, 65, 109, 110, 114, 127–8, 159, 171, 176, 178
audience development 7, 172, 177
audience engagement 23, 47, 64, 95, 99, 106, 107
audience expectations 37, 43, 22, 101, 170, 171
audience feedback 159–173
audience loyalty 30, 70
audience members 23–7, 29, 53–4, 127, 160
audience response 55, 57–9, 61, 70, 82, 111, 125, 149, 159, 161, 176;
    *see also* continuous audience response technology
audience segmentation studies 22–3, 27
authenticity 38, 50, 58, 11, 144, 148, 153–7
autobiography 131–3, 141, 144, 176

bands 14–15, 121, 123–4, 156
behaviour settings 101–6, 110–114
belonging 121–7, 144, 151, 175–8
Birmingham Music Archive 141, 143
bootleg recordings 153, 156–8

branding 16–17, 35, 131, 139
building regulations 40–41

clapping 86, 159
classical music 21, 22, 25–7, 29, 31, 62, 109, 121, 153, 156, 158–61
collaboration
    between performer-composer-audience 162,165, 167–8, 173
collective memory 150–151, 152, 156, 158
communication
    with audience 65–6, 106, 110, 160
    between performers 65, 121
communities of practice 122–3, 125–6
community 54, 31, 90, 96–7, 115, 121–8, 137–8, 142–5, 155, 175–6, 178
composition 101, 103, 161–4
concert rituals 1, 14, 21
conflict 109
continuous audience response technology 54, 3, 70–84, 161, 173, 178
co-performers 107–9, 121
coughing 2, 28
critics 48, 172
cultural prestige 144

dance 74–82
demographics 22, 31, 132, 178
digital archives 140, 143, 152

ecological psychology 101–2, 113
emotional response 57, 64, 71, 115–17, 119, 121, 125–7, 178
emotional significance 127, 142
England Rocks! 139, 140, 141, 145

Facebook *see* social media
fans 12, 15, 53, 92, 96–7, 127
festivals 115–26, 134, 139, 152

flow experience 90–92, 95–6, 98, 175
Friends' organisations 30, 32

health and safety 7, 45–6
heritage 122, 132, 138–41, 152

identity 9, 12–13, 115–16, 121–8, 138, 142, 158, 175–8
improvisation 70, 101,103, 105–14
informal learning 115; *see also* learning
instruments 101, 102, 103, 105, 108
interaction (performer–audience) 10, 11, 16, 29, 60–66, 83, 129, 149, 159–62, 168, 170, 176; *see also* communication

jazz 28, 70, 109, 153–6, 159
journeys 134, 136–38, 142, 145

learning 115, 122–3, 125–6, 170–71
legislation 39–41
listening at home 127, 154, 178
listening technology 2, 26
live music listening 10, 28–9, 36, 46, 64-5, 67, 92–8, 137, 144, 147–9, 153–4, 158–59, 161, 165–6, 175, 176, 178
Live Nation 9, 11
live recordings 152–8

mapping 131–41, 145, 147, 176
marketing 7–19, 178
mechanical recording 147, 152–5
memory 36, 96, 123, 127–8, 131–8, 140–51, 176
memory practices 149–50, 176–8
mobile phones 15, 89, 93–5, 99, 140, 157, 176,
music as product 12,156
music consumer 12–13, 147–8, 153, 155
musical cultures 151, 154
musical histories 128, 133–5, 138, 143–4, 151–2, 155, 176
musical influences 136–8
musical material 105, 107–8, 110–13
musical places 131–3, 136, 139, 141–5, 176
musicians 10, 101, 105–9, 117, 162

*Musicking* (C. Small) 1, 21–2
mythologization 147, 153, 155

new audiences 30, 160–61
nostalgia 36, 142, 150

online communities 90, 96–8, 128, 143, 148–52, 157, 175–6
online concert streaming 26–7, 148
opera 53, 59
orchestral music 25, 27, 59–64

performance 101, 108, 110–12, 114, 127, 134, 149, 155
performance context(s) 101, 104–9, 112–114, 120, 127, 137, 175
performance quality 26, 55–8,117, 129, 160, 161
performance technology 37, 11, 42–4, 48, 60
performers 28–9, 66, 101, 103,106, 108–10, 112, 114, 120, 121, 124, 168, 171
phonomusicology 153
popular music 35–6, 14, 37, 89–99, 109, 131–145, 154, 156, 158
post-performance discussion 159, 160, 162, 164–72
professional musician 121
programming 124
promoters 13, 17–19, 32, 41–3

recorded music listening 11, 62, 136, 142, 154–5
recording practice 128, 147, 158
refreshments 21, 35, 46, 104, 124
ritual 14, 16, 126, 138, 142, 160
rock music 131–2, 144, 153, 156

self-report 83, 116, 117
Small, C. *see Musicking*
smart phones *see* mobile phones
social media 2, 3, 14, 18, 58, 65–6, 71, 89–99, 127, 140, 147–50, 152, 157, 175
social interaction 83, 87, 127–8, 137, 142–3, 160

Strong Experiences with Music (SEM) 115–26, 178

talking 28–9, 33, 105, 159–60, 168
tickets 9, 12, 14, 67, 135–7, 149, 176
tourism 132, 138–9, 145
Twitter *see* Social media

venue 11, 35–50, 91, 105–6, 112–113, 120, 127, 139, 141, 143–4, 149, 175–6, 179

Woodstock Festival 42–3, 152

YouTube 49, 157